(Re)labeling

Linguistic Inquiry Monographs
Samuel Jay Keyser, general editor

A complete list of books published in the Linguistic Inquiry Monographs series appears at the back of this book.

(Re)labeling

Carlo Cecchetto and Caterina Donati

The MIT Press
Cambridge, Massachusetts
London, England

MIT Press books may be purchased at special quantity discounts for business or sales promotional use. For information, please email special_sales@mitpress.mit.edu

This book was set in 10/13 TimesLTStd-Roman by Toppan Best-set Premedia Limited. Printed and bound in the United States of America.

Library of Congress Cataloging-in-Publication Data is available.

ISBN: 978-0-262-02872-1

10 9 8 7 6 5 4 3 2 1

A Sara e Giuliano

Contents

Series Foreword

We are pleased to present the seventieth volume in the series *Linguistic Inquiry Monographs*. These monographs present new and original research beyond the scope of the article. We hope they will benefit our field by bringing to it perspectives that will stimulate further research and insight.

Originally published in limited edition, the *Linguistic Inquiry Monographs* are now more widely available. This change is due to the great interest engendered by the series and by the needs of a growing readership. The editors thank the readers for their support and welcome suggestions about future directions for the series.

Samuel Jay Keyser
for the Editorial Board

Acknowledgments

The joint work leading to this book started in the spring of 2006 and was intended as a short collaboration on a paper in which we were supposed to merge Carlo's talk at Incontro di Grammatica Generativa 32 (University of Florence, February 2006), which Caterina liked, and Caterina's talk at the InterPhases conference (University of Cyprus, May 2006), which Carlo liked. As it happened, things went differently. We can now say that we got acquainted with each other's work on labeling because an abstract was submitted to a conference but was never received, and this led Leonardo Savoia to do something unorthodox. Our thanks to Leonardo for doing that, although he was not aware of the consequences of his act.

Earlier and substantially different versions of the ideas discussed in chapters 2 and 3 have been published as Cecchetto and Donati 2010 and Donati and Cecchetto 2011. We have presented our work at numerous conferences and seminars, which we report in chronological order, because this book would simply not exist without input, criticism, and comments from the audiences at these events: Colloquium talk, University of Siena (July 2007); NELS (North East Linguistic Society) 38, University of Ottawa (October 2007); 18th Colóquio de Gramática Generativa, University of Lisbon (April 2008); Facing Movement Workshop, Pompeu Fabra University, Barcelona (August 2008); Ways of Structure Building Workshop, University of the Basque Country, Vitoria-Gasteiz (November 2008); Workshop on Head Movement, Hungarian Academy of Sciences, Budapest (August 2009); 20th Colóquio de Gramática Generativa, Pompeu Fabra University, Barcelona (March 2010); GLOW (Generative Linguistics in the Old World) in Asia 8, Beijing Language and Culture University (August 2010); Going Romance 24, University of Leiden (December 2010); Colloquium talk at École Normale Supérieure, Paris (March 2011); 21st Colóquio de Gramática Generativa, University of Seville (April 2011); GLOW (Generative Linguistics in the Old World) 34, University of Vienna (April 2011); Complex Sentences and

Beyond in Sign and Spoken Languages, Lichtenberg-Kolleg, Göttingen (October 2011); Islands in Contemporary Linguistic Theory Workshop, University of the Basque Country, Vitoria-Gasteiz (November 2011); Going Romance 25, Utrecht University (December 2011); Linguistics Colloquium, University of Chicago (February 2012); Generalizing Relative Strategies Workshop, University of Ghent (March 2012); Resumptive Pronouns Workshop, The Hebrew University of Jerusalem (June 2012); NELS (North East Linguistic Society) 43, City University of New York (October 2012); Colloquium talk, Harvard University (October 2012); Going Romance 26, University of Leuven (December 2012); 39th Incontro di Grammatica Generativa, University of Modena and Reggio Emilia (February 2013); Tokyo Conference on Psycholinguistics, Keio University (March 2013); GLUE (Generative Linguistics Urbis Æternae) 2, Rome (April 2013); Remnant Movement Workshop, University of Frankfurt (June 2013); International Congress of Linguists (ICL), University of Geneva (July 2013); Colloquium talk, University of Florence (November 2013); Going Romance 27, University of Amsterdam (November 2013); 36th Annual Conference of the German Linguistic Society (DGfS), Labels and Roots Workshop and Experimental and Theoretical Approaches to Relative Clauses Reconciled Workshop, University of Marburg (March 2014).

We went to quite a few conferences not only because we like to travel but also because we live in different cities (and, by the way, are happily married to Sara and Giuliano). Conferences were the occasion to work together and to prepare for the next conference and, ultimately, for this book. So, in addition to Skype, we must thank the many gardens, trains, buses, restaurants, cafés, airplanes, and streets around the world that hosted our brainstorming. Some places are still associated with linguistic issues. A problem found when working in 2007 in front of Santa Maria dei Servi in Siena still worries Carlo; the wi-fi of the bar in front of Ponte dell'Accademia in Venice allowed us to realize that a prediction we made was borne out by an obscure (for us!) particle in Chinese; the flight from Beijing to Amsterdam was entirely devoted to fighting against a problem that, although it anguished us for years, in the end turned out not to be a real problem. A bus from Ottawa to Montreal and the streets around Denfert in Paris were also quite inspiring.

We are grateful to the following people who read (parts of) this manuscript or discussed with us important aspects of the theory we wanted to propose: Klaus Abels, Adriana Belletti, Valentina Bianchi, Andreas Blümel, Chiara Branchini, Gennaro Chierchia, Noam Chomsky, João Costa, Roberta D'Alessandro, Marcel den Dikken, Naama Friedmann, Carlo Geraci, Giorgio

Graffi, Ciro Greco, Erich Groat, Teresa Guasti, Liliane Haegeman, Richard Kayne, Rita Manzini, Luigi Rizzi, Philippe Schlenker, Vassilios Spyropoulos, Markus Steinbach, Aleksandra Vercauteren, Mirta Vernice, Ming Xiang, four anonymous reviewers, and Anne Mark for her valuable help in editing this volume.

This book is dedicated to Sara and Giuliano, the two significant others of this long story.

Introduction

This book owes its title to a simple idea, whose many ramifications we will explore. In a nutshell, the idea is that words are special because they can provide a label for free when they merge with some other category. This special power of words is exemplified by the familiar head-complement configuration, as in (1).

(1) a. {saw, {a man}}

    b.

      saw   a man

Here, the structure that is created when the word (verb) *saw* and the phrase *a man* are merged receives a label from the verb—namely, it is a VP.

One idea that unifies the linguistic analyses presented in this book is that a word can provide the label for the newly created structure even in the case of Internal Merge (movement). This has important consequences, because movement of a word is special in one respect: it can "relabel" the structure, in the precise sense that the structure resulting from movement of a word can have a label different from that of the premovement structure. The new label is the one provided by the word that has moved. The simplest illustration is provided by free relatives, as in (2).

(2) I read what you read t_{what}.

In (2), the word *what*, which is a D, provides the label, so the structure *what you read* ends up being a DP, which is selected by the matrix verb *read*. We call cases like (2) *re*labeling cases because, metaphorically speaking, the movement of *what* turns a structure with label C (the premovement clause) into a structure with label D.

In this book, we will argue that relabeling cases triggered by the movement of a word are pervasive in the syntax of natural languages and that identifying them as such sheds lights on phenomena like relativization, islands and successive cyclicity, and Minimality effects.

We discuss the relabeling cases in the context of an explicit theory of labeling according to which the label results from the Probing operation (and not from Merge): more precisely, it is the probe that provides the label. A corollary is that, if no probe is present, the structure created by Merge remains label-less. We will show that this happens in a very restricted, yet important, set of cases.

The book is organized as follows.

Chapter 1 sets the stage for the theory of labeling that we endorse in this book. In order to claim that words have a labeling power, one must assume that (i) they have a theoretical significance and (ii) they are intrinsically endowed with a category to transmit. The correctness of these two assumptions, and ultimately of a traditional lexicalist stand, is discussed here in the light of a number of empirical and theoretical arguments. As we will explain, what is crucial for the analyses we will propose is the assumption that category determination is presyntactic. This we will express by saying that words enter syntax already equipped with a label. (Alternatively, one could say that, in order to enter into the syntactic derivation, a root must come bundled with a categorizing head.)

Having assumed that words enter into syntax with a category, in chapter 2 we explore their role in the syntactic structure. We first review the history of recent phrase structure theories, focusing on the X-bar schema and the departure from it in early Minimalist work. In particular, we discuss what we call the *symmetry problem*: a Minimalist notion of Merge is necessarily symmetric, a fact at odds with what appears to be needed for derivations to work—namely, labeled syntactic objects. We claim that the fundamental asymmetry of most syntactic objects comes, not from Merge itself, but from the independent operation of Probing, by which a feature (the probe) requires another feature (the goal). When Merge results from a probing operation, it yields a labeled syntactic object. The relevant notion of label and the algorithm relating labels to probes, which are the basic tools of all the analyses performed in the book, are given in (3) and (4).

(3) *Label*

When two objects α and β are merged, a subset of the features of either α or β become the label of the syntactic object $\{\alpha, \beta\}$. A label
   a. can trigger further computation, and
   b. is visible from outside the syntactic object $\{\alpha, \beta\}$.

(4) *Probing Algorithm*

The label of a syntactic object $\{\alpha, \beta\}$ is the feature(s) that act(s) as a probe of the merging operation creating $\{\alpha, \beta\}$.

(4) says that the label of any Merge output is always the feature asymmetrically triggering Merge. This simple algorithm can capture the core cases traditionally described by X-bar theory if every word is intrinsically a probe. If this is assumed, then a word, being a probe by definition, always activates the algorithm in (4), and its categorial feature provides the label for the output. For example, each time a head (= word) is externally merged with its complement, the head is bound to project, providing a label for the newly created object. Crucially, even when a word is *internally* merged, it projects. As noted earlier, this is what we call *re*labeling.

In chapters 3–5, we explore the empirical and theoretical consequences of these basic assumptions, in various areas: relativization structures, islands and successive-cyclic movement, and Minimality.

Chapter 3 is devoted to relativization structures, which indeed represent a traditional labeling puzzle, since relatives are clauses but have a nominal distribution. The switch from being a clause to being a nominal expression involves a labeling change (relabeling). We start with free relatives, where the application of the theory based on the definition of label and on the Probing Algorithm is most straightforward. We then turn to externally headed relatives, where the theory based on (3) and (4) derives the facts if it is coupled with a nonstandard analysis of noun complementation. We argue extensively that this analysis, by which nouns do not take complements the way verbs do, is welcome on independent grounds. We close chapter 3 by extending the labeling approach to two more relativization constructions, reduced relatives and internally headed relatives.

In chapter 4, we show that the relabeling approach sheds light on a classic problem investigated in the generative tradition at least since Ross's (1967) seminal dissertation: island constraints. The issue of island constraints is strictly related to the issue of successive-cyclic movement, since island effects plausibly arise whenever successive-cyclic movement is banned. Starting with this fact, we build on the idea that successive-cyclic movement creates a label-less layer that is destroyed later in the derivation. This idea is very natural in an approach that relates labeling and probing: since there is no obvious probe for successive-cyclic movement, there is no way to determine the label. Unprobed Internal Merge results in a structure with no label. As we will show, the label-less layer created by successive-cyclic movement is not compatible with relabeling (the operation that is responsible for relative clause formation). This allows us to explain why free relatives and full relative clauses are strong islands for extraction, and thus derive a central aspect of the Complex NP Constraint.

This account of island effects extends to adjunct structures like conditionals and *when*-clauses, as these can be reduced to free relatives. We also discuss the status of so-called peripheral adverbial clauses. We propose that these structures are the output of another possible instance of unprobed Merge: unprobed External Merge. Being unprobed, the merging operation attaching these clauses to the main clause yields a label-less syntactic object. This explains why peripheral adverbial clauses can only occur at the external boundary of the matrix clause (the resulting label-less layer is tolerated because it does not need to be selected). Furthermore, it explains why such clauses are islands (given their high positioning, *wh*-extraction out of them would be an instance of lowering movement).

Finally, chapter 4 deals with the other horn of the Complex NP Constraint: the impossibility of extracting out of what looks like a clausal complement of a noun. In our approach, which reduces strong islandhood to a conflict between relabeling and a label-less layer, nothing automatically explains this part of the Complex NP Constraint. We argue that this is a welcome consequence, because the degradation observed when a category is extracted out of a clausal complement of a noun is a spurious fact, due to a generalized garden path effect (a clausal complement of a noun is initially misanalyzed as a relative clause). This analysis is supported by crosslinguistic observations as well as by the results of two novel experiments monitoring the eye movements of participants reading minimally different relative clauses and clausal complements of nouns.

Chapter 5 focuses on another predicted property of unprobed *Internal* Merge, concerning Minimality. The difference between Internal Merge and External Merge is that when the merged element has already been merged once, it must be related to the internal copy, or, using traditional terminology, to the foot of the chain. This gives rise to intervention effects, which hold every time Internal Merge takes place, no matter whether it is probed or not.

When there is a probe, it naturally restricts the search of the copy, and only an element bearing the probed feature and c-commanding the copy intervenes and disrupts the derivation. This is classical Relativized Minimality. On the other hand, if no feature is probed, any element intervening and sharing *any* feature with the highest copy disrupts the computation. This is what we call *Gross* Minimality. We review three facts that, although they can be shown to be related, have so far lacked a unified account. These are the ban on preverbal subjects in direct questions in Italian and other Romance languages (and despite appearances in English as well!), subject-object asymmetries in relatives and questions in child grammar, and subject intervention in free relatives in Romance. We explain all these cases as instances of unprobed movement restricted, as our labeling approach predicts, by Gross Minimality. We also describe another characteristic of Gross Minimality that is expected under our approach: its effects should be gradient rather than categorical. In this way, we explain a number of fine-grained effects of the featural endowment of interveners in child grammar that have been described in the literature.

Chapter 6 concludes the book, opening possible directions for further investigation.

1 A Plea for Words

1.1 Introduction

In this initial chapter, we will discuss the very notion of "word" by exploring the feasibility of the view (often called *lexicalism*) that there is a neat division of labor between morphology and syntax. Morphology comes first and assembles morphemes into words, while syntax, which comes later, assembles the output of morphology (words) into phrases and sentences. Of course, according to the lexicalist view, there are some notions that are relevant for both morphology and syntax (say, agreement), since syntax and morphology do interface. However, these notions do not always match in the two components (e.g., the syntactic and morphological notions of agreement or head do not need to overlap), so a distinction should be maintained.

As recently as 10 or 20 years ago, a book like this would not have needed a chapter discussing the feasibility of the lexicalist view, since this view was largely (although not universally) accepted in formal linguistics work. However, nowadays there are very influential approaches that deny that a division of labor between syntax and morphology can be drawn. Typically, in antilexicalist models it is the existence of an autonomous morphology module that is denied, as expressed by the popular slogan "syntax all the way down." These models share the assumption that the same rules that are responsible for assembling words into phrases are responsible for assembling morphemes into words. If so, a word can no longer be defined as the output of morphology and the input to syntax, and there is room for such radical claims as "The concept 'word' has no theoretical significance in the grammar at all" (Julien 2007, 212) or "Lexicalism is dead, deceased, demised, no more, passed on..." (Marantz 1997, 202).

One "syntax-all-the-way-down" approach is Distributed Morphology, a framework that explicitly assumes that phrases are built directly out of morphemes, with no intervening notion of word (see Embick and Noyer 2007 and references cited therein for a presentation). Words are just a special class of phrases, and (ideally at least) no formal operation should refer to words by treating them as distinct from morphemes and phrases. However, Distributed Morphology is not the only framework that rejects the traditional assumption that syntax projects from the lexicon through words.[1] For example, a core principle of Nanosyntax (e.g., Ramchand 2008, Starke 2009) is that syntactic operations apply uniformly to the categories that traditional approaches would call morphemes, words, and phrases. In particular, in Nanosyntactic approaches words cannot be seen as the input to syntax, since words, and even morphemes, typically correspond to an entire subtree rather than to a terminal node.

A reason why antilexicalist approaches are popular is that syntax-all-the-way-down seems to be the null hypothesis. Everything else being equal, a theory that assumes just one set of rules for both "morphological" and "syntactic" operations is simpler than a theory that assumes two different set of rules. Also, it is clear that morphology contains generative rules of combination that appear prima facie very similar to syntactic rules. Still, the null hypothesis is not necessarily the right hypothesis, even more so if one takes seriously the thesis that the language faculty is modular. For example, to the best of our knowledge, no one has ever proposed that phonological and syntactic rules are one and the same, although syntax and phonology share some concepts (such as dominance and containment), the two modules interface, and a level in which syntactic and prosodic entities correspond has been proposed (see Nespor and Vogel 1986, Selkirk 1984).

This means that the issue of how modular syntax is with respect to morphology is to a large extent (as usual) a matter of empirical adequacy.

Obviously, our goal in this chapter is not to settle the question of whether lexicalism is right or wrong *in general*. Our more limited goal is to explore the feasibility of two assumptions that underlie the theory of labeling that we will introduce in chapter 2 and whose consequences we examine in the rest of the book.

(i) There are two separate modules for morphological and syntactic structures, and the output of morphological representations (for concreteness, call it *words*) is the input to syntactic representations.
(ii) A word, that which is delivered by morphology to syntax, is intrinsically endowed with a categorial feature.

Given their relevance for the theory of labeling that we will propose, we focus on (i) and (ii), while we do not discuss other aspects of antilexicalist approaches that are not directly relevant for us. For example, we remain neutral on whether syntactic terminals contain phonological material or just abstract syntactic features realized through late insertion when the relevant portion of the syntactic derivation is over. Similarly, it is not crucial for our proposal whether words are listed as such in the lexicon or only morphemes are.

To summarize, we investigate (i) and (ii) to show the feasibility of the assumption that a word, defined as the output of the morphology module, is endowed with a categorial feature when it enters syntax and may transmit it to the syntactic object that it contributes to forming.

We start with (i), which concerns the general architecture of the theory. Notoriously, this is slippery terrain, because global comparisons between theories are made difficult by the fact that the "everything else being equal" condition cannot be maintained. As a result, our conclusions about (i) will be somewhat open. Since (ii) is more specific, we believe evidence supporting or questioning it is easier to find.

1.2   No Morphology Module?

Some methodological considerations support the antilexicalist approaches that deny the existence of an autonomous morphology module. To begin with, as noted earlier, the claim that the same rules govern word formation and phrase formation is the null hypothesis. Furthermore, there is a fair amount of overlap between the vocabulary of morphology and the vocabulary of syntax (notions like noun, verb, head, singular/plural, and tense are relevant for both components), so assuming two separate modules introduces a certain amount of redundancy. If tenable, then, the antilexicalist model should be preferable.

However, there are reasons why until recently morphology was standardly assumed to be relatively autonomous from syntax, and why this view is still endorsed by influential scholars. In the following paragraphs, we present considerations supporting lexicalism, taken from important contributions by Ackema and Neeleman (2004) and Williams (2007).

Under syntax-all-the-way-down approaches, there is only one set of structure-building operations, which apply both to morphemes and to words, so properties and constraints holding at the word level should hold equally at the clausal level. Still, it is not difficult to come up with examples indicating that there are nontrivial differences between the two levels. Take the concept of "head," for instance. It is certainly tempting to conflate the syntactic and morphological notions of "head." However, as Williams observes, this raises the problem of explaining why in many languages, English being an obvious example, the head is positioned differently in the two systems. English words are head-final, whereas English phrases are head-initial. At a minimum, examples like these require weakening the strong claim that words are created out of morphemes by the same operation that creates phrases out of words. In doing so, they reduce the appeal of antilexicalist approaches.

Another potential concern is that, if what is normally called a phrase and what is normally called a word are similar objects (they are just two clusters of morphemes, with a different level of internal complexity), in principle a phrase should be able to head (in the technical sense of X-bar theory) another phrase, but this does not happen. (We return to this type of issue in chapter 2, which is entirely devoted to phrase structure theory.) So, some distinction between levels of complexity of clusters of morphemes seems necessary as far as X-bar theory is concerned, but introducing this distinction might be a tacit reinstatement of the notion of word.

In fact, "head" is not the only case where the word system (morphology) and the phrase system (syntax) display nontrivial differences concerning the same construct.

Another example discussed by Williams is *self*-anaphors. As is well-known (see Chomsky 1981 and much following work), an anaphor needs a local antecedent, but this does not need to be the sister node of a *phrasal* anaphor.

(1) John told stories about the destruction of himself.

However, the antecedent of a *lexical* anaphor must be its sister node. This is shown by the fact that the only meaning of (2) is 'John told stories about one's destruction of oneself'.

(2) John told self-destruction stories.

If anaphors in the word system behaved just like anaphors in the clausal system, in (2) *self*- should be able to take *John* as an antecedent, triggering the interpretation 'John told stories about the destruction of himself'. We mention this specific example because Williams claims that it reveals a fundamental difference between the morphological system and the syntactic system. The latter has nonlocal dependencies, while the former does not. Given that the existence of nonlocal dependencies (including movement) is a fundamental property of the syntax of natural languages, its absence in the word system raises a red flag for any attempt at reducing morphology to syntax.

A proponent of syntax-all-the-way-down approaches would reply by claiming that movement is indeed attested in word formation in other cases. Baker's (1988) syntactic analysis of noun incorporation is a classic example. Applied to English, this type of analysis amounts to saying that compound formation (as in, say, *city center*) results from movement of one word (here, *city*) that adjoins to another (*center*), much as in familiar cases of head movement in syntax—say, V to T. This would explain why head directionality appears to differ at the word and phrase levels without having to posit two separate notions of head. However, Ackema and Neeleman (2007) discuss several problematic cases for the hypothesis that complex words can be created by syntactic movement. One involves nouns like *driver*. Under a morphological analysis, *driver* is a complex noun, which, like any other noun, projects an NP in syntax (no matter how it was formed in morphology). Its argument is licensed through *of*-insertion, just as in the case of noncomplex nouns (e.g., *photo of Earth*); see (3a). However, under the movement analysis of *driver* (see (3b)), *drive* should start out in a VP. Since case is available for complements of verbs, the argument of *drive* is incorrectly predicted to appear in the accusative; that is, *of*-insertion is not expected.

(3) a. [$_{NP}$ [$_N$ drive-er] of a truck]
    b. *[$_{NP}$ [$_N$ [$_V$ drive]-er] [$_{VP}$ t_V [$_{NP}$ a truck]]]

Instances of head movement in syntax do not have any effect on case-assigning capacities. We illustrate this in (4) with Italian. (4a) shows the derivation of the complex noun *guidatore* (*guida(t)-ore* 'driver') under the analysis that word formation results from verb movement. In (4a), much as in English, *of*-insertion is necessary. (4b) is an indisputable case of verb movement, as shown by the fact that the verb has crossed the subject (the gerund *guidando* has moved to the left periphery, as happens in the so-called Aux-to-C construction; see Rizzi 1982). In (4b), *of*-insertion is not required (in fact, it leads to ungrammaticality).

(4) a. [$_{NP}$ [$_N$ [$_V$ guida(t)]-ore] *(di) [$_{VP}$ t_V [$_{NP}$ un camion]]]
        driv-er   *(of)   a   truck
    b. [$_C$ [$_V$ Guidando]] [$_{TP}$ tu t_V [$_{VP}$ t_V (*di) [$_{NP}$ un camion]]]
        driving   you   (*of)   a   truck
      'Since you were driving a truck…'

As Ackema and Neeleman observe, the syntactic approach might tackle the *of*-insertion problem by assuming that an incorporated head loses its case-assigning capacities, but this only shows that reducing morphology to syntax may require some ad hoc assumptions.

Another general point raised by Ackema and Neeleman concerns restrictions on syntactic operations, like the requirement that the landing site of movement c-command the base position and the fact that movement cannot occur out of islands. If a complex word is created via syntactic movement, this word-level operation should be sensitive to the same constraints. In contrast, if a complex word is formed in a separate morphology module, these restrictions are not expected to apply. As a matter of fact, nominal compounds can be interpreted in ways that are not compatible with a syntactic analysis. Take a hypothetical example like *drawer picture*. Since (at least in English) syntactic movement can take place out of complement position but not out of subject or adjunct position, the only interpretation for this compound should be the one resulting from the underlying configuration *picture of a drawer*; that is, the compound should indicate a picture that depicts a drawer. However, nominal compounds are interpreted quite freely: for example, given appropriate contexts, *drawer picture* can mean 'picture suitable for a drawer', 'picture that was attached to a drawer', and so on. At least for these interpretations, then, there must be a mechanism forming nominal compounds that does not depend on syntactic movement. This reduces the appeal of the syntax-all-the-way-down hypothesis, since a mechanism independent from syntax seems hardly avoidable at least in some cases.

Let us finally discuss and avoid a possible misunderstanding. Even if words can be defined as that which the morphological module delivers to syntax, there are cases where it is difficult to decide which sequence of morphemes counts as a word in a given situation. Sometime this difficulty is taken as an indication that the concept of word is unreliable in itself. For example, Julien (2007) seems to imply this when she notes that markers of tense, aspect, and modality in Haitian Creole are analyzed as prefixes on the verb by Sylvain (1936) but as auxiliaries by Spears (1990). So, the former scholar sees a single word where the latter scholar sees two separate words.

Of course, we do not deny that this type of difficulty may emerge, even more so in underdescribed languages. However, we think that this type of problem is not specific to the concept of word. Take the notion of verb phrase, which is a fundamental notion in syntax. It is not always easy to identify which sequence of words belongs to the VP. First of all, in languages that display a flexible word order, identifying the VP is not always straightforward. For example, in Saito 1985, now a classic work on Japanese syntax, the existence of the VP had to be argued for, instead of being simply assumed. Polysynthetic languages can pose an even bigger challenge, although, as discussed by Baker (1996), even in these languages affected objects form a tight construction with the verb. Even in a rigid word order language like English, identifying the VP can be nontrivial. Hornstein and Nunes (2008) discuss in great detail the consequences of the fact that standard tests like VP-fronting (see (5)), VP-ellipsis (see (6)), and substitution by *do so*–anaphora (see (7)) seem to identify either head + complement alone or head + complement + adjunct(s) as the maximal projection of the verb.

(5) a. John could eat the cake in the yard, and eat the cake in the yard he did.

   b. John could eat the cake in the yard, and eat the cake he did in the yard.

(6) John ate a cake in the yard with a fork and...
   a. Bill did too.
   b. Bill did in the hall.
   c. Bill did with a spoon.
   d. Bill did in the hall with a spoon.

(7) John ate a cake in the yard with a fork and...
   a. Bill did so too.
   b. Bill did so in the hall.
   c. Bill did so with a spoon.
   d. Bill did so in the hall with a spoon.

These examples show that deciding where exactly the boundary of the VP lies is not straightforward. In fact, VP-adjunction (and adjunction in general) is still an area in which general consensus is lacking (but see Hornstein 2009, Hornstein and Nunes 2008, and section 4.7 for some remarks). Consider also the debate over the VP-internal subject hypothesis (for a review, see Koopman and Sportiche 1991, McCloskey 1997) or over the existence of little v (e.g., Chomsky 1995b, Kratzer 1996).

All these issues, in part still open, concern the difficulty of defining clear boundaries for a central constituent such as V/vP. Notwithstanding these language-internal and crosslinguistic problems with VP identification, most researchers think that abandoning the notion of verb phrase would be like throwing the baby out with the bath water. We think the same for the notion of word. The fact that it may be difficult to decide exactly where the boundary of a word lies is not a strong argument against retaining this notion in the linguistic toolkit. Rather, it is the type of problem that should motivate linguistic research.

In this section, we considered the claim that there is no autonomous morphology module. Although this claim has the appeal of being the null hypothesis, even a pseudorandom selection of representative cases from the literature shows that it faces serious complications.

We do not think these complications show that the syntax-all-the-way-down hypothesis, although appealing, is necessarily wrong. Solutions can be given, but typically they require somehow loosening the idea that no separation exists between the morphology and syntax modules. All in all, it seems clear to us that the jury is still out on lexicalism, despite the ardent antilexicalist claims quoted above.

This leaves room for a proposal that builds on the notion that a word is what is delivered to syntax by a partially autonomous morphological module. We can now move to assumption (ii): the idea that words entering syntax are intrinsically endowed with a categorial feature.

1.3   Words Have an Intrinsic Category

In this section, we consider assumption (ii), repeated here.

(ii) A word, that which is delivered by morphology to syntax, is intrinsically endowed with a categorial feature.

The Categorization Assumption, a basic tenet of Distributed Morphology, can be seen as an explicit rebuttal to assumption (ii). Embick and Noyer (2007, 296) summarize this assumption as follows:

> [R]oots [to be identified with members of the traditional parts of speech such as nouns, verbs, and adjectives] never appear 'bare'; they must always be categorized by virtue of being in a local relationship with one of the category-defining functional heads (v, n, etc.)....In this way...so-called lexical categories...are always syntactically complex, consisting minimally of a Root and a category-defining functional head.

There is a sense in which the perspective of Distributed Morphology is exactly the opposite of the perspective we will assume in this book. We will argue that a word (be it a functional or an open class word) is intrinsically endowed with a categorial feature and can always transmit this feature to the structure in which it is inserted. On the contrary, under the Categorization Assumption, a root (which is Distributed Morphology's closest counterpart to the concept of open class word) receives a category from the structure it is inserted into, since intrinsically a root has no categorial feature.

In this section, we mainly (but not uniquely) use psycholinguistic arguments to support assumption (ii). First, we should clarify that our arguments are *not* the same type of argument traditionally used to support the psychological reality of words. For example, the following passage from Sapir (1921, 34) is often quoted as evidence that words have psychological reality:

> Linguistic experience, both as expressed in standardized, written form and as tested in daily usage, indicates overwhelmingly that there is not, as a rule, the slightest difficulty in bringing the word to consciousness as a psychological reality. No more convincing test could be desired than this, that the naïve Indian, quite unaccustomed to the concept of the written word, has nevertheless no serious difficulty in dictating a text to a linguistic student word by word; he tends, of course, to run his words together as in actual speech, but if he is called to a halt and is made to understand what is desired, he can

readily isolate the words as such, repeating them as units. He regularly refuses, on the other hand, to isolate the radical or grammatical element, on the ground that it "makes no sense."

At the end of this passage, Sapir adds the following footnote:

These oral experiences, which I have had time and again as a field student of American Indian languages, are very neatly confirmed by personal experiences of another sort. Twice I have taught intelligent young Indians to write their own languages according to the phonetic system which I employ. They were taught merely how to render accurately the sounds as such. Both had some difficulty in learning to break up a word into its constituent sounds, but none whatever in determining the words. This they both did with spontaneous and complete accuracy. In the hundreds of pages of manuscript Nootka text that I have obtained from one of these young Indians the words, whether abstract relational entities like English *that* and *but* or complex sentence-words like the Nootka example quoted above, are, practically without exception, isolated precisely as I or any other student would have isolated them. Such experiences with naïve speakers and recorders do more to convince one of the definitely plastic unity of the word than any amount of purely theoretical argument.

We believe that, suggestive as they are, these remarks are far from conclusive evidence for the issue at hand. First, they remain anecdotal, and, to the best of our knowledge, they have not been replicated (or, for that matter, proved wrong) in controlled experimental settings that are the gold standard in current psycholinguistic research. Furthermore, even if these findings could be replicated reliably, they would not necessarily indicate that the concept of word is needed to describe the linguistic competence of a speaker. As a matter of fact, the ability to segment speech into wordlike units does not necessarily tap the linguistic skills that are used in language production or comprehension, since word identification is a conscious, offline task that is susceptible to metacognitive strategies. Sapir's observations indicate that the notion "wordhood" is likely to play a role in a theory explaining why only certain sequences of morphemes are felt as natural and complete units by a speaker. However, word identification is not the same as speaking or comprehending. In order to conclude that the notion "wordhood" is necessary to describe linguistic (as opposed to metalinguistic) competence, we need to show that in online automatic language processing words, *by virtue of being words*, are processed differently from, say, morphemes or phrases.

We think there are several psycholinguistic observations of this kind, which support the idea that words (including open class words) have a privileged status with respect to other morphemes. These observations also suggest that words enter syntax with a category and may transmit it.

One piece of evidence involves language pathologies in which a brain-injured patient can speak using correct grammar, but cannot produce appropriate nouns (anomia; see Miceli, Giustolisi, and Caramazza 1991) or verbs (averbia; see Ardila and Rosselli 1994). Crucially, these are category-specific deficits, as they affect the production of only verbs or only nouns. For example, patients with anomia cannot produce nouns for objects they are familiar with even if they have a preserved morphosyntax in general and in the nominal domain in particular. Similarly for patients with averbia.

These disorders are a challenge to the Categorization Assumption, at least in its strongest form, since, under that theory, category determination for a certain root is reduced to the syntactic environment in which that root is inserted. One example can illustrate this point. Patient EBA (see Shapiro and Caramazza 2003 and references therein) appears to have a preserved nominal syntax but is extremely impaired at naming nouns, as measured by her performance on the Boston Cookie Theft picture. We reproduce this picture in figure 1.1 (taken from the Boston Diagnostic Aphasia Examination; see Goodglass and Kaplan 1983) together with EBA's verbal description in (8).

(8) EBA: Oh Lordy, she's making a mess. She let the thing go, and it's getting on the floor. They're stealing something. He's falling; he's gonna hurt himself. She's cleaning these things. She's looking at him falling, and she's gonna get some of the stuff he's giving her.

Figure 1.1
The *Cookie Theft picture* (Goodglass and Kaplan 1983). Copyright permission granted by Pro-Ed, Inc., Texas.

It is not obvious how the Categorization Assumption can explain why patients like EBA have a selective noun deficit with no concurrent syntactic breakdown at the DP level. As a matter of fact, the deficit cannot have to do with root retrieval in general, since it is category-specific. Nor can it be a deficit in nominal syntax, since nominal syntax is preserved, at least to the extent that one can judge from the patient's performance (including the complex sentence (8)). This leaves little room for rejecting the traditional view that words enter syntax already equipped with a category. In fact, the dominant view in clinical linguistics is that "spared naming and comprehension of nouns in the presence of impaired naming and comprehension of verbs in some patients, and the opposite pattern by other patients, indicate that one of the organizing principles of the lexical system concerns the grammatical class of words" (Hillis and Caramazza 1991, 2081).

So, a first potential challenge for the Categorization Assumption coming from clinical linguistics is posed by patients with preserved syntax but category-specific deficits. A second is posed by patients who display the mirror-image pattern: impaired syntax but preserved production of nouns or verbs. Several agrammatic patients have been described who cannot produce grammatical sentences, but can unproblematically produce nouns and verbs in isolation in repetition or picture-naming tasks. For example, Friedmann and Grodzinsky (1997) report patients who show no problem in repeating inflected verbs in isolation but are impaired at completing a simple sentence by producing the correctly inflected form of the verb. In Friedmann and Grodzinsky's study, the patient listens a source clause like *Yesterday the boy walked* (in Hebrew) and is expected to complete the target sentence *Tomorrow the boy...* by producing the verb *walk* in the future tense (in Hebrew). If a root must be inserted into a syntactic context in order to receive a grammatical category, this pattern of dissociation between production in isolation and production in a sentence is not really expected, as agrammatic patients should not be able to produce the syntactic environment that would categorize roots to begin with.

In principle, there are ways to make the findings from clinical linguistics compatible with the Categorization Assumption. For example, one might claim that the piece of structure that "categorizes" a root (say, the v or n abstract head) is so minimal that it is present even in the very impoverished production of agrammatic patients. In the same vein, one might argue that the deficit of patients like EBA only affects the category-defining functional head that transforms the root into a noun, while leaving the rest of the DP unaffected. While this move is a possible reaction to the clinical findings, it would make the Categorization Assumption virtually unfalsifiable.

As priming effects have been widely used to investigate the structure of the human mental lexicon, they can also be used to confront the Categorization Assumption. Most research concentrates on semantic priming (which is typically facilitating) and orthographic priming (which is typically inhibitory) in lexical decision or in reading tasks. However, the role of the grammatical class (verb, noun) to which primes and probes belong has also been considered. One conclusion is that words sharing the same root facilitate each other even if they belong to different grammatical classes (nouns and verbs); this clearly demonstrates that *at some level of processing* the representation of the common root is unmarked for grammatical class (Deutsch, Frost, and Forster 1998). This result is consistent with the Categorization Assumption, but also with other theories that assume rules of word formation in the lexicon/morphology. However, Crepaldi (2007) reports results showing that semantic priming may be constrained by grammatical class: for example, a noun facilitates reading of a semantically related noun but a verb does *not* facilitate reading of a semantically related verb. As prime and probe are words in isolation, this introduces another challenge for the Categorization Assumption: under this assumption, it seems necessary to say that the category-defining functional head accompanies a word even if the word appears without a syntactic context, as in priming studies.

In language acquisition, as well, there is evidence suggesting (at least prima facie) that words have a privileged status and enter syntax already equipped with a categorial label. Obviously, children start speaking by uttering words rather than morphemes or phrases. More relevantly, children seem to distinguish among open class words, as they produce nouns before verbs, and verbs before adjectives (see, e.g., Caselli, Casadio, and Bates 2001). Earlier mastery of the category "noun" has also been reported in comprehension studies (see Waxman and Booth 2003), as 11-month-olds categorize invented nouns as referring to objects in the immediate environment but cannot categorize other invented words (e.g., adjectives) as referring to different classes of meaning (say, salient properties of objects). Unless it is postulated that children start with a totally different system from adults, the Categorization Assumption requires saying that, when children produce their first isolated nouns (at about 12 months), they master at least the skeleton of the DP structure. While this is not impossible, it is not immediately consistent with the observation that children produce their first DPs of determiner + noun form in canonical DP positions only a year and a half later, at age 2;6 (Valian 1986) and have a defective DP structure (e.g., they can omit determiners) until age 3 (e.g., Guasti et al. 2008).

This evidence from language acquisition is reinforced by studies of very special cases of child production, home-sign systems. As extensively studied by Goldin-Meadow and colleagues (see Goldin-Meadow 2011 for a review), profoundly deaf children who are not exposed to sign language and do not receive (successful) speech therapy, do not develop a complete language. However, they invent gesture systems with a stable, albeit very limited, lexicon, and their multigesture production shows some regularities. In particular, in a single-case study Goldin-Meadow et al. (1994) report that a deaf child (David) maintained a distinction between nouns and verbs in his early production. He did so by using one set of gestures as nouns and a separate set as verbs. Later (starting at age 3:3), David could use the same gesture as noun and verb, but he distinguished the two uses by altering the form of the gesture and its position in a gesture sentence. At this age, David also showed mastery of the category adjective. So, the observation that a distinction between noun and verb is attested before the two-word stage is replicated in the very atypical circumstance in which the child is developing only a rudimentary linguistic system. (In this specific respect, home-sign systems are not dissimilar from pidgins, where the basic part-of-speech distinctions are well-attested, despite the absence of a stable clausal syntax.)

What most of the cases we have reviewed have in common is that categorial distinctions (at least those concerning verbs, nouns, and adjectives) are well-attested even when the syntactic structure that is supposed to be responsible for category determination is not detectable, as in language pathology and in very early stages of the acquisition of complete and incomplete linguistic systems. The Categorization Assumption might postulate the existence of an invisible syntactic structure responsible for category determination, but it requires independent justification that is difficult to find.

Another general consideration suggesting that words are lexical units equipped with an intrinsic category is that, when words move and the immediate environment in which they occur changes, they retain the category they have in their base position. Consider a sentence with *wh*-splitting like (9) in French.

(9) Combien   faut-il   que j'achète de livres?
    how.many needs-it   that I buy   of books
    'How many books should I buy?'

Plausibly, in this sentence *combien* 'how many' keeps its category (say, that of a quantificational determiner) in its displaced position, even if it is no longer in a DP environment. The most straightforward prediction of approaches that claim that words are provided with a category only as a function of the syntactic structure into which they are inserted is that there should be cases where words change category when they move in isolation. However, we know of no cases like that. Of course, scholars who deny that words have an intrinsic label have an obvious way out: namely, assuming that what appears to be movement of a bare word is in fact movement of the larger (albeit invisible) structure that categorizes the word (say, v, n, etc.). While this is possible, the burden of proof should be on these scholars. Furthermore, the concern we expressed earlier comes up again—namely, that the proposal might become unfalsifiable.

We mention the permanence of a word's category under movement because it is crucial for the many cases of (re)labeling that we will look at in this book. Constructions like free relatives and many others show that, far from *receiving* a category in the displaced position, the word *transmits* its own category to the structure it is inserted into when it moves.

1.4 Conclusion

This chapter sets the stage for the theory of labeling we will endorse in this book. A key feature of the theory is that words are special in at least one respect: when they merge with another category, they can provide the label for the newly formed object. This is immediately visible in familiar head-complement configurations, but we will show that the same labeling power of words is responsible for the creation of relativization structures of many different types. The labeling power of words will be captured in our framework by a rule called the Probing Algorithm, which we introduce in chapter 2 and continue discussing throughout the book.

However, in order to claim that words have a labeling power, one must assume that (i) they have theoretical significance and (ii) they are intrinsically endowed with a category to transmit. The feasibility of these two assumptions is what we discussed in this chapter. We do not hope to have convinced all readers that (i) and (ii) are necessarily the right assumptions. However, we hope to have amassed enough evidence to convince even the skeptical reader that a version of lexicalism that postulates a relative independence of the morphology module from the syntax module should be given a chance. For the sake of this skeptical reader, we should stress once more what is not negotiable in our approach and what is less central. What cannot be dispensed with is the assumption that category determination is presyntactic. In our view, this assumption is most naturally expressed by saying that the bundle of features that constitutes the output of the morphology module (a word, in our pretty traditional, perhaps old-fashioned terminology) contains a categorial feature.

However, the idea that category determination is presyntactic can be expressed in different ways. For example, as one reviewer pointed out, we might also assume that a root must enter into the syntactic derivation bundled with a categorizing head. We do agree that assuming a categorizing head, which crucially operates before syntax kicks in, is consistent with the relabeling approach that we will pursue, as long as this unit (the root plus the categorizing head) is recognized as having labeling properties.

Be that as it may, that words (in the sense just introduced) come with a category on their sleeve is the starting point of our story. Let us see where this leads.

2 Labels from X-Bar Theory to Phrase Structure Theory

2.1 Introduction

In chapter 1, we explained why we stick to the traditional assumption that the concept of word is a genuine primitive of the theory of grammar. In this chapter, we explore how words enter syntax and how they combine to form phrases and clauses. In other terms, we deal with a traditional topic in the theory of syntax: phrase structure theory.

The chapter is organized as follows. We first review the recent history of phrase structure theory, focusing in particular on the X-bar schema (section 2.2) and its abandonment in early Minimalist work (section 2.3). We then discuss two basic problems with the Minimalist definition of Merge: what we call the *symmetry* problem (the fact that simple Merge does not yield any automatic notion of head and projection; section 2.4) and the *linearization* problem (the difficulty of integrating a Linear Correspondence Axiom approach to word order into bare phrase structure theory; section 2.5). We then discuss whether labels should be defined *internally*, as part of the syntactic computation, or whether they are only needed *externally*, at the interface for interpretation. We argue for an internal definition (section 2.6) and discuss two labeling algorithms that have been proposed in recent years (sections 2.7 and 2.8), showing that they cannot qualify as an automatic device yielding labeled syntactic objects from a symmetric Merge operation. We finally propose a new algorithm, the *Probing Algorithm*, which assigns a central role to words (section 2.9). We claim that the introduction of this algorithm solves the problems previously encountered and at the same time makes some interesting and novel predictions. We close this chapter (section 2.10) by anticipating some of these predictions, which will be thoroughly discussed in the rest of the book.

2.2   The X-Bar Schema

The Government-Binding approach to the lexicon-syntax interface (see Chomsky 1981) was very simple and straightforward, in that it assumed two ingredients as primitives. One was the Projection Principle (Chomsky 1986), which states that properties of words are projected into the syntactic structure. The other was the X-bar schema (Chomsky 1970, Jackendoff 1977), according to which this projection is filtered by a rigid, universal, and hierarchical structure, reproduced in (1).

(1)

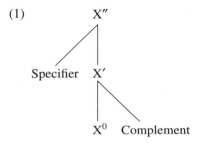

This schema means that each word can head a phrase, projecting its categorial and other features upward at most two levels. Moreover, each phrase is headed by a word. Each component other than the maximum and minimum levels is optional. The schema is stated as a primitive and a universal, the atom of any syntactic structure. The only uncontroversial variable was the order of head and complement, which could vary from language to language (this is the Head Parameter; Stowell 1981, Travis 1984).

This approach has several advantages. First, the schema posits a single discrete model for any syntactic structure, allowing immediately for the infinite recursion property of natural languages. Second, it posits a fundamental asymmetry in phrase structure, identifying one element as the head, the "leading element" of any group of words. Third, it allows important typological predictions concerning word order variation and its tendency toward systematicity.

However, an approach like this cannot be maintained given a strong Minimalist stand. In Minimalist theorizing, the Inclusiveness Condition (Chomsky 1995b, 225) requires that syntax only deals with lexical entries and their properties, without adding any other object during the computation. However, the X-bar schema violates this condition: it preexists any lexical entry and filters the direct interface between lexicon and syntactic computation. Bar levels are particularly problematic. What are they? They are not lexical properties in any obvious sense but they display a specific syntax, so under the Inclusiveness Condition they should be discarded.

Moreover, the rigidity of the schema imposes a number of spurious or vacuous projections: in particular, a word cannot enter a syntactic derivation without projecting a phrase structure. This implies a great departure from the minimal assumption: even elements that really look like words, like *what* or *he*, must be analyzed as projecting into a phrase, which is nevertheless invisible and empty in most cases, as illustrated in (2).

(2)   D″

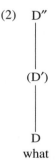

(D′)

D
what

Another problematic aspect of X-bar theory, even though it is probably less evident, concerns the notion of "head." This notion has a double life. On the one hand, a head is intended as the atom of any syntactic computation— namely, a bundle of features with a privileged status, possibly because it is merged as such from the lexicon (or numeration in more modern terminology). Under this conception, the term *head* is a close synonym of the term *word* or *lexical item*. In this book, we will abandon this opaque use of the term *head* and replace it with *word*. However, in X-bar theory, the term *head* also refers to a technical notion: it indicates the center of the phrase—that is, the category from which the entire phrase receives its core properties. This second notion of *head* is close to the notion of *label* (which is the term we will use here). In X-bar theory, a head in the first sense is also a head in the second sense, whence the use of the same term for two distinct, although to a large degree extensionally overlapping, concepts. However, this ambiguity is not innocuous, as we will show.

Much of the research on Merge, labels, and the like in the past 20 years can be described as an attempt to eliminate the X-bar schema while keeping some of its results—in particular, the Projection Principle and the asymmetry in phrase structure between the "leading element" (the head) and the categories with which it combines. We now turn to this research.

2.3   Bare Phrase Structure: Dealing with Inclusiveness

A crucial step toward eliminating bar levels from the set of theoretical objects is so-called *bare phrase structure*, a proposal by Chomsky (1995a,b), who builds on Muysken's (1982) relational view of phrase structure. In particular, Chomsky (1995b, 242) proposes that projection levels should be interpreted as pure descriptions of some structural configurations. More precisely:

(3) *Minimal projection* (X^0)
   A minimal projection is a category that does not project at all (a word).
   Maximal projection (X'')
   A maximal projection is a category that does not project any further.
   Intermediate projection (X')
   An intermediate projection is a category whose status is neither minimal nor maximal.

This approach, while minimally departing from X-bar theory, is already quite different. Importantly, here projection levels do not violate the Inclusiveness Condition, as syntax makes no reference to them. This approach also eliminates all the spurious or vacuous projections that were standard under the rigid view, in which a word X could not enter syntax without projecting all the way up to X''. By using relational definitions, a head in the sense of X-bar theory can be defined as a minimal nonmaximal projection. But unless a word combines with other material, there is no way to tell whether it is minimal or maximal. It is indeed both. Donati (2006) explores this property to derive the syntax of free relatives, typically headed by a minimal/maximal projection; we will return to this in section 3.2.

   In fact, early Minimalist work was somewhat inconsistent on how radical the elimination of the X-bar apparatus should be. On the one hand, Chomsky (1995b, 242) claimed that "there are no such entities as XP (X^{max}) or X^0 (X^{min}, terminal element)...though we may use these as informal notations." On the other hand, Chomsky (1995b) himself did not just use these concepts as "informal notations"; rather, he invoked them in the definition of core grammatical conditions. A notable example is the Chain Uniformity Condition (Chomsky 1993), which states that a chain must be uniform with regard to its phrase structure status. This condition was intended to prevent cases in which a head (intended in the X-bar sense) moves to a specifier position (intended in the X-bar sense). Hence, the X-bar theory notion of head survived in the early Minimalist period through its relational reformulation, not just as a taxonomic concept but as a component of the theoretical apparatus. It is not obvious that this was of any good to the theory, since the Chain Uniformity

Condition proved to be problematic (see Nunes 1998 for early discussion, and chapter 3 for many cases that are at odds with such a condition).

Another case in which the spirit of bare phrase structure theory would require a major departure from X-bar theory involves head movement. Under X-bar theory, it was unproblematic to state specific conditions for head movement (say, a tighter version of locality expressed via the Head Movement Constraint; see Travis 1984). However, this should not be possible under a strict version of bare phrase structure, since the X-bar apparatus is no longer available and purely relational definitions do not provide a rigid notion of head.

All in all, while the transition from X-bar theory to bare phrase structure was conceptually appealing, it raised various problems. Let us start with the most serious one: the *symmetry* problem.

2.4 The Symmetry Problem

The simplest definition of Merge is "combine," a binary operation putting two elements together. This is a clearly symmetric operation that does not yield any head—that is, any prevalence of one element over the other. Merge yields as its output something as simple as $\{\alpha, \beta\}$.

However, there is overwhelming evidence that a symmetric output is not desirable. When two linguistic elements are merged, typically one takes priority over the other. One aspect of the problem concerns projection: a syntactic object is typically hierarchically organized, with one of the two merged categories determining the distributional and interpretive properties of the object created by Merge. So, what is needed in addition to Merge is something that forces one of the two elements to project, or, in newer terms, to provide a label. Some asymmetry needs to be built into Merge or into its output. This is the aspect of the necessarily (a)symmetric output of Merge that we call the *labeling* problem, to which this book is basically devoted from section 2.7 on. However, the symmetry problem has another aspect as well, the *linearization* problem, which we deal with briefly in the next section.

2.5 The Linearization Problem

Kayne's (1994) Linear Correspondence Axiom (LCA), the algorithm that determines linearization of purely hierarchical syntactic structures, was explicitly formulated in X-bar theory terms (in fact, it can be seen as an attempt to derive some fundamental properties that in X-bar theory are simply stipulated). As the LCA translates asymmetric c-command into linear precedence, it is at odds with a purely symmetric operation like Merge.

In recent years, many proposals have tried to reconcile the LCA with the symmetric nature of Merge. The basic idea is that some asymmetry needs to be imposed on syntactic structures for linearization to be possible.

The weaker form of this idea posits this asymmetry requirement as a condition on Phonetic Form (PF). Symmetric syntactic objects (i.e., structures that c-command each other) can be generated by syntax. However, they must be destroyed by PF through movement operations, whose output is a structure where one object asymmetrically c-commands the other (see Moro 2000 and Barrie 2011 on Dynamic Antisymmetry; see, also Guimarães 2000 and others on "rolling movement").

This weak antisymmetric approach is attractive in that it is compatible with a minimal definition of Merge as an operation yielding symmetric syntactic objects, relegating asymmetry to a requirement holding at the PF interface. However, we see at least two problems. First, this approach presupposes that Merge can be symmetric but that movement must introduce an asymmetry. However, under the strictest Minimalist view, movement is just another instance of Merge, one in which α is merged with a category β that is contained within α—so technically, movement is Internal Merge. If movement is Internal Merge and Merge is symmetric, movement cannot have a rescuing symmetry-breaking role. Second, even if the unification of Merge and movement is not accepted, the weak antisymmetric approach can solve only one part of the symmetry problem, since it does not help with the labeling aspect. In principle, labeling determination has nothing to do with linearization: linearization does not tell how a label arises from an operation as simple as Merge.

The stronger version of the linearization proposal fares better from this point of view: it simply states that syntactic objects must be asymmetric, and it forces Merge to apply only to asymmetric pairs of objects. To obtain this result, a number of ways have been proposed to create asymmetric structures from simple symmetric Merge by employing so-called *Self-Merge* (Guimarães 2000, Kayne 2009). In particular, Self-Merge plays a role in avoiding the symmetry problem when two words merge: if one of the two merges with itself, an asymmetric structure results, as illustrated in (4).

(4) $\alpha \beta$
     $\{\alpha, \alpha\}$
     $\{\beta \{\alpha, \alpha\}\}$

Self-Merge can be effective in allowing a formulation of the LCA that is compatible with the simplified apparatus of bare phrase structure. It also introduces the required asymmetry into syntactic objects without complicating the definition of Merge. Although Self-Merge may seem like a technical device contrived to solve the conceptual problem of explaining the presence of asymmetry where symmetry is expected, we think the Self-Merge option is interestingly exploited in the framework of antilexicalist "realizational" morphology (Adger 2013, Boeckx 2008a). For example, Adger assumes that each lexical entry is a simple root, which must merge with a functional label in order to enter a syntactic derivation. This provides the required asymmetry and labels the structure to begin with.

Still, we do not adopt this type of approach. First, it can be argued to be at odds with the spirit of the proposal that Merge itself is a simple, symmetric operation. Second, and more importantly for us, this proposal is deeply embedded in an antilexicalist view that we do not accept for the reasons discussed in chapter 1. If we believe that what drives syntax is words, stipulating that a word needs to undergo Self-Merge in order to enter a syntactic derivation is an unjustified departure from the minimal assumption. In other terms, Self-Merge appears to be completely gratuitous.

All in all, the approach to linearization based on the LCA cannot be easily combined with bare phrase structure. Although this is a very interesting area of investigation, we will not dwell on it in the remainder of this chapter, focusing instead on the labeling part of the symmetry problem.

2.6   Projection = Labels: Defending an Internal Definition

The intuition of the notion "label" is that a group of words retains some of the properties of one (and only one) of the words that make up the group. This asymmetry in the output of Merge plays a role in many components of grammar. It plays a role at the interfaces. At the PF interface, if word order is a matter of postcyclic linearization, the notion of head may play a crucial role. But it also plays a role at the LF (Logical Form) interface. Semantic selection is sensitive to the notion of head, just to mention the most salient of these relations.

Even more centrally, though, labels are usually considered to be needed in the syntactic computation. In the standard view, the one implemented in the Projection Principle, a syntactic derivation is driven step by step by lexical properties. At the first step of the derivation, these are directly encoded in the word itself, but the other steps appear to be no different. In general, what a label does is to divide words and their features into two categories: the ones that survive and remain active in the next step of the derivation, and those that do not.[1] The one that remains active, as Chomsky (2008, 141) puts it, "selects and is selected."

Each SO [syntactic object] generated enters into further computations. Some information about the SO is relevant to these computations. In the best case, a single designated element should contain all the relevant information: the label (the item "projected" in X-bar theories; the locus in the label-free system of Collins 2002). The label selects and is selected in EM [External Merge], and is the Probe that seeks a Goal for operations internal to the SO: Agree or IM [Internal Merge].

More explicitly, we can define a label as in (5).

(5) *Label*
    When two objects α and β are merged, a subset of the features of either
    α or β become the label of the syntactic object {α, β}. A label
    a. can trigger further computation, and
    b. is visible from outside the syntactic object {α, β}.

Given the definition in (5), Merge can remain symmetric and minimal. Furthermore, the Inclusiveness Condition is respected since the label is no new object to be inserted into the derivation. On the contrary, a label is a subset of the features that are already present in the derivation. For example, if a verb is merged with a direct object, some feature of the verb (typically its categorial feature) will become the label of the newly formed syntactic object. However, now there is a burden on the computation. In fact, given α and β, two syntactic objects merged together, something in the computation must be able to select one of them as the survivor, the label. This has to be done efficiently, by minimal search. The quest for the proper algorithm(s) able to determine the label for each syntactic object has been at the heart of much debate in recent years. We will summarize it in the next two sections.

First, though, we need to discuss the exact nature of labels, and in particular whether they are to be defined *internally*, as a core aspect of syntactic computation, as in the traditional approach stemming from Government-Binding Theory, or *externally*, as in a recent proposal by Chomsky (2013), who claims that labels are only needed at the interface for the interpretation of syntactic objects. As noted earlier, labels seem to play some role in interpretation. The issue then is whether they also play a role in syntax, or whether one must assume that they are purely an interface condition.

We believe the external definition of label is very questionable. First of all, the evidence that labels have a role in interpretation is not overwhelming: the same syntactic category can correspond to various semantic types (a DP can correspond to an individual, a generalized quantifier, or a property; a proposition can correspond to a CP or a DP; a predicate can correspond to a VP, an NP, or an AP; and so on). Furthermore, a label can simply be ignored at the semantic interface (e.g., the PP *of John* is interpreted in *their painting of John* much as the DP *John* is interpreted in *They painted John*). So, at best a label imposes some loose constraints on how a syntactic object is interpreted.

On the contrary, we believe the evidence for the *internal* definition is much more substantial. Without a label, it is difficult to build both a theory of External Merge, explaining how a syntactic object merges with certain other categories, and a theory of Internal Merge, predicting intervention restrictions on movement. To begin with, the notion of syntactic label is really at the core of the fundamental idea that syntactic categories are distributional—that is, that the features of a given element of a group determine the distribution of the group itself. On a more technical plane, it is difficult to explain how selection can drive Merge if labels only play a role at the interface. A syntactic notion of label can explain straightforwardly why *He told John* is acceptable (*John* has the right label to satisfy the selectional requirements of the verb *told*), while **He spoke John* is not (*John* has the wrong label for the selectional requirements of the verb *spoke*). Without a syntactic label, we would be forced to assume that both derivations are equally well-formed in syntax and that **He spoke John* is interpretively defective.

A label-less syntax would also have trouble accounting for well-known restrictions on movement. Here, we exploit Adger's (2013) illuminating discussion of simple examples like (6).

(6) Anson's cat arrived.

Suppose there is a feature in T that probes the closest D feature. In a label-less syntax, the complement of V would bear no information that could ensure that [Anson's cat] counts as the closest D-related object, and we would incorrectly predict generalized possessor raising to be possible, yielding (7) for (6).

(7) *Anson's arrived cat

In other words, "label-less structures effectively predict that a DP in the specifier of another DP will always be more prominent for syntactic relations outside the latter DP. That prediction does not seem, in general, to be correct" (Adger 2013, 16).

There are three reasons why Chomsky (2013) has proposed the external definition of labels, which we are questioning here. The first has to do with what Chomsky calls the strong Minimalist thesis and the related attempt to reduce the narrow syntactic component as much as possible, relegating as many linguistic properties as possible to interface conditions. While we agree in principle with the methodological correctness of this attempt, we believe, for the reasons we mentioned, that labels belong to the core part of grammar that cannot be dispensed with and cannot be relegated to the interface.

Furthermore, a syntactic definition of label does not imply a departure from the strong Minimalist thesis. Quite the opposite: labels, as we said, are a device stripping off features from words, and as such represent a computationally efficient procedure. They are thus good candidates for those "third factor properties" (Chomsky 2005) imposed on language by more general non-language-specific computational principles.

A second and more specific reason why Chomsky tries to expunge labels from syntax is related to a computational paradox that arises in his account of successive-cyclic movement. We will discuss this paradox in section 4.3: see also the end of section 2.7.

Third, the internal and external definitions of label make very different predictions on one important question that will be relevant in this book: namely, which types of syntactic object can remain label-less (if any). If labels are needed internally for computation to proceed, every syntactic object will need a label except the root, where the computation ends. Root clauses are thus predicted not to need a label under the internal definition of label. On the other hand, under the external definition, labels are needed only at the interface, so a label is needed at the end of the cycle, when the structure is sent to interpretation. So if there is a point where a label is indisputably needed, it is the root clause, where the computation ends. It follows that the internal and external definitions of label make opposite, not just different, predictions. Importantly, we will propose an analysis of successive-cyclic movement (chapter 4) and of root structures in adult and child grammar (chapter 5) that fulfills the predictions of the internal definition of label regarding which syntactic objects can be label-less.

2.7   The Head Algorithm (or Words Are Special)

Chomsky (2008) observes that the computation must be able to determine the label of each syntactic object by minimal search. Let us consider the first labeling algorithm he proposes, given in (8), which we will call the *Head Algorithm*.

(8) *Head Algorithm*
   In {H, α}, H a lexical item (LI), H is the label.

This algorithm has a strong intuitive basis: if there is an asymmetry between the two elements that are merged, and one of them is structurally simpler, then it is automatic for the system to distinguish the two elements and select one: specifically, by minimal search, it selects the one that is structurally simpler, and that one becomes the label. This is the lexical item, the word.

This algorithm is also consistent with a lexicalist point of view. We are assuming that words are different, as they are the input to syntax. Therefore, they must be easily recognizable as such. This is not completely trivial, though. How can we distinguish a word from a bundle of features that is not a word—say, a morpheme? Chomsky (2008) claims that words come with a special feature (the "edge feature"), which is the very property that prompts them to enter the syntax and combine with other linguistic elements. This edge feature is the fuel of each syntactic derivation, since it forces words to combine in phrases and clauses. The edge feature is also what distinguishes a word from a label. Recall how we defined a label: in the canonical case, when two categories merge, a subset of the features of one of them become the label of the newly created object. The label (the temporary root node) is what selects and is selected. Since a label is the output of Merge (albeit an indirect one mediated by the Probing operation, as we will argue), a label can never be a word, so it cannot have the edge feature.

While we will adopt this approach to distinguish words from morphemes and phrases, we consider the term *edge feature* infelicitous. As Boeckx (2008a) observes, the so-called edge feature is very different from formal features, which are checked throughout the derivation and enter agreement relations. Therefore, we will refrain from using this name, although we will stick to the intuition that words are special, because a word qua word can always provide the label ("project," in traditional terms) when it is merged with another category.

The next question is what features of the word provide the label when the word "projects." For the time being, we assume that the categorial feature of the word is always among the features that become the label of the newly created syntactic object.

Let us take stock. Each word has a property that forces it to combine with other linguistic elements. In this sense, the Head Algorithm in (8) is on the right track. However, it is possible to show that (8) is at the same time too restrictive and too powerful.

Rephrased in X-bar terms, (8) claims that a head always projects. To see how (8) works, consider (9), a case of External Merge of a word with a syntactic object. By virtue of (8), the object generated by merging the word with the syntactic object receives the label of the word itself (i.e., a subset of its features; see (5)).

(9)   read   *read the book*

However, any kind of Merge involves labeling. If by Merge we mean not only External Merge but also Internal Merge (i.e., movement), then we expect (8) to work indistinguishably in cases like (9) and in cases where movement is involved. Consider (10), where a simple word is internally merged to a syntactic object.

(10)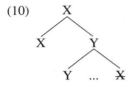

By (8), X provides the label. Thus, (10) illustrates an interesting consequence of (8) when applied to Internal Merge: it predicts that what is traditionally called head movement has the property of modifying the label of its target. *Head movement has a relabeling power.* We will return to this consequence and discuss whether it is desirable or not. For the time being, we observe that this is a case where (8) might be too powerful.

However, (8) is also too restrictive, since it does not provide the computational system with an automatic device for labeling all core cases of syntactic objects created by Merge. While we might expect labeling to be not always deterministic, leaving some work to the interfaces, (8) alone would result in too much indeterminacy. Let us look at some cases of undesirable indeterminacy in detail.

First of all, a system working with only the Head Algorithm in (8) would have nothing to say about the very first step of any derivation, when two words are merged, as in (11).

(11) {saw, John}

This would result in a weird grammar, in which any computation automatically runs at least two parallel derivations given any pair of words, depending on which word provides the label. Chomsky (2005) acknowledges this problem but claims that a multiple Spell-Out system like phase theory ensures that the "wrong" derivation will crash early enough. Still, the system would introduce the computational burden of maintaining two parallel derivations up to the next higher phase even in trivial cases like (11), which are not temporarily ambiguous in any reasonable sense.

A more problematic case systematically arising in a grammar containing only (8) is illustrated in (12), a configuration where the external argument is merged with VP (or vP, in a more elaborated structure).

(12)   *the boys read the book*

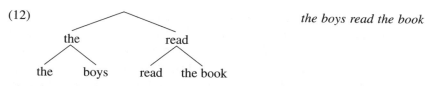

In (12), two objects are merged, but neither of them is a word. (8) might be taken to mean that the resulting object does not have any label, but this is clearly an unwanted result. Alternatively, a system with (8) as its only labeling algorithm might be taken to mean that labeling cannot be decided in such cases. This is equally unsatisfactory.

To handle cases like (12), Chomsky (2013) adopts an idea underlying Moro's (2000) Dynamic Antisymmetry: (12) is a case of undesired symmetry, so it must be destroyed by some kind of movement. In fact, Chomsky suggests a similar approach for another case of undesired symmetry (lack of labeling): the intermediate step of successive-cyclic movement of a *wh*-phrase. He speculates that the reason why a *wh*-phrase must evacuate its intermediate landing site is that the node created by its first movement step is unlabeled, being symmetric.

The idea that unlabeled nodes can be generated but must be destroyed is potentially interesting, and in chapter 4 we will use a version of it for analyzing the intermediate step of successive-cyclic movement. However, we see several problems with adopting this idea in the form that Chomsky suggests. First, the proposal is patently countercyclic. In fact, if what destroys symmetry and creates a label is movement, the symmetric structure lacking a label (say, Spec,vP) will remain in place until the landing site of movement (say, Spec,TP) becomes available. But, in order for the derivation to reach the point where Spec,TP is created, the structure without a label (Spec,v) should be selected. However, this is impossible under the definition of label given in (5) (a label selects *and is selected*). Although we believe that there are ways out, we will argue that the countercyclicity problem can be fixed only by assuming that the role of movement in destroying symmetry is merely indirect (see section 4.3). The only alternative would be to assume that labels play no role in syntax and are only needed at the interface. However, we have already found this hypothesis lacking (section 2.6).

Another problem is that the movement that destroys the symmetry at the Spec,vP level creates another point of symmetry at the Spec,TP level. After all, even the configuration created by the movement of the external argument is a case in which two objects are merged but neither of them is a word. Therefore, the Head Algorithm in (8) cannot decide the label. It seems that the problem is sneaking in through the window after being pushed out the door.

Of course, the tacit assumption is that the symmetry problem can be more easily fixed at the Spec,TP level since in this case (Internal) Merge has been probed. Still, if Probing can fix the symmetry problem with Internal Merge, the most economical option would be for Probing to also fix the symmetry problem with External Merge at the Spec,v level. The labeling approach that we develop in section 2.9 does exactly this.

An alternative that Chomsky considers is the same one mentioned for First Merge (of two words), as in (11): either category in (12) can label the syntactic object, but the interface will filter out the incorrect labeling. But this proposal would be inconsistent with the very idea of having a labeling algorithm: if the algorithm is effective in only one configuration ({word, syntactic object}) out of the three configurations Merge can generate (the other two being {word, word} and {syntactic object, syntactic object}), it is basically of little use.

Finally, the Head Algorithm in (8) yields wrong or at least suspect results in a number of contexts where a word is merged with a syntactic object, as illustrated in (13) and (14) for External Merge and Internal Merge, respectively. Recall that once we give up X-bar theory and if we believe in words, we have no alternative but to analyze atomic elements like *he* or *what* as words, in the absence of strong evidence for a more complex analysis.[2]

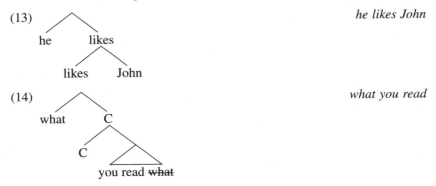

(13)   *he likes John*

(14)   *what you read*

Given (8), in both (13) and (14) the label should be provided by the lexical head. This is clearly wrong in the case of (13), which is interpreted as a clause, not as a DP. It is a controversial result in the case of (14), which can be interpreted as clausal in nature, not (necessarily) as a DP.

2.8 The Movement Algorithm

The previous quick review of some representative cases of Merge clearly shows that a system that contains only (8) as a labeling algorithm is unsatisfactory. Chomsky (2008) was aware of these problems, and this is why he indeed proposed a second algorithm, adding (15) to (8).

(15) If α is internally merged to β forming $\{\alpha, \beta\}$, then the label of β becomes the label of $\{\alpha, \beta\}$.

The algorithm in (15) is meant to avoid any problem with labels of internally merged structures. It ensures that "in all movement operations, it is always the target that projects," a standard assumption in the generative grammar of the past 40 years. A configuration immediately captured by the algorithm in (15) is (16).

(16)   *which book did you read*

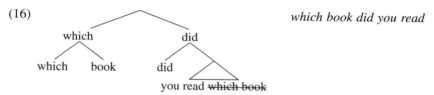

Given X-bar theory, which assumed a rigid structure preexisting movement and lexical insertion, the condition holding that the target always projects came for free. Movement was assumed to be "substitution," where the displaced element substituted for an empty node. Hence, the label for the structure was already given and movement was predicted not to have any effect on the structure itself. This is illustrated in (17).

(17)

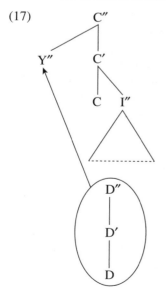

There are several problems with adding (15). First, in a Minimalist frame-work, where there is no structure prior to syntactic operations and the only operation responsible for movement *and* for structure building is Merge, there is simply no place for the notion of substitution. Second, (15) actually stipu-lates that External Merge is different from Internal Merge, an ad hoc residue of a movement theory. Third, having two algorithms is not desirable in a Minimalist framework. Fourth, introducing (15) into the system, with all the theoretical costs just mentioned, is not even empirically adequate. It solves the problems with syntactic objects involving movement (those represented in (16)), but not the other problems: neither the First Merge problem illustrated in (11), nor the problem illustrated in (12). We end up with two algorithms and two separate Merge operations, and we still have indeterminacies. Clearly, we need something better.

In the next section, we will propose an alternative view of labeling deter-mination that appears to do a much better job. In a sense, this book can be seen as an exploration of the consequences of the view of labeling introduced in the next section.

2.9   The Probing Algorithm

Suppose that Merge does not impose any asymmetry. Any application of Merge combining two distinct objects is possible. Suppose also that Merge is free, costless, and replicable *ad libitum*. A consequence of this simple view seems to be the impossibility of deriving a label, as discussed above.

However, Merge is not the only syntactic operation involved in creating syntactic structure. There is another operation that plays an equally crucial role: namely, *Agree*—or, as it is also called, *Probing*. Probing is an operation by which an unvalued feature (a probe) finds a matching feature (a goal), giving it a value. Here is Chomsky's (2004, 113) definition:

(18) Call H a *Probe* P, which seeks a *Goal* G within XP; P = H
     c-commands G.... If the P-G relation satisfies the relevant conditions,
     then uninterpretable features of P, G delete.[3]

What is important here is that Probing, in contrast to Merge, is indeed intrinsi-cally asymmetric. To put it simply, it is the probe that needs a goal and seeks for it, not vice versa.

Before we proceed, we need to comment on one aspect of (18): namely, on the fact that an uninterpretable feature of the probe deletes as a result of the Probing operation. In our view, the question of what feature is interpretable is potentially slippery, since it depends on the semantic model that is assumed.

A safer notion, commonly used in more recent Minimalist work, is the opposition between valued and unvalued features. In many cases, this opposition is easier to detect. For example, there is a clear basis for saying that the subject DP values the agreement features of the verb, rather than the other way around.

Having clarified this, we pursue the notion that, since Probing is clearly asymmetric, it is natural to derive the asymmetry of syntactic objects not from the structure-building operation Merge, which is flat, but from Probing. In order to do so, we need just one more assumption: namely, that Probing itself is the trigger for (most) Merge operations. This can be obtained in a straightforward way. It is not controversial that Probing plays a role in movement (Internal Merge) operations, where the probe is the (possibly indirect) trigger of movement. Although Probing can take place long-distance, it is typically associated with movement, with the goal internally merging to the phrase headed by the probe.

Next, consider that a selectional configuration like (19) can be naturally interpreted as Probing.

(19) {saw, John}

Although no structural asymmetry is built into the syntactic object created by Merge in (19), there is an asymmetry in the lexical properties of the two words involved (i.e., in their features). A classical way to describe this asymmetry is to say that *John* saturates *saw*, and not vice versa. We can frame this asymmetric relation between the two members of a merging pair in terms of a probe-goal relation: *saw* has an unvalued feature (a selection feature)—a probe—that is valued by some feature(s) of *John*, the goal.

The case of External Merge of the external argument to the vP, illustrated in (12), does not seem fundamentally different. The functional category v must assign a theta-role; therefore, it can be seen as the probe of the merging operation.

Capitalizing on this extensive interpretation of the concept of Probing, we propose the following algorithm:

(20) *Probing Algorithm*
    The label of a syntactic object {α, β} is the feature(s) that act(s) as a probe for the merging operation creating {α, β}.

Because (20) is quite natural, it is no surprise that several authors have proposed very similar approaches. For example, Adger (2003, 91) reduces selection to a probe-goal relation and defines the head as the element that selects in any merging operation. The Probing Algorithm is also reminiscent of Pesetsky and Torrego's (2006) Vehicle Requirement on Merge. Boeckx (2008a, chap. 3) discusses labeling in detail, reaching similar conclusions.

Before we discuss the cases that were problematic given Chomsky's (2008) labeling algorithms, let us make explicit an important consequence of what we have said so far. We have assumed that words exist and that they are special entities. We have proposed formalizing "wordhood" in syntax by assuming that words come with a special property, which forces them to merge with other material. If this is so, and if words are intrinsic probes qua words, they always activate the Probing Algorithm. This means that a word can always label the syntactic object it contributes to forming. With this in mind, we now review all the cases discussed in preceding sections.

2.9.1 Head-Complement Configurations, Simple Case

Consider (9), repeated in (21). Here, *read* unambiguously labels the structure because (i) *read* is a word, hence a probe by definition, and (ii) *read* selects (i.e., probes) *the book*.

(21)   read   *read the book*

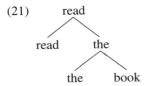

2.9.2 Head-Complement Configurations, First Merge Case

Recall that the configuration in (11), repeated in (22), cannot be satisfactorily treated under Chomsky's (2008) system including only the Head Algorithm in (8), which must allow for parallel derivations until the first step of Spell-Out.

(22) {saw, John}

We think there is better approach to this problem, which we call the *double-probe approach*. We assume there is no labeling indeterminacy in (22), because although both merged elements are words (hence intrinsic probes), *saw* is a double probe, being also a selector: if a double probe "wins" over a single probe, *saw* labels the structure, as is desirable.

2.9.3 Labeling Ambiguities

Now consider (13) and (14), repeated in (23) and (24), involving a head and a complex syntactic object.

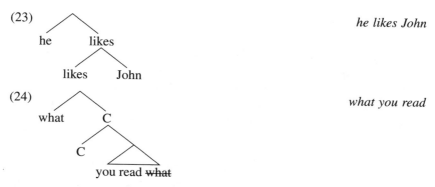

(23)   *he likes John*

(24)   *what you read*

What (23) and (24) have in common is that they involve Internal Merge of a word with a probing syntactic object. Therefore, in this configuration, neither the internally merged word (*he* in (23) and *what* in (24)) nor the probe of the movement operation (T in (23) and C in (24)) clearly wins as the label. If there is no clear winner, there are three logical possibilities: (i) neither category provides the label, (ii) both the internally merged word and the probe of the movement operation provide the label, or (iii) either the internally merged word or the probe of the movement operation provides the label. As we will show in detail in chapter 3, possibility (iii) correctly describes what happens in configurations like (24): a labeling ambiguity arises, and either the word labels the structure (being an intrinsic probe) or the syntactic object does (being the probe of the operation). As for the configuration in (23), see Cecchetto and Donati 2010, where we argue that cases where the pronoun provides the label are indeed attested (these include small clauses in identity sentences). So, the configuration in (23) might be a labeling ambiguity case. Although we cannot discuss this issue in this book, chapter 6 contains some speculative remarks.

Regarding possibility (i)—namely, that the resulting object remains without a label—see chapters 4 and 5, where we argue that label-less objects, although not altogether excluded, have a very restricted distribution. We return to the issue of the no-labeling option for (24) in chapter 5.

Finally, we refer the reader to the insightful discussion by Citko (2008), who defends possibility (ii), the option that two categories can provide the label at the same time. Citko adopts an analysis in terms of what she calls "Project Both" to capture properties of comparative correlatives and of extended projections in the sense of Grimshaw 1991. Again, while the Project Both option might be instantiated in other cases, it does not apply in (23) and (24), as will be evident in the following chapters.

2.10   Conclusion

We conclude this chapter with two general observations that relate it to the rest of the book.

The first observation concerns the notion of head. We have already said that in X-bar theory, the notion of head had a double life. It was intended both as the atom of any syntactic computation (namely, a bundle of features with a privileged status; in this sense, *head* is a close synonym of *word* or *lexical item*) and as the category from which the entire phrase receives its core properties (in this sense, *head* is a close synonym of *label*). Of course, in canonical cases, a head in the first sense is also a head in the second sense, whence the use of the same term. However, this ambiguity is not innocuous. For example, there are cases in which a category is a head in the first sense but not in the second. A simple example is the configuration following movement of what looks like a word—say, movement of *what* in (25).

(25) I wonder what you cooked.

In (25), *what* is a head, if *head* means 'word', but is not a head, if *head* means 'the category from which the entire phrase receives its core properties' (in traditional terms, *what* does not project in (25)). This tension is solved in X-bar theory by postulating that *what* is not really a word, but a phrase with an invisible structure. Sometimes, one becomes so accustomed to a certain stipulation that one stops seeing it as a stipulation. Still, positing an invisible structure each time what looks like a word does not provide a label is undesirable. Of course, there are cases in which there is reason to believe that a word is indeed embedded into an invisible structure, but we need specific evidence to assume this.

Assuming the Probing Algorithm, we can stick to the slogan "A head is a head is a head." In particular, we assume that nothing prevents a word from transmitting its label when it is internally merged. In chapter 3, we will argue extensively that this is a welcome consequence. For example, although *what* does not provide the label in (25), it does so in the free relative in (26).

(26) I devoured [$_D$ what [$_C$ you cooked]].

The derivation illustrated with (26), where a word is internally merged and provides the label, will be the main topic of this book. We will show that this operation is not restricted to free relatives but is much more general. It is therefore convenient to have a name for this operation, and we will call it *relabeling*.

A terminological clarification is in order here. Typically, when Merge takes place, a new label must be determined, since the structure is extended. Take (26). The word *what* is merged with the syntactic object with label C and, by virtue of being a word, provides the label D. Of course, the label C previously determined is unaffected by this operation. So, the operation we call relabeling does not *change* the label that was attributed to an object in a previous step of the derivation. Relabeling means that a newly merged word provides a label that is not the same label the structure had at the previous stage of the derivation. In (26), the label switch is from C to D, but we will note cases where the switch is from C to N or from C to P.

A second general observation is this: the fact that Merge typically results from a Probing operation does not imply that it has to. Chomsky (2008) has proposed that Merge, either External or Internal (movement), is a costless operation that applies freely. While Chomsky's claim is intuitive in one sense, it is puzzling in another. The intuitive basis of Chomsky's reasoning is that, since Merge is the fundamental structure-building operation, it must be costless; otherwise, silence should be preferred to speech. However, the claim that Merge applies freely cannot be true in a strict sense. If Merge were totally free, anything would go and massive overgeneration would occur, clearly an undesirable result. In fact, Chomsky (2008, 2013) does not propose that Merge is totally unconstrained, as he assumes that it must conform to "third factor principles"—very general principles that, although they are not specific to the language faculty, may determine the general character of attainable languages. These include principles of efficient computation, like the No-Tampering Condition, which states that Merge of α and β leaves the two merged syntactic objects unchanged, and the Inclusiveness Condition, which states that syntax only deals with lexical entries and their properties, without adding any other object during the computation. However, we suspect there must also be *linguistic* constraints governing unprobed Merge, since it seems to be a fact that Merge is typically associated with Probing, although Merge and Probing are conceptually distinct and may apply independently of each other.

We think that the approach to labeling we have proposed can naturally explain why Merge is typically (although not obligatorily) associated with Probing. In fact, the Probing Algorithm in (20) severely constrains the application of free (=unprobed) Merge, because according to (20), each time Merge is *not* probed, its output will have *no* label. This is true both for External Merge and for Internal Merge.

But, given (5), an object without a label has a very restricted distribution: it cannot be selected, and no further computation can take place inside it. Given these restrictions, do label-less objects actually exist? One obvious candidate is clauses (another candidate is the structure resulting when an adjunct is merged to the clausal spine; see Hornstein 2009 and section 4.7). Clauses are very special objects, in that they can be root structures, and in this sense they are unique among all the syntactic categories. This peculiarity of clauses may entail another peculiarity: arguably, root clauses (=sentences) do not need labels. Given (5), if labels are needed for a derivation to proceed (labels can trigger further computation) and feed External Merge (through selection), when a structure neither is embedded nor triggers further computation, it needs no label. We will explore this consequence of our system in chapter 4, where it will play an important role in the explanation of successive-cyclic movement and of strong island effects, and in chapter 5, where we will discuss phenomena related to Minimality in root and embedded contexts.

3 Relativization as a Case of Relabeling

3.1 Introduction

In the previous chapters, after defending the lexicalist position that words are the input to syntax, we proposed a theory of labeling that stays close to the Minimalist quest for simplification. However, the proof of the pudding is in the eating, and the validity of a theory of labeling can be fully evaluated only by confronting it with actual linguistic phenomena in which label attribution plays a crucial role. In this chapter, we deal with a classic topic: relativization structures. The reason should be apparent: relative clauses are puzzling because they are clauses but have a nominal distribution, a fact that has to do with labeling. The step from being a clause to being a nominal expression involves labeling change. We will refer to this change as *relabeling*.[1]

We begin in section 3.2 with free relatives, where application of the theory based on the definition of label and on the Probing Algorithm, repeated in (1) and (2), is most straightforward.

(1) *Label*
   When two objects α and β are merged, a subset of the features of either α or β become the label of the syntactic object $\{\alpha, \beta\}$. A label
   a. can trigger further computation, and
   b. is visible from outside the syntactic object $\{\alpha, \beta\}$.

(2) *Probing Algorithm*
   The label of a syntactic object $\{\alpha, \beta\}$ is the feature(s) that act(s) as a probe for the merging operation creating $\{\alpha, \beta\}$.

In section 3.3, we switch to externally headed relatives, showing that the theory based on (1) and (2) derives the basic properties of this construction, if it is coupled with a nonstandard analysis of noun complementation. We will argue extensively that this analysis is welcome on independent grounds. In section 3.4, we show that the theory based on the idea of (re)labeling can handle reduced relatives. In section 3.5, we deal with internally headed relatives, mostly by focusing on Italian Sign Language (LIS). Section 3.6 concludes this chapter.

There are two relative structures that we will not deal with in this chapter, though. The first is nonrestrictive relatives; the second is amount relatives (Carlson 1977, Grosu and Landman 1998), in which the relative clause specifies the number/amount of the entities/stuff denoted by the head noun. These constructions have semantic properties that are largely independent from and orthogonal to the syntax of relabeling, so we leave them out of the picture.

3.2 Free Relatives

An interesting consequence of the system based on the Probing Algorithm is that, since the label is provided by the probe, there can exist cases of labeling "conflict," or ambiguity, if more than one probe triggers the relevant merging operation. One case is a labeling ambiguity that arises in so-called free relatives.

Consider the structure in (3).

(3)   *what you read*

(3) is derived by internally merging the word *what* to the edge of a clause. The result is an ambiguity between two probes. *What*, being a word, is by definition a probe and can provide the label. On the other hand, C, being the probe of the merging operation, can also provide the label (see Bury 2003, Citko 2008, Donati 2006, Iatridou, Anagnostopoulou, and Izvorski 2001, and Larson 1998 for similar analyses; see Donati and Cecchetto 2011 for a full elaboration of the present analysis; see also Chierchia and Caponigro 2013 for a semantic implementation).

This kind of labeling "conflict" never arises when a phrase is internally merged, as in (4).

(4)   C   *what book you read*

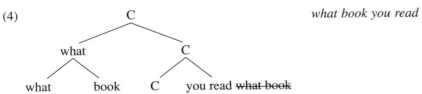

Here, Merge holds between two syntactic objects, and no ambiguity arises: by the Probing Algorithm in (2), C (the probe of the merging operation) labels the entire construction.

The prediction is that the minimal difference between (3) and (4) should be reflected in the distribution and interpretation of the two structures: more precisely, (3) is predicted to have two possible labels, while (4) has a single labeling possibility. This prediction is borne out by the systematic ambiguity of a phrase like *what you read*. This phrase can be interpreted as a free relative and be embedded under a verb selecting a DP, as in (5).

(5) I read what you read/a book.

However, it can also be interpreted as an indirect interrogative clause and be embedded under a verb selecting for a clausal complement, as in (6).

(6) I wonder what you read/if the sun will shine tomorrow.

Crucially, no ambiguity at all, either in interpretation or in distribution, arises when phrasal movement is involved. As shown in (7), the structure resulting from phrasal movement can only occur in environments appropriate for clauses and can only be interpreted as a simple interrogative.

(7) a. I wonder what book you read.
    b. *I read what book you read.

As a further clarification, let us stress that, under the relabeling approach, it is *not* necessary to assume that the embedded C is featurally distinct in (8a) and (8b)—say, because it is interrogative in the former but not in the latter. On the contrary, we assume that C has the same featural specification and can attract the *wh*-category by regular *wh*-movement in both cases. What changes between the two sentences is only the resulting label, C in (8a) and D in (8b). This suffices to explain the different distribution and interpretation, with no need to assume that C is different.[2]

(8) a. I wonder what you cooked.
    b. I devoured what you cooked.

Simple as it is, this analysis faces at least two objections. The first concerns the fact that the Probing Algorithm predicts that any *wh*-word should be able to relabel the structure and trigger a free relative interpretation, while, at least prima facie, free relatives are more restricted than expected. However, as discussed in detail by Caponigro (2003) and Van Riemsdijk (2006), crosslinguistically free relatives are quite widespread.

An example of the unexpectedly limited distribution of free relatives is their alleged impossibility with *who* in English. In fact, many (but not all) speakers find free relatives with *who* unacceptable when *who* is the subject of the free relative. Still, for many speakers free relatives with *who* improve considerably when *who* is the object. ((9) and (10) are from Caponigro 2004, 40.)

(9)   ??[Who couldn't sleep enough] felt tired the following morning
(10) I will marry [who you choose].

Furthermore, free relatives with counterparts of *who* are totally natural in most of the 29 languages Caponigro considers in his survey.[3]

Importantly, the analysis in terms of relabeling can easily explain some unexpected gaps in the paradigm of free relatives crosslinguistically. We start with Italian, where *chi* 'who' free relatives are allowed but *cosa* 'what' free relatives are impossible.

(11) *Cosa è successo è terribile.
       what is happened is terrible

As Caponigro (2003, 26) observes, a revealing hint toward explaining the ban against *cosa* free relatives is the double nature of the Italian word *cosa*, which, in addition to being used as the *wh*-word meaning 'what', translates the English word *thing*. The consequence is that *cosa*, in addition to being what looks like a *wh*-word (see (12)), can also be the restriction of the *wh*-determiner *che* (see (13)).

(12) Cosa è successo?
       which is happened
       'What happened?'

(13) Che cosa è successo?
       which thing is happened
       'What happened?'

Suppose that, even when it is introduced by no overt determiner, as in (12), *cosa* is the restriction of a null determiner, possibly because it carries a residue of the lexical meaning 'thing'. Despite appearances, then, in (11) *cosa* is a phrase, not a word, and the underlying structure of (11) is (14), which is equally unacceptable.

(14) *Che cosa è successo è terribile.
       which thing is happened is terrible

Crucially, in the relabeling approach, only a word (not a phrase) can provide the N label. If *cosa* is a phrase, the relabeling approach thus explains why *cosa/che cosa* can be used in questions (see (12) and (13)), but not in free relatives (see (11) and (14)).

In the same way, we can explain a further (neglected) gap in the paradigm of free relatives in Italian. One way to ask a direct question involves the use of the *wh*-determiner *che* alone.

(15) Che   è   successo?
     which is happened
     'What happened?'

It is only natural to assume that in this case *che* introduces a null N; that is, (15) would be structurally identical to (14) but for the fact that N is null in (15). If so, we predict that *che* should not be able to enter the free relative construction, since, once again, what looks like a *wh*-word is in fact a *wh*-phrase. This prediction is confirmed by the ungrammaticality of (16).

(16) *Che   è   successo è   terribile.
      which is happened is terrible
      'What happened is terrible.'

This amounts to saying that Italian *che* is more similar to English *which* than to English *what*. Notice in fact that *which* in English has a comparable distribution. Although *which* can appear alone in questions, as in (17a), it is legitimate to assume that it always occurs in a complex structure involving a nominal restriction (akin to *one*), as represented in (17b).

(17) a. Which do you want?
     b. [which [~~one~~]] do you want

If *which* always heads a phrase, it should not be able to introduce a free relative construction: not being a word, it does not have a "relabeling power." This is indeed the case, as (18) shows.

(18)   *Which happened is terrible.

The syntax of *wh*-elements is notoriously intricate in French (see, e.g., Hirschbühler and Bouchard 1985, Obenauer 1994), and this is not the place for a thorough analysis of their distribution in questions and free relatives. We simply point out that a similar gap is observed in French free relatives as well. While they are perfectly productive with *qui* 'who', they cannot be introduced by an equivalent of *what*; that is, they cannot be introduced either by *quoi* or by *que*.

(19) a. *Qu'il   m'a   dit est terrible.
         which he me has told is   terrible
         'What he told me is terrible.'
     b. Que t'a-t-il   dit?
         what you has he told
         'What did he tell you?'

(20) a. *Concentre-toi sur quoi tu   dois te   concentrer.
        focus-you   on what you must you focus
        'Focus on what you must focus.'
   b. Sur quoi tu   dois te   concentrer?
      on   what you must you focus
      'On what must you focus?'

The fact that the distribution of *que* and *quoi* in French follows the same pattern as the distribution of *che* and *cosa* in Italian (available in questions, impossible in free relatives) encourages a similar explanation: they are not simple words, but heads of a more complex phrase, and as such they cannot relabel a clause, giving rise to a free relative.

Another interesting question concerns *wh*-words like *when*, *how*, and *where*. Given the Probing Algorithm, we expect these words to be able to introduce free relatives. And in fact, we think they do (*why* is an interesting exception, which we will consider in section 4.6.2). We analyze adverbial clauses like the (b) examples in (21), (22), and (23) as cases of free relatives (these are what Caponigro (2003) calls PP-like free relatives). The (a) examples are included to illustrate the by now familiar labeling "ambiguity."

(21) a. I wonder how you prepared your job talk.
   b. I will prepare my interview how you prepared your job talk.

(22) a. I wonder where he will tell me to go.
   b. I will go where he will tell me to go.

(23) a. I wonder when you will leave.
   b. I will be sad when you will leave.

We postpone a proper analysis of this type of free relative to section 4.6.1, since in chapter 4 we will focus on strong island effects and this type of free relative is the prototypical case of a strong island. For now, suffice it to say that free relatives introduced by *when*, *how*, and *where* do exist, as one expects under the relabeling approach to relativization.

The relabeling approach to free relatives has another important advantage. To the best of our knowledge, while there are in-situ interrogatives, there are no in-situ free relatives, although both constructions involve the same *wh*-words. We can straightforwardly explain this difference between interrogatives and free relatives. Consider (24), where we use English words to create a fictitious free relative in a hypothetical *wh*-in-situ language.

(24) *I buy [you like what].

The verb *buy* in (24) needs to select a DP but, if *what* remains in situ, the category with which *buy* merges is not of the right kind (it is a TP, not a DP).

Note that movement of *what* at LF (Logical Form) cannot help, under the standard assumption that selectional requirements must be checked cyclically. Therefore, the nonexistence of in-situ free relatives is just a consequence of the relabeling of the *wh*-movement involved.[4]

A related case concerns the ungrammaticality of free relatives in which the *wh*-word takes a restriction that is stranded in situ. These structures might appear to be incorrectly ruled in by the Probing Algorithm in (2). In (25), *which* is a word, and as such it can provide the label. The probe of the movement is C, which can also provide the label given (2). The structure should be ambiguous (an indirect question or a free relative), but it is quite ungrammatical.

(25) *which you read [~~which~~ book]

However, a natural explanation is available for the ungrammaticality of (25) and similar sentences. What rules out (25) is not that something goes wrong with labeling, but that subextraction of the *wh*-determiner out of the *wh*-phrase is illicit (more specifically, as we argue in Cecchetto and Donati 2010, the derivation in (25) implies a locality violation: the *wh*-D moves, crossing the label D of the *wh*-phrase, but the label is closer to C than the *wh*-D is). As a reviewer notes, ceteris paribus, cases like (25) should be acceptable in languages that permit Left Branch Extraction. In those languages, the counterpart of [which you read book] should be acceptable as a free relative, while the counterpart of [which book you read] should still be unacceptable as a free relative. In section 3.5, we will discuss relatives in Italian Sign Language (LIS) as a possible instantiation of this case.

A second objection that can be raised against our analysis is the existence of a class of free relatives that appear to allow phrasal *wh*-movement. These are *ever*-relatives, illustrated in (26).

(26) I will buy whichever book you will buy.

In Donati and Cecchetto 2011, we denied that *ever*-relatives are free relatives and offered an alternative analysis in terms of externally headed relatives. In other words, we argued that (26) is structurally closer to (27) than to (28).

(27) I will buy the book you will buy.

(28) I will buy what you will buy.

As already pointed out in a neglected paper on Italian (Battye 1989), there are at least three properties that single out *ever*-relatives, or their Italian counterpart, *unque*-relatives. First, *ever*-items can have an absolute use. In other words, they do not need to appear in a relativization structure. Ordinary free relatives by definition cannot have an absolute use. (Examples (29)–(32) are provided by Chierchia and Caponigro (2013, 7), who build on the proposal advanced in Donati and Cecchetto 2011 to develop a semantic analysis of *ever*-relatives.)

(29) a. John would go out with whichever woman.[5]
     b. Gianni uscirebbe   con   qualunque donna.
        Gianni would.go.out with whichever woman

(30) a. *John would go out with which/what (woman).
     b. *Gianni uscirebbe   con   quale (donna)/chi.
        Gianni would.go.out with which (woman)/who

Second, *ever*-items can occur with the complementizer introducing headed relatives, while, again, ordinary free relatives cannot.

(31) a. John would read whichever book that he happened to put his
        hands on.
     b. Gianni legge qualunque libro che gli   capita tra le mani.
        Gianni reads whichever book that to.him comes in the hands

(32) a. *John would read which/what (book) that he happened to put his
        hands on.
     b. *Gianni legge quale/quanto (libro) che gli   capita
        Gianni reads which/what (book) that to.him comes
        tra le   mani.
        in the hands

Third, an *ever*-item can cooccur with a relative pronoun, while an ordinary free relative cannot.

(33) a. Whichever boy to whom I speak keeps telling me the same thing.
     b. Qualunque ragazzo a cui   parlo   mi dice la stessa cosa.
        whichever boy   to whom (I) speak me tells the same   thing

(34) a. *Which/What (boy) to whom I speak keeps telling me the same
        thing.
     b. *Quale (ragazzo)/Chi a cui   parlo   mi dice la stessa cosa.
        which (boy)/who   to whom (I) speak me tells the same   thing

The natural hypothesis is that *whichever* and *qualunque* are regular (free choice) determiners (see Chierchia 2013) and that the phrases they introduce are regular DPs. This explains why, although modification by a relative clause is possible (as with other determiners), it is not required (hence the absolute use in (29)). The other peculiarities illustrated above can be explained in the same vein: if *ever*-items head ordinary quantificational DPs, we expect them to be able to occur in headed relatives, hence naturally followed by a complementizer or a relative pronoun.

A reviewer asks what explains the contrast between (35) and (36), given that we are assuming that (35) is a headed relative much like (36).

(35 Bill will eat whichever dish wins the contest.

(36) *Bill will eat the dish wins the contest.

We do have an explanation for this contrast, which we will outline in section 3.3, after we present our analysis of externally headed relatives.

To conclude our discussion of *ever*-relatives: we acknowledge that *whatever* appears to have a more restricted distribution than *whichever*. In particular, while *whatever*-phrases followed by the complementizer *that* can easily be found with a random Google search, (37) being an example, they are usually judged ungrammatical.

(37) (*)Consider that the value of whatever house that stands on any lot is
         derived in large part from the perceived value of other, comparable
         houses in the neighborhood.

Ultimately, the differing behavior of *whatever* and *whichever* must have to do with the fact that *which* is obligatorily transitive, while *what* can appear without a restriction. We cannot further elaborate on this aspect of the distribution of *ever*-items here.

One final observation before we turn to headed relative clauses. Some languages, like Italian, French, and Spanish, have constructions introduced by complex expressions of the form "demonstrative + relative" (*quello che* in Italian, *ce qui* in French, *lo que* in Spanish). These constructions are functionally similar to the free relatives we have considered so far, but they are syntactically very different. In particular, the element introducing them is never a *wh*-element, so they are never ambiguous with interrogatives. Furthermore, a complementizer-like element follows the demonstrative.[6] Hence, these structures must be considered a special case of headed relatives in which the head is a null NP and the external determiner is something like a demonstrative or a pronominal.

It has been suggested (see Chomsky 2013) that all free relatives should be analyzed in this way, crucially involving a silent D external head responsible for their nominal interpretation. This might look attractive at first in the light of an archaic English construction, illustrated in (38), in which the *wh*-element *which* is preceded by a determiner-like element *that*.

(38) That which we call a rose / By any other name would smell as sweet. (*Romeo and Juliet* II, ii, 1–2)

However, this analysis does not stand up to closer scrutiny. First of all, the *wh*-elements that appear in these "demonstrative + relative" structures are *not* the same ones that can open a free relative. This is clear in English from example (38) containing *which*, not allowed in free relatives.

(39) *which we call a rose

The same split in the *wh*-paradigm is found in Romance. In Italian, for example, *cui* 'which' is allowed in the "demonstrative + relative" structure, but is not grammatical in free relatives; *quanto* 'how' is grammatical in free relatives, but it is not allowed in the "demonstrative + relative" structure (40).

(40) a. quello di cui   ti   ho   parlato
         that of which to.you (I) have told
         'what I told you about'
     b. *quello di quanto ti   ho   parlato
         that of how   to.you (I) have told

As a generalization, we can say that the *wh*-elements occurring in free relatives are a subset of those occurring in questions (Caponigro 2003, 2004), not of those occurring in headed relatives. On the contrary, the *wh*-elements occurring in the "demonstrative + relative" construction correspond to those occurring in headed relatives. Furthermore, only a subset of free relatives could be analyzed by postulating an abstract "demonstrative + relative" structure, since free relatives introduced by *wh*-words like *when, how,* and *where* obviously resist this type of analysis, being adverbial rather than nominal.

Finally, an analysis taking relatives introduced by a simple *wh*-word at face value is certainly more parsimonious than an analysis postulating a structure that is invisible in most cases.

Let us now turn to externally headed relatives.

3.3 Externally Headed Relatives

Consider the following sentences:

(41) The boy that I will never forget has arrived.

(42) The boy who I will never forget has arrived.

Although externally headed relatives like those in (41) and (42) have been systematically investigated for 40 years in the generative tradition, their correct analysis is still very much open. In particular, one aspect that remains controversial is the best way to capture the fact that the relative clause "head" seems to play a double role in the overall structure. For example, the "head" *(the) boy* in (41) and (42) is a constituent of the matrix clause, but at the same time it seems to satisfy the selectional requirements of the predicate internal to the relative clause.

At least three main devices have been proposed in the generative tradition to account for this construction (see Bianchi 2002 for a historical survey). According to the raising approach (see, e.g., Bhatt 2002, Bianchi 1999, Donati and Cecchetto 2011, Kayne 1994, Vergnaud 1974), the "head" is inserted directly in the relativization site and moves to a position external to the relative clause (see (43a)). Under a second approach illustrated in (43b), which can be called the (null) operator approach, the relative clause "head" is not transformationally related to the gap inside the relative clause. Instead, a relative pronoun (which is overt in (42) but remains phonologically null in (41)) moves to Spec,CP, leaving a trace in the gap position, and is identified with the relative clause "head" (see Chomsky 1981 and Browning 1987 for two variants of this approach). A third approach, the matching analysis (Chomsky 1965, Cinque 1978, Hulsey and Sauerland 2009, Kayne 1975, Sauerland 2003), is illustrated in (43c). Under the matching analysis, as under the raising analysis, the gap inside the relative clause is transformationally related to the category that has moved to the left periphery of the relative clause. However, this category is phonologically deleted under (near) identity with the external head. According to the matching analysis, then, the internal head and the external head are *not* part of a movement chain, but are related by whatever mechanism links an elided constituent and its antecedent in ellipsis cases. (For concreteness, in (43a–c) a movement chain is indicated by inserting a trace, while ellipsis-type deletion is indicated by crossing out the category that goes unpronounced.)

(43) a. the boy [that I will never forget t_{boy}]
     b. the boy [Op_i that I will never forget t_{Op}]
     c. the boy [~~boy~~ that I will never forget t_{boy}]

The raising analysis illustrated in (43a) has an obvious advantage over the null operator approach illustrated in (43b): it explains the relation between the gap and the "head" with no need to introduce a special mechanism, since the existence of transformations is well-attested in constructions distinct from relative clauses. The raising analysis is also more parsimonious than the matching analysis illustrated in (43c), since the latter postulates the occurrence of a transformation *and* of deletion under (near) identity. Furthermore, an ample literature has pointed out empirical advantages of the raising analysis (see Bianchi 1999 for an extended discussion). These advantages can be summarized as follows: the head of the relative clause behaves as if it occupied the position of the gap inside the relative clause with respect to various diagnostics. For example, as observed in Vergnaud 1974 and much following work, the acceptability of (44) suggests that at some level the external head, *(the) headway*, occupies the argument position inside the relative clause, under the assumption that idiomatic expressions like *to make headway* must form a unit at some level of representation.

(44) The headway that John made is commendable.

In the same vein, starting with Doron 1982 it has been observed that (some types of) relative clauses admit a *de dicto* reading. For example, the *de dicto* reading of (45) can easily be explained if the external head has left a copy (trace) in the gap position, where it is in the scope of the intensional verb *to seek*.

(45) John will find the woman that he seeks.

The facts in (44) and (45), together with other reconstruction facts that we will consider in section 3.3.4, have led various researchers to embrace the raising analysis. Still, this analysis encounters some well-known problems. In this section, we will show how they can be fixed, if the relabeling perspective based on the Probing Algorithm is adopted.

First, however, let us clarify one aspect of the raising analysis that does not seem controversial. Following Kayne (1994) and especially Bianchi (1999), we take for granted that the determiner that introduces the head noun is inserted *after* the relative clause has been created by the occurrence of the relevant transformation; in other words, the determiner that introduces the head noun is never located inside the relative clause. This is strongly suggested by the fact that the external determiner must take wider scope than a quantifier inside the relative clause. In (46a), for example, the existential quantifier must have wide scope, while (46b) shows that the same quantifier can take narrow scope in the corresponding simple clause. (These Italian examples are modeled after Bianchi 1999, 40.)

(46) a. Un compito   che ho   distribuito a ogni   studente
        an assignment that (I) have given   to every student
        (era troppo difficile). ($\checkmark \exists \forall$ *$\forall \exists$)
        was too   difficult
        'An assignment that I gave to every student was too difficult.'
     b. Ho   distribuito un compito   a ogni studente. ($\checkmark \exists \forall$ $\checkmark \forall \exists$)
        (I) have given   an assignment to every student
        'I gave an assignment to every student.'

The impossibility of the ∀∃ reading in (46a) follows if the indefinite determiner is merged outside the relative clause, after the "head" of the relative clause has raised, under the standard assumption that a relative clause is a strong island (this explains why the universal quantifier is trapped inside the relative structure and cannot take wide scope).

3.3.1   A Relabeling Analysis for Externally Headed Relative Clauses

A severe critique of the raising analysis is due to Borsley (1997), who mentions several problems. One is particularly serious and relevant for our purposes. This problem concerns word order in *wh*-relatives. Assuming that *wh*-elements such as *which* are determiners, the raising analysis directly predicts that in *wh*-relatives, after raising of the relative clause "head," the order should be as shown in (48), not (47).

(47)   the man which John saw

(48)   the [[which man] John saw ~~which man~~]

Proponents of the raising analysis have discussed this problem and proposed various solutions that include some stipulations. To derive the correct word order, many assume an unmotivated movement of *man* in (47) stranding the determiner *which*, a movement that moreover has the property of turning a specifier (the NP *man*) into something accessible to selection by an external head (the D head *the*). Iatridou, Anagnostopoulou, and Izvorski (2001) capture this by postulating that the moved category can project (this is assumed by Bhatt (2002) as well). However, this solution generates a problem at a more general theoretical level: more familiar instances of movement (e.g., *wh*-movement, raising, passive movement) never involve a projecting movement. In all these cases, it is the target that projects. Therefore, it is necessary to explain why the moved category can project only in relative clauses, and not in many other movement cases.

While this was never explained in the previous literature, it is straightforwardly predicted under the perspective on (re)labeling based on the Probing Algorithm discussed in chapter 2. Under the Probing Algorithm, any word has the power to transmit its label both in the case of External Merge and in the case of Internal Merge (movement), because it is an intrinsic probe. As discussed earlier, one case in which a word "projects" in a movement configuration is free relatives. Ordinary relatives are just another case of this sort. Consider a *wh*-relative like (49). Under a version of the raising analysis such as Bianchi's (1999) or Kayne's (1994), the first step of the derivation (see (50a)) is obvious. However, (50a) is problematic in two respects. First, the word order is wrong, as we just mentioned. Second, the label of the structure with which the external determiner combines is equally wrong, since determiners combine with an NP, not with a CP. Clearly, the desired configuration is something like (50b), but the problem is how to get from (50a) to (50b)—that is, how to derive the "projecting nature" of the movement of *man* (postulated, but not explained, in Bhatt 2002 and Iatridou, Anagnostopoulou, and Izvorski 2001).

(49) the man which John saw

(50) a. [DP the [CP [DP which man] John saw ~~which man~~]]
      b. [DP the [NP man [CP [DP which ~~man~~] John saw ~~which man~~]]]

However, assuming the Probing Algorithm, the "projecting nature" of the movement of *man* in (50) *is* predicted: *man* is a word; therefore, it is an intrinsic probe and can provide the label when it is externally merged with CP. So, the noun *man* "relabels" the structure and allows it to combine with the external determiner.

It is worth comparing the derivation of a free relative with the derivation of a *wh*-relative. In both cases, the crucial point is that a word "projects" when it is internally merged (i.e., moved). The main difference is that the moved word is a determiner in a free relative, while it is a noun in a (*wh*-) relative.

(51) a. *Free relative*   b. Wh-*relative*

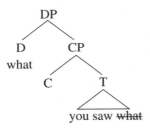

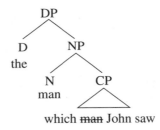

Wh-movement takes place both in free relatives and in *wh*-relatives, but in the former *wh*-movement is the relabeling movement, while in the latter it is only the first step of the relativization process. After *wh*-movement has taken place in a *wh*-relative, the relabeling movement of N applies.

We assume that the landing site of the movement of N is a dedicated position in the left periphery (see Rizzi 1997), although we do not undertake a cartographic exploration, since it is not crucial for our investigation of relativization as a case of relabeling. From now on, we will refer to our approach as the *relabeling analysis*, since the crucial ingredient of this approach is that relatives result from movement of a word, which has the power to "nominalize" the clause by labeling it.

A question naturally arises at this point: what is the trigger of the final, and crucial, labeling movement of the head noun? The noun here has no specific morphological marker that might be probed by the complementizer. On the other hand, as noted above, the result of N-raising is to provide the external determiner with an object satisfying its selectional requirements (through relabeling).

In Donati and Cecchetto 2011, we argued that the satisfaction of selectional requirements is indeed the trigger of the N-raising, and we called this type of operation *selection-driven movement*. We argued that the existence of selection-driven movement is indeed expected under the unification of Internal and External Merge. This is why: it is uncontroversial that selection is responsible for structure-building operations (with the exception of (some) adjuncts; see section 4.7 for discussion). Typically, selection involves an element taken from the numeration and a syntactic object already formed in the computational space. If selection is a type of Probing, as we have been assuming, this amounts to saying that an element taken from the numeration can probe an element in the computational space and trigger External Merge. Under the unification of Internal and External Merge, it also triggers *Internal* Merge.

We will not discuss the properties of selection-driven movement further, because in this book we will eventually adopt an alternative account. We will argue that raising of the head noun in relatives is simply *not* probed, and that its output is nevertheless labeled given the labeling power of the raised word. However, we will examine this possibility only after offering a comprehensive theory of unprobed movement, since it is obvious that unprobed movement can be assumed only if it is severely restricted on general grounds (allowing unprobed movement across the board would lead to massive overgeneration). We will take up this discussion again in section 5.6, when, after introducing unprobed movement, we return to free relatives and compare them with other relativization structures.

3.3.2 The "Missing" Internal Determiner (and a Couple of Other Problems)

Borsley (1997) points out another problem for the raising analysis: in *that*-relatives, a determiner appears to be missing. As a matter of fact, two determiners are predicted to be involved: the one internal to the relative clause, corresponding to the *wh*-determiner; and the external one, selecting the entire relative NP. However, only the latter surfaces in *that*-relatives (as witnessed by the ungrammaticality of (52)).

(52) *the the man that I saw

While Borsley's point is well-taken, we suspect that the solution to this problem might vary from language to language and be subject to parameterization. For example, in Donati and Cecchetto 2011, we assumed, following

Bianchi (1999), that a determiner is stranded in the base position of the head noun, before this raises and projects.

(53) [DP the [NP man [CP that I saw [DP D ~~man~~]]]]

This analysis works very well for the Romance and Semitic varieties where the stranded D is visible and assumes the form of a resumptive pronoun (see Borer 1984, Doron 1982, and much following work).

(54) *Substandard Italian*
　　un ragazzo fortunato che gli　　hanno　　regalato un sogno
　　a　boy　　lucky　　that to.him (they) have given　a　dream
　　'a lucky boy, who they gave a dream to'

(55) *Hebrew*
　　Tasimi madbeka al ha-safta　she ha-yalda menasheket ota.
　　put　sticker　on the-granny that the-girl　kisses　　her
　　'Put a sticker on the granny that the girl kisses her.'

However, this analysis is less natural for varieties where resumptive pronouns are not visible. For the latter cases, a different analysis may capitalize on the nominal nature of complementizers, which has been observed at least since Rosenbaum 1967. If a complementizer has a double life as a determiner, it is possible to assume a derivation for *that*-relatives that differs minimally from the derivation of the *wh*-relative in (50b). For example, in the English relative *the man that John saw*, one can assume that the DP *that man* moves to the periphery of the relative clause, where the relabeling movement of N starts off.

(56) the man that John saw
　　a. [DP the [CP [DP that man] John saw ~~that man~~]]
　　b. [DP the [NP man [CP [DP that ~~man~~] John saw ~~that man~~]]]

Of course, this analysis fixes the "missing determiner problem," since there *is* a determiner inside the relative clause (this is what is usually analyzed as the complementizer *that*).

　　Two questions immediately arise: What triggers the movement of the DP to the left periphery of the relative clause? And why is *that* the only determiner allowed in *that*-relatives?

　　Notice that the former question does not arise with the minimally different *wh*-relatives, since there is an obvious morphological trigger for the movement of the *wh*-phrase (the *wh*-feature). We speculate that the answers to the two questions might be the same. Suppose that the movement of *that man* to the left periphery in (56) is triggered by a morphological feature related to the nature of *that* as a demonstrative. If so, one does not expect a nondemonstrative determiner to pop out, much as one does not expect a non-*wh*-determiner to pop out in a *wh*-relative.

The difference between a *that*-relative and a *wh*-relative might be even smaller in languages like Italian and French, where the complementizer (*che* and *que*, respectively) has the same form as a *wh*-word (see Kayne 1976 and Manzini and Savoia 2003 for two different views on the *wh*-nature of complementizers like *che* and *que*). In these languages, basically the same analysis might be given to *that*-relatives and to *wh*-relatives: the relevant phrase undergoes *wh*-movement to the left periphery, where the relabeling movement of N starts off.

Note that if the complementizer in externally headed relatives is reanalyzed as the determiner stranded by the noun that relabels the structure, it becomes obvious why a complementizer is impossible in *wh*-relatives.

(57) *the boy who that left

(57) is ruled out by whatever condition prevents the noun *boy* from being introduced by two determiners at the same time.[7]

This analysis raises many interesting questions for other embedded clauses, since, if the complementizer is a determiner in relative clauses, it becomes possible to assume that it is a determiner in complement clauses as well. We mention some interesting work in this respect (Arsenijević 2009a, Kayne 2010, Manzini and Savoia 2003, 2011), but we do not elaborate on this issue here, since this would lead us too far away from the analysis of relabeling configurations. We will return to more general issues of clausal complementation in chapter 4.

Yet another parametric option for the internal determiner is found in Spanish, in the construction illustrated in (58a), an alternative to the *that/che* construction just discussed (58b).

(58) a. el   hombre con el   que quiero   irme[8]
          the man   with the that (I) want to.leave
      b. el   hombre con que quiero   irme
          the man   with that (I) want to.leave
          'the man with whom I want to leave'

Arregi (1998) convincingly argues that the derivation of (58a) is as sketched in (59).

(59) el hombre con el que quiero irme
      a. [$_{DP}$ el [$_{CP}$ [$_{PP}$ con el hombre]$_j$ [que quiero irme ~~con el hombre~~]]]
      b. [$_{DP}$ el [$_{NP}$ [$_{NP}$ hombre] [$_{CP}$ [$_{PP}$ con el ~~hombre~~] que quiero irme ~~con el hombre~~]]]

In (59), the full PP *con el hombre* is first moved to the edge of the clause, from which position the head *hombre* is subextracted to relabel the structure, leaving the preposition and the determiner stranded.

The idea is thus that Spanish has two options: the option in (58b), where *que* is a determiner and is pied-piped to the edge of the clause (as in the English case in (56)), and the option in (58a), where an independent determiner *el* is inserted and *que* has full C status.

All in all, while different languages might adopt different strategies, it is fairly clear that there is crosslinguistic evidence for a D-like element inside the relative clause.

We summarize the various crosslinguistic options for the "missing determiner" in relative clauses in (60). Notice that the "D external" option in the fourth column is the one instantiated in free relatives, where a determiner moves from a clause-internal position to the edge of the clause, relabeling it as a DP. We will argue in section 3.5 that this option also derives at least some internally headed relative clauses, notably in Italian Sign Language (LIS).

(60) *Realizations of the internal determiner in relatives*

D in situ	D *wh* in CP	D in CP	D external
silent: ?	*wh*-relatives (English, Italian, etc.)	*el que* (Spanish)	free relatives
resumptive (Hebrew, substandard Italian)	*que/che* relatives (Romance)	*that*-relatives (English)	relatives in Italian Sign Language (LIS)

Finally, like other versions of the raising analysis, the relabeling approach to relative clauses can deal with the case mismatch problem raised by Borsley (1997). He observes that in sentences like (61) the very same DP should receive two cases: nominative in the relative clause and accusative in the matrix clause (in languages with morphological case, the DP is assigned the "matrix" case).

(61) I saw the man that ~~man~~ left.

This case mismatch problem receives a natural explanation under our analysis: in fact, in both *wh*-relatives and *that*-relatives, we assume there are two DPs that share the same noun head. The internal DP receives nominative in (61), and the external DP receives accusative.

We briefly mention here a further potential problem for the raising analysis—namely, antireconstruction effects illustrated by the contrast between

(62a) and (62b). Principle C effects are supposed to be stronger in sentences like (62a) than in sentences like (62b).

(62) a. ?? Which report that John$_i$ is incompetent did he$_i$ submit?
 b. ? Which report that John$_i$ revised did he$_i$ submit?

Chomsky (1995b) and Lebeaux (1989) argue that (62b) is better because the R(eferential)-expression is contained in a relative clause and because relative clauses, being adjuncts, can be late-merged. In (62a), the R-expression is contained in a complement clause, a position that would block late merging. Clearly, this type of explanation is not compatible with the raising analysis, since the relative clause is nothing like an adjunct under the latter analysis (in fact, the relative clause is the *necessary* source position of the external head). In fact, the contrast between (62a) and (62b) is not that sharp, and it has even been proposed that antireconstruction effects in general are spurious (Lasnik 2003, chap. 9). We do think there is something real in the contrast between (62a) and (62b), although we do not adopt the Chomsky/Lebeaux approach. We postpone discussing these cases until section 4.4.3, which is devoted to clausal complementation and clausal adjunction.

It is time to take stock. According to the relabeling analysis for externally headed relatives, the crucial step of the derivation is the movement of a noun, which, by virtue of being a word, can relabel and nominalize the structure according to the Probing Algorithm.

Our next goal is to cope with what looks like an obvious counterexample: in many cases, the nominal constituent that is modified by the relative clause is not a simple noun, but a phrase. Putting it in other terms, the "head" of the relative clause does not need to be a head (in the sense of phrase structure theory; i.e., a word). To give just one example:

(63) the [[destruction of the city] which you witnessed]

The next section is devoted to this issue. In fact, as we will show, far from being a problem for the relabeling analysis, the pattern of relative clauses with a phrasal "head" turns out to support it.

3.3.3 Relative Clauses with a Phrasal "Head" (or Noun Complementation Is Not Noun Complementation)

The problem raised for the relabeling analysis by structures like (63) should be clear enough. Under the Probing Algorithm, even if *destruction of the city* moves, it cannot relabel the structure, which keeps the wrong CP label as shown in step (64b) of the derivation and therefore cannot be selected by the external determiner.

(64) a.   [$_{DP}$ the [$_{CP}$ [$_{DP}$ which destruction of the city] you witnessed [~~which destruction of the city~~]]]

     b.   *[$_{DP}$ the [$_{CP}$ [$_{NP}$ destruction of the city] [$_{CP}$ [$_{DP}$ which [~~destruction of the city~~] you witnessed [~~which destruction of the city~~]]]]]

In fact, we have only one way out, if we want to keep the gist of the relabeling analysis. Namely, we must assume that whatever material modifies the head noun (*of the city* in (64)) can (and must) be late-merged, after the head noun has moved and has "relabeled" the structure. In this section, we extensively defend this admittedly unorthodox assumption.

The idea that adjuncts can be merged late in the derivation is not particularly contentious. The reason is that adjuncts are exempted from the Theta-Criterion, which forces arguments to be inserted into the derivation as early as the predicates they receive a theta-role from.[9] We acknowledge that the idea that arguments of the noun can be late-merged is much more controversial. Therefore, we present extensive evidence showing that they (including phrases like *of the city* in (64)) never behave like proper complements; rather, they behave like adjuncts (see Adger 2013 for an articulate defense of this view).

3.3.3.1 Omissibility

In the verbal domain, one key test for distinguishing elements that obey the Theta-Criterion (arguments) from elements that do not (adjuncts) is that the former are obligatorily expressed while the latter can be omitted.[10] With "complements" of nouns, the situation is sharply different. So, although *They destroyed yesterday* is not acceptable because the complement is not expressed, *The destruction was awful* is acceptable, although the "complement" is not expressed here, either. In fact, to maintain the approach stemming from Chomsky 1970 that takes nouns to be able to assign theta-roles just as verbs do, it is necessary to postulate that the Theta-Criterion behaves differently depending on whether it applies to nouns or to verbs. However, this is a brute stipulation and should be avoided if possible.

There are accounts that deny that a distinction between argument and adjunct can be drawn in the nominal domain and that argue that nouns cannot assign theta-roles. Typically, these accounts are framed in Davidsonian terms (Dowty 2003 and Higginbotham 1985 are two classic references, but see also Hale and Keyser 2002 and Kayne 2009 for the view that nouns cannot take complements). Such accounts are in the same spirit as our assumption that the modifier of the head noun of the relative clause is always an adjunct-like element.[11]

3.3.3.2 Constituency Tests

In the clausal domain, standard constituency tests indicate that the verb and the internal object form a minimal constituent. For example, in (65a) *did that* replaces the complex constituent *bought a house*. However, (65b) is not even interpretable, although it should be acceptable if *did that* could replace the group of words *John bought* (excluding the internal argument *a house*), under the reading 'John bought a house but he bought no car'. The strong deviance of (65b) is explained by the fact that the unit formed by subject + verb *excluding the internal argument* can never be a constituent, under well-established assumptions on clause structure.

(65) a. John bought a house and Mary did that too.
     b. *John bought a house but did that no car.

Observations of this kind are at the heart of generative approaches and motivate a condition called the Verb-Object Constraint by Baker (2009). As Baker argues, this condition is one of the best candidates for a language universal.

If we apply the same constituency tests to the unit formed by the noun and the "complement," the results are quite different (we thank Chiara Branchini for pointing out the relevance of this observation). For example, in Italian, the proform *quello* 'that (one)' can replace the unit formed by determiner + noun, crucially excluding the "complement" of the noun (see (67)). The same point is illustrated in (68) for English.

(66) Ho   visto *la foto*   di Gianni.
     (I) have seen the picture of Gianni
     'I saw the picture of Gianni.'

(67) Ho   visto *quella* di Gianni.
     (I) have seen that   of Gianni

(68) I have already seen *the picture* of John, but I haven't yet seen *that* of Mary.

We acknowledge that this evidence may not be conclusive, because one cannot exclude the possibility that in (67) and (68) the pronoun "replaces" the entire DP out of which the "complement" of the noun has (vacuously) moved.

In fact, assuming the raising analysis for relative clauses, a vacuous movement of this type might be necessary for cases where the pronoun "replaces" the determiner plus the relative clause head, but not the relative clause itself. Consider a conceivable derivation of (69c). (69a) illustrates the by now familiar derivation of a *wh*-relative under the relabeling analysis. (69b) illustrates vacuous extraposition of the relative clause, while in (69c) the proform *that* stands for the structure out of which vacuous extraposition has taken place.

(69) a. the [book [which book you like most which book]]
    b. the [book *t*] [which book you like most which book]
    c. that which you like most

However, the complication introduced by vacuous extraposition may be avoided with other constituency tests. Take fronting. The unit formed by determiner + noun can be fronted (say, for contrastive focus), while the alleged complement of the noun is stranded (see (70) in Italian, which is fully natural with a short break before the PP *di Gianni*).

(70) NESSUN AMICO ho   incontrato *t* di Gianni.
     no   friend (I) have met   of Gianni
     'NO FRIEND I met, of Gianni.'

Crucially, fronting the determiner plus the head of the relative clause but not the relative clause itself results in ungrammaticality. This is shown by (71), which is ungrammatical under any intonational contour (we use a negative quantifier to exclude a nonrestrictive reading).

(71) *NESSUN AMICO ho   incontrato *t* a cui   ho   parlato.
     no   friend (I) have met   to whom (I) have talked

We interpret the contrast between (70) and (71) in the following way. In (71), vacuous extraposition of the relative clause is not possible, probably because the information structure associated with contrastive focus is incompatible with the information structure associated with extraposition. Under the raising analysis, this is all that is required to explain the ungrammaticality of (71). *Nessun amico* 'no friend' is not an autonomous constituent excluding the relative clause. However, (70) is grammatical, and it seems plausible to assume that, if vacuous extraposition is blocked in (71), it must also be blocked in the very similar (70). So, what has moved in (70) must be the constituent *nessun amico*, excluding the PP *di Gianni*, showing that determiner + noun form a unit that excludes the "complement" of the noun.

    All in all, the most straightforward interpretation of the pattern reported in this section is that at some level of representation there can be a constituent formed by determiner + noun, crucially *not* including the "complement" of the noun. This is expected if the "complement" can be late-merged to the constituent formed by determiner + noun. This finding introduces a sharp asymmetry between the nominal domain and the verbal domain, where there is evidence that the direct object cannot be late-merged to the constituent formed by verb + subject. This means that we have found independent evidence for the hypothesis, which plays a crucial role in the relabeling analysis of relatives, that the alleged complement of the noun is not a proper complement.[12]

3.3.3.3 Islandhood
Another familiar way to distinguish arguments from adjuncts is based on their island status. In the verbal domain, there is an argument/adjunct asymmetry in that adjunct clauses are islands for extraction, while extraction from argument clauses is much easier. Again, we observe a fundamental difference in the nominal domain, where the argument/adjunct asymmetry is much weaker, since both relative clauses and "complement clauses" of the noun are islands. This pattern is captured by the Complex NP Constraint (Ross 1967). Since adjuncts to the noun and "complements" of the noun pattern alike with respect to islandhood, a common analysis in terms of late Merge may be on the right track. This common pattern might be less solid than usually considered, but let us stick to the standard generalization at this stage. We will offer a critical and detailed discussion of the Complex NP Constraint in section 4.4.

3.3.3.4 The Ne-Cliticization Pattern
In this section, we discuss an independent argument in favor of the hypothesis (required by the relabeling analysis) that the "complement" of the head noun of a relative must be late-merged. This argument is based on the pattern of *ne*-cliticization in relative clauses in Italian. One of the uses of the clitic *ne* in Italian is illustrated in (72). In (72), ne is a proform for the PP *della riunione* 'of the meeting'; that is, it is the "complement" of the noun *riassunto* 'summary'.

(72) a. Ho   scritto un riassunto della riunione.
         (I) have written a   summary of.the meeting
         'I wrote a summary of the meeting.'
     b. Ne ho   scritto un riassunto.
         of.it (I) have written a   summary
         'I wrote a summary of it.'

However, if the PP to which *ne* corresponds modifies the "complement" of the head noun of a relative clause, *ne*-cliticization becomes sharply ungrammatical.[13]

(73) a. Ho   letto un riassunto della riunione che tu   hai   scritto.
         (I) have read a   summary of.the meeting that you have written
         'I read a summary of the meeting that you wrote.'
     b. *Ho   letto un riassunto che tu   ne   hai scritto.
         (I) have read a   summary that you of.it have written

Our account directly predicts the ungrammaticality of (73b) and similar sentences. *Ne*-cliticization is impossible because any modifier of the head noun *riassunto* 'summary' (including the clitic material) can be merged only after the head noun has moved to the left periphery and relabeled the structure. This means that the surface position of the clitic *ne* is lower than the position in which it is inserted into the derivation. So, the derivation of (73b) involves a lowering movement, and this explains the deviance of the sentence.

Notice that the ungrammaticality of (73b) is not due to a general ban against moving the category out of which *ne* is extracted. In fact, *ne*-cliticization is possible if the DP where the clitic initially is located moves for reasons other than relativization. In (74) the movement of the DP is due to passivization, and in (75) it is an ordinary case of *wh*-movement. In both cases, *ne*-cliticization is felicitous.

(74) Un riassunto ne   è stato scritto [~~un riassunto ne~~].
     a   summary   of.it is been written
     'A summary of it was written.'

(75) Quanti   riassunti   ne   sono stati scritti   [~~quanti riassunti ne~~]?
     how.many summaries of.it are been written
     'How many summaries of it were written?'

The acceptability of (74) and (75) is expected in our system, since the "complement" of the noun does *not* need to be merged as late as the final phase, in the general case. It *must* be late-merged that high only if it attaches to the head of the relative clause; otherwise, relabeling could not take place. In (74) and (75), early Merge of the clitic "complement" when the DP occupies its base position is possible, since no relabeling is involved in passivization and interrogatives. Accordingly, these sentences do not involve any lowering movement of the clitic.

3.3.3.5 *Extraction of the Modifier of the Relative Clause Head*

In this section, we discuss a final argument supporting the hypothesis that the "complement" of the head noun of a relative clause is late-merged after the head noun has relabeled the structure. But first, let us avoid a possible misunderstanding. One problem that the raising analysis does *not* have is incorrectly predicting strong island effects when the head noun is extracted from a relative clause. Canonical cases of island violations involve extraction *out of* the complex NP formed by the head noun + the relative clause (in section 4.4, we return to the islandhood of complex NPs and show how the relabeling analysis can deal with it). By definition, the movement of the head of the relative clause takes place *inside* the complex NP. Therefore, no generalized island effect is expected. However, there are special cases in which the traditional version of the raising analysis predicts an island effect, which is crucially not observed. Consider a sentence like (76) in Italian.

(76) Di quale ragazzo hai   incontrato un amico che ora è in
     of which boy   (you) have met   a   friend that now is in
     carcere?
     jail
     'Of which boy did you meet a friend who is now in jail?'

(76) is as acceptable as its simpler counterpart (77).

(77) Di quale ragazzo hai   incontrato un amico?
     of which boy   (you) have met   a   friend
     'Of which boy did you meet a friend?'

However, under a traditional version of the raising analysis (76) should be ungrammatical, since *di quale ragazzo* 'of which boy' has been extracted out of a relative clause and relative clauses are an island for extraction, as shown by (78). (Bianchi (1999) discusses the problem raised by (76) and offers some possible solutions.)

(78) *Di quale ragazzo hai   incontrato un amico che ha
     of which boy   (you) have met   a   friend that has
     parlato di quale ragazzo?
     spoken

However, the relabeling analysis, which assumes that any modifier of the relative clause is late-merged, does not suffer from the problem that affects the traditional raising analysis. Under the relabeling analysis, (76) is licit because the position where *di quale ragazzo* is externally merged is outside the relative clause. Hence, no island effect is expected.

In this section, we have presented three general arguments (omissibility, constituency tests, and islandhood) suggesting that in general nouns do not take complements the same way verbs do. Furthermore, we have discussed two pieces of evidence (*ne*-cliticization and extraction of the modifier of the relative clause head) showing that the modifier of the head noun of the relative clause is late-merged after the head noun has relabeled the structure. In the next section, we further defend the relabeling analysis by considering reconstruction effects in detail.

3.3.4 Reconstruction Effects

As we already mentioned, one classical argument that has been used to support the raising analysis for externally headed relatives is the presence of reconstruction effects: namely, the observation that from an interpretive point of view the head noun behaves as if it were in the position of the gap inside the relative clause. The raising analysis captures these effects very naturally, since it is possible to say that they are triggered by the presence of a copy of the relative clause head in the base position (see Chomsky 1995b for the idea that reconstruction effects support the copy theory of movement). We assume that any version of the raising analysis (including the relabeling analysis) can straightforwardly explain the occurrence of reconstruction with respect to idiom interpretation and the *de dicto* reading, illustrated in (44) and (45). Other reconstruction facts are more complex and display some inconsistencies, as shown by the considerable literature on reconstruction effects in relative clauses. Let's consider these effects in some detail.

3.3.4.1 *Principle C Reconstruction*
A first important puzzle concerning reconstruction effects in relative clauses was noticed by Munn (1994). Munn pointed out that Principle C effects do not arise in sentences like (79), where the R-expression is contained within the modifier of the head noun. This is surprising, since the corresponding question (80) seems to violate Principle C.

(79) the picture of Bill$_i$ that he$_i$ likes

(80) *Which picture of Bill$_i$ does he$_i$ like?

The contrast between (79) and (80) is a problem for a "classical" version of the raising analysis, which assumes that what raises in (79) is the phrase *picture of Bill*. However, the grammaticality of (79) is no surprise under the relabeling analysis. In this approach, the material that modifies the head noun *picture* must be late-merged after N-raising; otherwise, relabeling cannot take place. Therefore, no Principle C effect is expected, since no trace/copy of the modifier is present in the gap position of the relative clause to begin with. The relabeling analysis also offers a solid basis for explaining why (80) is worse than (79). The difference has to with (re)labeling. In (79), the moved category (*picture*) labels the structure, and this *forces* late Merge of any modifier of the noun. However, in (80) the *wh*-phrase does not label the structure, so earlier Merge of *of Bill* in a previous phase inside the relative is not blocked. It is this derivation that is responsible for the degraded status of (80) with respect to (79).

While the vast literature on reconstruction effects in relative clauses (see, e.g., Bianchi 1999, Cecchetto 2006, Munn 1994, Safir 1999, Sauerland 2003, Vergnaud 1974) has focused on the contrast between (79) and (80), it has neglected the sharp contrast between (81) and (82).

(81) the professor of John$_i$'s that he$_i$ always praises

(82) *the professor$_i$ that he$_i$ always praises

(81) is identical to (79) in the relevant respect: *of John's* must be late-merged after N-raising; otherwise, relabeling cannot take place. Hence, no Principle C effect is expected. However, it is easy to reduce the very degraded status of (82) under the relevant interpretation to a Principle C effect, given the ungrammaticality of (83).

(83) *He$_i$ always praises that professor$_i$.

The relabeling analysis relates the very degraded status of (82) to the ungrammaticality of (83) most straightforwardly: the head noun *professor* in (82) raises out of the DP *that professor* (see section 3.3.2), so there is a copy of this DP inside the relative clause. It is this copy that triggers a Principle C effect.

(84) *[$_{DP}$ the [$_{NP}$ professor [$_{CP}$ [that ~~professor~~]$_i$ he$_i$ always praises [~~that professor~~]$_i$]]]

All in all, the diagnostic based on Principle C effects strongly supports the relabeling analysis in which a noun, never a noun phrase, raises and becomes the external head. Note that saying that (82) is ruled out as a Strong Crossover violation would be just restating the point that we are making. Any desirable theory should try to unify Principle C and Strong Crossover, given that they exclude the same configuration. Call it Principle C effect or Strong Crossover effect, the ungrammaticality of (82) is evidence that the noun *professor* was in the position of the gap before reaching its Spell-Out position. The grammaticality of (81) is evidence that the PP *of John's* was not.

3.3.4.2 Principle A and Variable Binding Reconstruction
A reconstruction argument often used to support the traditional version of the raising analysis involves Principle A—specifically, the absence of Principle A effects in sentences like (85).

(85) The picture of himself [that John likes *e* most] (was never on display).

Note that the grammaticality of (85) is *not* expected under the relabeling analysis, which assumes that *of himself* must be late-merged. How can we explain data like (85)? Following Bianchi (1999) and Cecchetto (2006), we question the diagnostic based on Principle A and claim that data like (85) are not reliable evidence in favor of *syntactic* reconstruction. Cecchetto (2006, 17) offers the acceptability of (86) in support of this view. (86) is a case where the absence of a Principle A effect in a relative clause not only can but *must* be treated as a case of binding without c-command.

(86) La descrizione di se stesso [che ~~descrizione~~ aiuterebbe Gianni a
     the description of himself   that   would.help Gianni to
     passare l'esame] (non è stata presa in considerazione dalla
                                   commissione).
     pass   the exam (was not considered by the committee)

The acceptability of (86) cannot be due to the fact that the anaphor *se stesso* 'himself' is interpreted in the position of the gap; that is, (86) cannot be a case of syntactic reconstruction. This is so because the position of the gap (the subject position of the relative clause) is not c-commanded by the alleged antecedent of the anaphor (*Gianni*).

In the same vein, Safir (1999, 595) provides example (87), where the anaphor *himself* cannot be directly bound by its intended antecedent (*the rock star*) either in its surface position or in the alleged reconstructed position. In neither position is *the rock star* or *himself* in a local configuration, because another potential binder intervenes (*his wife, she*).

(87) The rock star said that his wife would not identify which pictures of himself she had defiantly sent to the tabloids.

We conclude that the absence of Principle A effects when the anaphor is inside a modifier of the relative clause head does not indicate that syntactic reconstruction has taken place (which in turn would suggest that the modifier has moved out of the relative clause together with the head, contra what the relabeling analysis allows). So, what is responsible for the acceptability of these cases?

Before we answer this question, let us look at another argument often used to support the traditional version of the raising analysis—namely, the possibility of variable binding in sentences like (88). Variable binding is not expected in (88) under the relabeling analysis, since *of his* must be late-merged in a position not c-commanded by *every boy* (recall that *every boy* cannot undergo QR (quantifier raising) out of the relative clause; see (46)).

(88) The relative of his$_i$ that [every boy]$_i$ likes lives far away.

However, as Cecchetto (2006) observes, an interesting pattern emerges if one avoids *picture*-NPs and focuses on NPs with a simpler argument structure, since the latter NPs contain a noun that derives from an unaccusative verb. While variable binding is easy in (89), it is much more difficult in (90). The same contrast holds between (91) and (92) in Italian, where there is clear evidence that the noun *fallimento* 'failure' is unaccusative (see Cecchetto 2006 for further discussion).

(89) The one accident of his$_i$ that everyone$_i$ remembers is the one that affected him$_i$ first.

(90) ??The one accident of his$_i$ that everyone$_i$ remembers affected him$_i$ first.

(91) Il proprio$_i$ fallimento che nessuno$_i$ dimentica è quello che è
the self's failure that nobody forgets is the.one that is
avvenuto per primo.
happened first
'His own failure that no boy forgets is the one that happened first.'

(92) ??Il proprio$_i$ fallimento che nessuno$_i$ dimentica è avvenuto
the self's failure that nobody forgets is happened
per primo.
first

(89) and (90) are minimally different, and the complex DP that contains the relative clause (*the one accident of his that everyone remembers*) is actually identical in both sentences. So, if the bound variable reading in (89) were due to reconstruction of the phrase *accident of his*, we would expect the same reading to arise in (90), contrary to fact. The only difference between (89) and (90) is that the former is an identity sentence while the latter is a subject-predicate sentence. This makes the contrast between (89) and (90) highly reminiscent of the contrast illustrated in (93) and (94) (this type of contrast was originally identified by Geach (1964)). Geach observed that a quantified expression can bind a pronoun outside its syntactic scope in the identity sentence (93), while the same reading is much harder in the subject-predicate sentence (94).

(93) The woman [every man]$_i$ loves is his$_i$ mother.

(94) ??The woman [every man]$_i$ invited to the party came without him$_i$.

Much following literature (e.g., Jacobson 1994, Sharvit 1999) has shown that variable binding without c-command (called in this literature "indirect binding") is possible in a restricted set of cases, crucially involving identity sentences. We will not go into the issue of indirect binding any further, except to point out that contrasts like the one in (89) and (90) support an indirect binding analysis for the alleged cases of variable binding reconstruction in relative clauses. If a mechanism of semantic reconstruction is assumed for variable binding, it is only natural to extend it to the absence-of-Principle-A cases mentioned above.

In this section, we have discussed reconstruction effects in externally headed relatives. The relabeling analysis can easily explain the occurrence of reconstruction with respect to idiom interpretation and the *de dicto* reading, much like other versions of the raising analysis. However, the facts concerning Principle C are compatible only with the relabeling analysis, which prescribes the reconstruction of the head noun but not of its modifiers, not with more traditional versions of the raising analysis. Finally, we discussed murkier cases involving Principle A and variable binding reconstruction and argued that they should be better treated as cases of semantic reconstruction.[14]

3.3.5 Fighting with Hydras

In this section, we touch on a challenge for the analysis of relative clauses, which was first pointed out by Perlmutter and Ross (1970, 350). This is how they phrase the problem:

[C]onsider the sentence

[(95)] A man entered the room and a woman went out who were quite similar.

...The grammaticality of [(95)] raises a serious problem, for what is the antecedent of the relative clause in [(95)]? It cannot be either *a man*

[(96)] *A man who were quite similar entered the room and a woman went out.

or *a woman*

[(97)] *A man entered the room and a woman who were quite similar went out.

Neither of these singular noun phrases can serve as the antecedent of a relative clause whose predicate (*similar*) requires an underlying plural subject, and whose verb (*were*) is inflected to agree with a plural subject in surface structure. The only possible antecedent of the relative clause in [(95)] would seem to be the discontinuous noun phrase *a man...(and) a woman*. But how can a discontinuous noun phrase be the antecedent of a relative clause? No analysis of relative clauses that has yet been proposed in the theory of generative grammar is able to account for sentences like [(95)]. Their existence thus presents the theory with a new paradox.

It is probably fair to say that relative clauses with a discontinuous antecedent, or *hydras*, as they have also been called, are still puzzling after more than 40 years, although various attempts have been made to account for them (see, e.g., Link 1984, Suñer 2001, Vergnaud 1974). In particular, hydras are a direct challenge to the family of raising analyses that the relabeling analysis belongs to, since it is difficult to imagine what the source position of the discontinuous antecedent can be. Hydras may appear to be less problematic for the (null) operator approach illustrated in (43b), since this approach dispenses with the assumption that the relative clause "head" is transformationally related to the gap inside the relative clause. Still, even assuming the (null) operator approach, the question arises how the null operator can be identified with a discontinuous "head."

We acknowledge that we do not have a definitive solution to the challenge posed by hydras. However, we suspect that the problem is more general and that the solution must be found outside the realm of relative clauses. In fact, a case somewhat reminiscent of the hydra problem is illustrated by simple sentences like (98).

(98) A man and a woman are entering that restaurant.

In (98), at least superficially, there is no plural DP that the verb can agree with. However, a plural category must be syntactically represented, at least if one wants to stick to the hypothesis that verb agreement is a syntactically governed phenomenon.

As Moltmann (1992) observes, there is evidence that the plural category that must be syntactically represented must exhaust all conjuncts if more than two are present. (99) has only the interpretation, contrary to world knowledge, according to which marriage is a three-person deal.

(99) #a child, a man, and a woman who were married

There are different approaches to the syntax of coordination, from multidimensional analyses to more conservative approaches, and each of them might deal with hydras in different ways. We sketch one possible direction.

Suppose that for data like (98) and (99) we adopt the approach that has been developed for another construction, the Big DP analysis of clitic doubling (e.g., Belletti 1999, Boeckx 2003, Cecchetto 2000, Torrego 1995, Uriagereka 1995), according to which the clitic heads a projection that hosts the doubled category in its Spec (we use X-bar terminology for concreteness). So suppose that the coordinated DPs are also merged with a plural D head, which provides the label as illustrated in (100).

(100) a. [$_{Big\ DP}$ [a man and a woman] D_{pl}]
       b. [$_{Big\ DP}$ [a child, a man, and a woman] D_{pl}]

This type of analysis explains the agreement pattern in (98), since a plural D is syntactically represented. It also explains the exhaustivity effect in (99), since there can be just one head in the Big DP representing the coordinated DPs occupying the Spec position.

If this type of analysis is on the right track, it can be expanded to cases of hydras like (95). The Big DP headed by *who* might move from the subject position to the left periphery of the relative clause. From this position, the usual relabeling movement might take place across the board, raising *man* and *woman*.

(101) [$_\text{Big DP}$ [(a) man and (a) woman] who] $t_\text{Big DP}$ were quite similar

In this section, we fought with hydras, a notoriously dangerous task. Although we indicated a possible line of attack, our main observation is that hydras are a facet of the more general problem of representing syntactic coordination. So the ultimate solution to the problem of hydras in relatives depends on what theory of coordination is chosen.

3.4 Reduced Relatives

In our theory of relativization, the crucial role is played by the nominal head and its relabeling movement, and not, say, by *wh*-movement or the C area. Reduced relatives (e.g., *the woman drinking coffee*) are a case in which relativization is completely dissociated from C and *wh*, as predicted.

Reduced relatives are found in many languages. They can be considered "relatives" in that they contain a verb phrase modifying a head noun, but they seem to be "reduced" in that they contain no complementizer or relative/ *wh*-element and they present a verbal form that is not (fully) inflected for tense. In our view, this kind of structure is interesting because it shows that relativization does not necessarily require a full clausal level. Here, our analysis of reduced relatives crucially diverges from others that identify them with full-fledged relative CPs (e.g., Kayne 1994; but see Bhatt 2006 for an analysis close to the one presented here). Let us show how this analysis works, given our (re)labeling framework.

Notice, first, that reduced relatives appear to be severely constrained. They can only be subject relatives, never object relatives.

(102) a.   the man eating the apple
      b. *the apple the man eating

In English, reduced relatives contain either a present participle, as in (102a), or a past participle, as in (103).

(103) the philosopher admired (by Marx)

Past participle reduced relatives are even more constrained: in English, they are fully productive only with passive verbs (see (103)), while they are marginal with unaccusatives (see (104)). They are impossible with transitive verbs in the active voice and with unergative verbs (see (105) and (106), respectively).

(104) ?the philosopher arrived yesterday

(105) *the philosopher opened the window

(106) *the philosopher phoned yesterday

Reduced relatives with a past participle are fully productive in Italian as well.

(107) la   ragazza amata   da Gianni
      the.FEM girl.FEM loved.FEM by Gianni
      'the girl loved by Gianni'

(108) il   ragazzo   arrivato   ieri
      the.MASC boy.MASC arrived.MASC yesterday
      'the boy arrived yesterday'

As extensively discussed by Burzio (1986), Italian reduced relatives are grammatical with both passive and unaccusative verbs (see (107) and (108), respectively), while, as in English, they are totally ungrammatical with unergative and transitive verbs in the active voice (see (109) and (110), respectively).

(109) *il   ragazzo aperto   la   finestra
       the boy   opened the window

(110) *il   ragazzo telefonato ieri
       the boy   phoned   yesterday

Let us first consider reduced relatives with a past participle. Given the strong similarity in structure and meaning between these and full relatives, it would be desirable to offer as unified an account as possible for both structures. We claim that the relabeling approach can do the job.

Consider our derivation of (103), sketched in (111). It is pretty clear that the head of a reduced relative (here, *philosopher*) is external, since it precedes the verb, much like the head noun in a full relative. By the usual reasoning, we assume that movement of N from its argument position to its derived position relabels the structure, conveniently providing the external determiner with the NP it needs to select.

(111) the [$_{NP}$ philosopher [$_{VP}$ admired ~~philosopher~~]]

The derivation in (111) is parallel to the derivation of a full relative except in two respects. The first difference is the landing site of N-raising VP periphery in reduced relatives, CP area in full relatives. The second difference is that in (111) there is no visible D inside the structure that gets relabeled. Recall from section 3.3.2 that we analyzed the complementizer in full relatives as the D stranded by the N that undergoes relabeling movement, and we discussed crosslinguistic evidence for the existence of an internal determiner stranded in the clause. However, no such D is visible in reduced relatives. We take this fact at face value and, instead of assuming a null D in ad hoc fashion, we claim that in (111) the participle *admired* is merged directly with the bare noun *philosopher*. Of course, this has consequences. In languages like English and Italian, a transitive verb cannot assign accusative to bare singular nouns (it is not crucial for us to take a position on the precise mechanism of accusative assignment/checking, since any theory should account for the fact that singular bare nouns are not proper assignees of accusative case in these languages). This explains why reduced relatives are possible only with unaccusative and passive verbs. If the verb does not need to assign accusative, the noun can be merged to V and then move and relabel the structure, satisfying the selectional requirement of the external D. The noun will receive a case together with the external D.

The interpretation of a structure like (111) shows pretty clearly that the noun that is modified by the reduced relative receives a theta-role from the past participle. Under our analysis, this means that the noun satisfies the selectional requirements of the verb. More specifically, this means that theta-role assignment is not necessarily restricted to DPs. This does not seem problematic, since there is independent evidence that nouns can receive theta-roles: this is what happens with adjectives. Adjectives such as *nice* and *ugly* do assign a theta-role to the noun they modify. The same mechanism holds here. V and N merge;. V probes N for selection and assigns it a theta-role. As far as labeling is concerned, when V and N merge, the syntactic object they create has the label V: while both V and N are probes (being words), V is a double probe (being also a selector; see section 2.9.2).

The similarity of the structural configuration obtaining between the noun and the adjective in an ordinary DP and between the noun and the past participle in a reduced relative offers a basis for explaining why the past participle behaves as an *adjectival* passive in reduced relatives. For example, a past participle can display superlative morphology in a reduced relative (see (112)), but not in the corresponding full relative (see (113)).

(112) un uomo amatissimo da tutti
       a   man   loved.much by everyone

(113) *un uomo che venne amatissimo da tutti
        a   man   that was   loved.much by everyone

The fact that N and V are in a local configuration in reduced relatives is the basis for explaining why they agree in gender and number in Italian (see (107) and (108)), much as adjectives and nouns do in this language.

The same analysis applies to reduced relatives with an unaccusative past participle, although we do not know why this type of reduced relative is fully productive in some languages (e.g., Italian) but only marginal in other languages (e.g., English).

This relabeling account straightforwardly explains why reduced relatives with transitive verbs in the active voice are not possible (see (105)). As we said, NPs (as opposed to DPs) can merge only with unaccusative/passive verbs, since these do not need to assign case. By Burzio's Generalization, a verb that does not assign accusative case does not express an agent argument either.

For reduced relatives with present participles in English, which are allowed with any kind of verb, a different analysis is required. We illustrate our proposal in (114). Here, the noun *philosopher* is externally merged and projects according to the Probing Algorithm, but we assume that nothing goes wrong with theta-role assignment, since the vP contains a PRO in argument position.

(114)   D   *the philosopher admiring Marx*

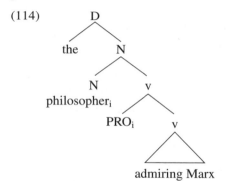

The reason for this different analysis (and different distribution) is apparent: PRO can occur in a phrase headed by a *present* participle, as shown by the grammaticality of (115), but it cannot occur in a phrase headed by a *past* participle, as shown by the ungrammaticality of (116).

(115) [PRO Admiring Marx] is dangerous.

(116) *[PRO Admired Marx] is dangerous.

The assumption that PRO occupies subject position in structures like (114) can shed light on why reduced *object* relatives with a present participle are not allowed.

(117) *The philosopher Marx admiring (writes obscurely).
     (Intended interpretation: 'The philosopher who Marx admires writes obscurely.')

We assume that (117) is ruled out by whatever explains why PRO cannot occupy object position.

The account of reduced relatives we have proposed has three welcome features: (i) it is minimally different from the analysis of full relatives, without stipulating a full-fledged silent clausal structure; (ii) the impossibility of past participle reduced relatives with active transitive verbs and ergative verbs follows straightforwardly; and (iii) it explains the restriction of reduced relatives to subject relatives.

To the best of our knowledge, no alternative account exists that combines these three features.

3.5 Internally Headed Relatives: The Case of LIS

An advantage of (any version of) the raising analysis is that it accounts for the existence of internally headed relative clauses, which simply realize overtly what the raising analysis takes to be the underlying structure of externally headed relative clauses. One example of an internally headed relative and of the corresponding externally headed structure is given in (118), from Japanese (the "head" noun is italicized). This feature of the raising analysis should not be underestimated. While the raising analysis can explain the existence of two related relativization strategies by simply assuming that the "head" can raise at different points (before or after Spell-Out), alternative approaches have a harder time explaining why relativization can be realized through two different structures. ((118) is from Shimoyama 1999, 147.)

(118) a. Yoko-wa   [[Taro-ga   sara-no   ue-ni   oita] *keeki*]-o
         Yoko-TOP   Taro-NOM   plate-GEN on-LOC put   cake-ACC
         tabeta.
         ate
         'Yoko ate a piece of cake which Taro put on a plate.'
      b. Yoko-wa   [[Taro-ga   sara-no   ue-ni   *keeki*-o
         Yoko-TOP   Taro-NOM   plate-GEN on-LOC cake-ACC
         oita]-no]-o   tabeta.
         put-NOMINALIZER-ACC ate
         'Yoko ate a piece of cake which Taro put on a plate.'

Interestingly, when the relative clause head *keeki* 'cake' does not move (namely, in the internally headed relative in (118b)), the nominalizer particle *no* surfaces in the right periphery of the relative clause. This particle is not present when *keeki* moves. In our relabeling approach, this can be interpreted as indicating that in (118a) *keeki* moves to the structural position that is occupied by the nominalizer particle in (118b). The particle is not needed in (118a), since the movement of *keeki* can relabel the structure by turning it into a nominal constituent. Interestingly, this correlation between head-internal relatives and nominalizer particles is not restricted to Japanese, but is widely attested cross-linguistically (see Comrie 1981, Keenan 1985).

Rather than pursuing the typological dimension further, we will focus here on just one case of internally headed relative clauses, those in Italian Sign Language (LIS). Our relabeling approach allows us to identify in LIS another case of linkage between nominalizer and internal head, which differs in interesting ways from the case of Japanese internally headed relatives.

We take LIS relative clauses to be internally headed, as shown in detail by Branchini and Donati (2009) (see Cecchetto, Geraci, and Zucchi 2006 for a correlative analysis, though). (119) is an example. Following standard practice, we indicate signs in capital letters. Coindexing between two signs indicates that they are articulated in the same region of the signing space, and in turn this means that they are coreferential. For simplicity, we do not indicate the nonmanual marking (roughly speaking, a raised eyebrow) obligatorily occurring with PE and possibly extending to the entire preceding clause (see Branchini 2007 on this).

(119) [PIERO CONTRACT$_i$ SIGN DONE   PE$_i$] GIANNI
    Piero   contract   sign   ASPECTUAL.MARKER PE   Gianni
    FORGET
    forget
    'Gianni forgot the contract that Piero signed.'

The relative clause, which always comes first, is closed by an element, glossed as PE here, which is a determiner also found in other contexts with a clear demonstrative function (see Branchini 2007). Since LIS is a fairly consistent head-final language at least as far as functional heads are concerned, the area where PE is located corresponds to the C area.

What is interesting about LIS is that evidence exists that PE is not directly merged in that position; rather, it moves there from head-internal position. In other words, PE starts as the determiner of the head (it is the "internal determiner" we discussed extensively in section 3.3.2) and moves to the C area. The evidence is that (i) PE obligatorily agrees in space with the head noun, as indicated by coindexing in (119), and (ii) PE can optionally be realized in situ, as illustrated in (120), where it appears next to the noun CONTRACT.[15]

(120) [PIERO CONTRACT$_i$ PE$_i$ SIGN DONE]   GIANNI
    Piero   contract   PE   sign   ASPECTUAL.MARKER Gianni
    FORGET
    forget
    'Gianni forgot the contract that Piero signed.'

So, it is very tempting to interpret movement of PE as yet another instance of a relabeling movement: D moves to C and relabels the structure, turning the clause into a (complex) DP, namely, a relative clause. Under this analysis, LIS fills a gap in the typology of relativization strategies we have discussed so far: a LIS relative is sort of a free relative with a full head. The movement of PE is indeed very similar to the movement involved in free relatives, being the movement of a D head. However, the PE-clause can also be considered a full relative, since it contains a full NP "head." While in full relatives in languages like English or Italian, N is extracted out of the DP, in LIS the relabeling movement of D strands the "head" noun in its base position.[16]

A relabeling analysis of PE movement makes one interesting prediction: the structure should be ambiguous, being a case of labeling "conflict." Under the Probing Algorithm, PE can provide the label because it is a word and thus an intrinsic probe; but the probe of the movement of PE is C, which can also provide the label. This prediction appears to be confirmed by data like (121), which we discuss in Cecchetto and Donati, in press a.

(121) PIERO CONTRACT SIGN DONE   PE GIANNI
       Piero   contract   sign   ASPECTUAL.MARKER PE Gianni
       FORGET
       forget
       'Gianni forgot that Piero signed the contract.'

(121) is minimally different from (119). In fact, if one looks only at the order of signs, the two sentences might appear to be the same. However, there is a difference: in (121), unlike in (119), PE is not articulated in the same position in space as CONTRACT (indicated by the absence of coindexing between CONTRACT and PE). Our informants argue that PE does not refer to the noun CONTRACT in (121); rather, it refers to the entire clause PIERO CONTRACT SIGN DONE 'Piero signed the contract' (Cecchetto and Donati, in press a). So, the PE-clause is interpreted as a relative clause in (119) but as a factive complement clause in (121), as the different translations indicate.

Notice that PE is not a *wh*-element (see Cecchetto, Geraci, and Zucchi 2009 for discussion of how the *wh*-feature is expressed in LIS). Therefore, the labeling ambiguity between (119) and (121) is not exactly the same one found in the free relative/embedded question alternation: the PE-clause can be either a relative clause (when PE projects) or an embedded complement clause (when C does). Still, the ambiguity that arises between a D label and a C label is exactly what one expects under the Probing Algorithm.

3.6   Conclusion

In chapter 2, we proposed a theory of labeling that has among other things an interesting corollary: namely, that words can label the structure they merge with, no matter whether they are moved there or inserted there for the first time. In this chapter, we have capitalized on this feature of our labeling theory to derive a full-fledged theory of relativization. We analyzed in turn several relative constructions: free relatives, externally headed relatives of various kinds, reduced relatives, and internally headed relatives. The idea that underlies our approach to relative structures is quite simple: the defining (and puzzling) property of relatives—namely, that they are (possibly reduced) clauses with a nominal distribution—comes for free if a word (with label N or D) can relabel the structure it is internally merged to. This minimally simple analysis requires a significant change of perspective on noun complementation, though. In particular, it is necessary to abandon the idea that nouns take complements the way verbs do. However, we have reviewed several independent pieces of evidence supporting this change of perspective.

In chapter 5, after providing some background information about the possibility of unprobed movement, we will return to free relatives and to an issue that we had to leave open—that is, the trigger of the relabeling movement of N in externally headed relatives. Finally, in section 5.4 we will conclude our discussion of relativization structures by discussing a feature of child grammar that has attracted much attention in recent years: the fact that children comprehend and produce object relatives much later than subject relatives. We will offer an explanation for this asymmetry within the (re)labeling approach.

But before dealing with these remaining issues concerning relativization, we must examine another interesting development of the (re)labeling approach. As we will show in chapter 4, this approach can shed new light on a classic topic in the theory of syntax: successive-cyclic movement and island effects.

4 Successive-Cyclic Movement and Its Constraints: Cyclicity and Islands

4.1 Introduction

In this chapter, we show how the (re)labeling approach can shed light on the nature of long-distance *wh*-movement and of island constraints.

A standard assumption in the generative tradition is that long-distance *wh*-movement proceeds successive-cyclically; that is, it advances by intermediate steps through designated clause positions. The underlying intuition supporting this analysis is that splitting long-distance movement into shorter steps reduces the computational cost associated with the derivation and makes it "manageable."

However, the related assumption—that there are intermediate steps of movement that are (i) obligatorily vacated and (ii) apparently unprobed—is problematic for the current theory of movement and derivation, and always has been. A recent family of proposals attempts to explain the first property of the intermediate step, its intrinsic instability, as a problem of labeling (see, e.g., Chomsky 2013). The idea, in a nutshell, is that this step is label-less, hence cannot be tolerated, hence needs to be destroyed through further movement. However, this line of approach has nothing to say about the second property of the intermediate step, the apparent lack of a trigger.

We think we can do better by sticking to the facts and by claiming that the intermediate step of a successive-cyclic movement is indeed unprobed. Importantly, we can derive the intermediate step's instability *from this very fact*. An unprobed movement yields an unlabeled syntactic object (due to the Probing Algorithm). An unlabeled syntactic object cannot be seen from the exterior and hence cannot be embedded. It is thus unstable in embedded contexts, giving rise to successive steps of movement.

But does it make sense to assume that Merge can be unprobed? We need to answer this important question in order to be sure that a labeling account of successive-cyclic movement is not just a trick, but a reasonable solution. This will be our starting point in this chapter.

We first discuss unprobed movement and its distribution (section 4.2). We then return to successive-cyclic movement, explaining in detail how to derive its properties within the (re)labeling approach (section 4.3). Given these necessary premises regarding successive-cyclic movement, we show that our approach to (re)labeling can also shed light on a problem investigated in the generative tradition at least since Ross's (1967) seminal dissertation—namely, island constraints. As we show in detail (section 4.4), the label-less layer created by successive-cyclic movement is not compatible with relabeling, the operation that is responsible for relative clause formation. This allows us to explain why free relatives and full relative clauses are strong islands for extraction. That extraction from relatives is not possible is the first horn of Ross's Complex NP Constraint. In section 4.4, we also deal with the other horn of the Complex NP Constraint: the impossibility of extracting out of what looks like a clausal complement of a noun. In our approach, which reduces strong islandhood to a conflict between relabeling and a label-less layer, nothing automatically explains this part of the Complex NP Constraint. We argue that this is a welcome consequence, because the degradation observed when a category is extracted out of a clausal complement of a noun is a spurious fact, due to a generalized garden path effect (a clausal complement of a noun is initially misanalyzed as a relative clause). This analysis is supported by the observation that in languages where this garden path effect does not arise, because clausal complements of nouns are never temporarily ambiguous with relative clauses, extraction from clausal complements is indeed allowed. Furthermore, we present experimental evidence confirming the existence of garden path effects with clausal complements of nouns (section 4.5).

We show that the account of island effects in relative clauses extends to adjunct structures like conditionals and *when*-clauses, as these can be reduced to free relatives (section 4.6). We also discuss the status of "peripheral adverbial clauses" in the sense of Haegeman 2003, 2010a (section 4.7). As peripheral adverbial clauses cannot be reduced to free relatives, we propose that these structures are the output of another possible instance of unprobed Merge: unprobed External Merge. Being unprobed, the merging operation attaching these clauses to the main clause yields a label-less syntactic object. This explains why peripheral adverbial clauses can only occur at the external boundary of the matrix clause (the resulting label-less layer is tolerated because it does not need to be selected). Furthermore, it explains why such clauses are islands (given their high positioning, *wh*-extraction out of them would be an instance of lowering movement).

We then return to the status of modifiers of the noun that other approaches consider to be complements, and we discuss to what extent it is possible to extract out of them (section 4.8). Section 4.9 concludes the chapter.

4.2   Can Merge Be Free?

Let us start by repeating the two conditions of our theory of labeling, since they will play a pivotal role in the discussion of successive-cyclic movement and of island effects. These are the notion of label (1) and the Probing Algorithm (2).

(1) *Label*

When two objects α and β are merged, a subset of the features of either α or β become the label of the syntactic object $\{\alpha, \beta\}$. A label
a. can trigger further computation, and
b. is visible from outside the syntactic object $\{\alpha, \beta\}$.

(2) Probing Algorithm

The label of a syntactic object $\{\alpha, \beta\}$ is the feature(s) that act(s) as a probe of the merging operation creating $\{\alpha, \beta\}$.

What (2) says is that the label of any Merge output is always the feature asymmetrically triggering the merging operation. However, the fact that Merge typically results from a Probing operation does not imply that it has to. For example, Chomsky (2008, 137) claims that Merge, either External or Internal (movement), is a costless operation applying freely:

As has long been recognized, the most elementary property of language—and an unusual one in the biological world—is that it is a system of discrete infinity consisting of hierarchically organized objects. Any such system is based on an operation that takes *n* syntactic objects (SOs) already formed, and constructs from them a new SO. Call the operation *Merge*. Unbounded Merge or some equivalent is unavoidable in a system of hierarchic discrete infinity, so we can assume that it "comes free," in the present context.

The intuition underlying Chomsky's claim is quite clear and hardly avoidable, as there is a sense in which the basic structure-building operation Merge must be costless; otherwise, silence should be preferred to speech (or to signing, in the visuospatial modality of language). However, there is also a sense in which the claim that Merge applies freely cannot be accepted. If the claim were correct, there would be no space to develop a theory of grammatical *constraints*. This would be clearly wrong, since we know that there are well-defined constraints on both Internal and External Merge and that, typically, Merge *is* triggered.

In order to avoid this prima facie contradiction, it is useful to notice that the combination of (1) and (2), while not blocking the application of free (=unprobed) Merge, severely constrains it. In fact, (2) implies that each time Merge is *not* probed, its output will have *no* label. This is true both for External Merge and for Internal Merge. But, given (1), an object without a label has a very restricted distribution: it cannot be selected and no further computation can take place inside it.

Given these restrictions, do label-less objects actually exist? One obvious candidate, at least if one assumes the internal definition of label that we defended in section 2.6, is clauses (another candidate is the structure resulting when an adjunct is merged to the clausal spine; see Hornstein 2009 and section 4.7). Clauses are very special objects, in that they can be root structures, and in this sense they are unique among all syntactic categories. This peculiarity of clauses may entail another peculiarity: arguably, root clauses (=sentences) do not need labels. Given (1), labels are needed for a derivation to proceed (labels can trigger further computation) and feed External Merge (through selection). So, when a structure is not embedded and is complete, it needs no label.

This uniqueness of clauses is what underlies the idea that clauses are phases (i.e., cycles). Consider the definition of a phase as a syntactic object *that cannot be modified by further computation* (Chomsky 2013, 42) and is complete enough to exit the derivation: this definition is close to saying that a phase is an acceptable label-less object.

Assuming a derivational perspective, the fact that root clauses do not need labels also has consequences for the derivation of (some types of) subordinate clauses. For example, there is a stage in the derivation of (3) when the finite embedded clause is a matrix clause (this is before this clause is embedded).

(3) John believes that Mary is smart.

At that stage of the derivation of (3), a label is not necessary, although a label becomes necessary when the clause is embedded. This fact will play a central role in our account of successive-cyclic movement in the next section.

Another consequence of the idea that root clauses can remain label-less is that they can host unprobed instances of movement. Consider (4), in which we signal the presence of a label-less node by using the empty set notation (this is just a convenient way to indicate a label-less layer and should not be interpreted as the presence of any special type of label).

(4) [ø a book [c Mary likes ~~a book~~]]

In (4), the element that is moved is a phrase, not a word, and thus cannot qualify as a probe. Since the target C is not visibly endowed with any morphological feature, there is no direct evidence that it probes the moved phrase either; hence, it is natural to assume that *a book* is internally merged by an application of unprobed (free) Merge. The structure is thus unlabeled. Assuming the internal definition of label, this is not a problem insofar as the structure is a root structure.

If we are on the right track, there should be cases of "dislocation" or "topicalization" that are restricted to the root and are not possible in embedded contexts. In fact, such cases are reported for a variety of languages (see the literature on "root transformations" stemming from Emonds's (1976) seminal work; Bianchi and Frascarelli 2010 on the English/Romance asymmetry in the distribution of topics; and Albrecht, Haegeman, and Nye 2012 for an overview). For example, Cinque (1977) distinguishes between hanging topics and Clitic Left Dislocation because the former are allowed only in matrix contexts. This is illustrated by the contrast between (5a) and (5b). Note that, following Cinque, in (5) we use a hanging topic DP that corresponds to an indirect object in order to distinguish between the hanging-topic construction and Clitic Left Dislocation (Clitic Left Dislocation would require a dislocated PP).

(5) a. Giorgio, penso   che gli   abbiano   nascosto la   verità.
         Giorgio (I) think that to.him (they) have hidden   the truth
         'Speaking of Giorgio, I think that they did not tell him the truth.'
    b. *Penso   che Giorgio gli   abbiano   nascosto la   verità.
         (I) think that Giorgio to.him (they) have hidden   the truth

A similar type of "topicalization" that can target only the root is right-dislocation in strict head-final languages like Japanese and Turkish. We illustrate this with Turkish data from Kural 1997, 501, but the situation is identical in the relevant respect for Japanese (see Cecchetto 1999b, Takano 2014, Tanaka 2001). The discourse-neutral word order in Turkish is shown in (6). (7a) illustrates a licit case of right-dislocation to the root, while (7b) shows that embedded right-dislocation is ungrammatical.

(6) Ayşe   [Ahmet'in   öğrencilerle   konuştuğu]nu
    Ayşe.NOM Ahmet-GEN students-with speak-PAST-3SG-ACC
    biliyor.
    know-PRES.3SG
    'Ayşe knows that Ahmet spoke with the students.'

(7) a. Ayşe   [Ahmet'in   konuştuğu]nu   biliyor
         Ayşe.NOM Ahmet-GEN speak-PAST-3SG-ACC know-PRES.3SG
         öğrencilerle.
         students-with

b. *Ayşe   [Ahmet'in   konuştuğu]nu   öğrencilerle
Ayşe.NOM   Ahmet-GEN speak-PAST-3SG-ACC students-with
biliyor.
know-PRES.3SG

Left dislocation, as distinct from topicalization in English, is another construction that is restricted to the root, according to Lasnik and Uriagereka (1988). Left dislocation is illustrated in (8), and topicalization in (9).

(8) a. John, Mary likes.
    b. *I think that John, Mary likes.

(9) a. John, Mary likes him/that man.
    b. I think that John, Mary likes him/that man.

One could of course postulate that an abstract morphological feature triggers the relevant movement in all these cases, but this move would have an ad hoc flavor and would also require stipulating that the relevant feature be present only in the matrix C. On the other hand, taking the absence of a morphological trigger at face value can explain why these constructions are allowed only at the root, at least if one adopts the theory of labeling expressed in (1) and (2): a root clause can host an unprobed movement since it does not need a label; an embedded clause cannot, because it cannot tolerate being unlabeled.

One might object that there are languages that manifest an overt topic morphology, so assuming an abstract topic morphology in (5)–(9) and equivalent sentences in other languages is not particularly costly; this amounts to the usual move of postulating that a morphological feature that is overt in one language can be null in another. However, if we look at the one language whose topic morphology has been studied in detail, Gungbe, it emerges that our way of approaching topic constructions is justified. Aboh (2003, 311) explicitly argues that topic constructions that are morphologically marked in Gungbe are the counterpart of Italian Clitic Left Dislocation structures and not of Italian hanging topics. Therefore, data from Gungbe are consistent with the idea that, while Clitic Left Dislocation is morphologically triggered, as assumed in the cartographic tradition (see Rizzi 1997, among many others), hanging topic formation is not. If there is no trigger, the node to which the hanging topic is attached is label-less, and this explains its restriction to root contexts. Similarly for right-dislocation in Japanese and Turkish and for English left-dislocation (adopting Lasnik and Uriagereka's (1988) terminology).

4.3   Successive-Cyclic Movement

What about embedded clauses? Embedded clauses by definition need a label, since they are targets of selection (which is a type of probing in our system). This should entail that unprobed movement to the periphery of embedded clauses is impossible. However, assuming a derivational perspective, there is a step of the derivation in which embedded clauses *are* root clauses. This is when they have not yet been selected. At this stage, they do not need a label and can host unprobed instances of movement, as we have already mentioned. It is from this tension, we claim, that the instability of the intermediate step of successive-cyclic movement arises. But let us first review the theory of successive-cyclic movement in the current literature.

That movement must proceed successive-cyclically is stipulated in the current generative framework in the Phase Impenetrability Condition (PIC) in (10).

(10) *Phase Impenetrability Condition*
    The complement of a strong phase α is not accessible to operations at the level of the next highest strong phase β; only the head and the edge of α are. (adapted from Chomsky 2001)

The background assumption is that once generated, certain syntactic objects, called phases, cannot be modified by further computation.[1] That the derivation proceeds phase by phase is expected in a framework that takes seriously the issue of computational complexity, as it captures the intuition that once a part of the derivation is over, its internal details can be "forgotten." Supposedly, this alleviates the computational burden. The simplest version of phase theory would assume that, when the computation internal to a phase is over, only the phase's label remains accessible. This is what we will propose in a moment. The classical definition of the PIC, (10), is more complex than this, since it introduces a distinction between the edge and the complement of a phase and postulates that the edge of a phase remains accessible as late as when the next highest strong phase head enters the derivation.

Before we illustrate how the system based on the PIC works, we must say what counts as a phase, since the way the PIC works critically depends on this. Chomsky (2001) claims that all CPs, transitive vPs (and possibly DPs) are phases. However, since the PIC is introduced to capture successive cyclicity and since the evidence for successive-cyclic movement targeting Spec,vP is mainly theory-internal (with the important exception of Legate's (2003) discussion of *wh*-reconstruction effects, QR, parasitic gaps, and the Nuclear Stress Rule as evidence for vP phases), we will focus here on CP phases and on how the PIC derives the fact that long-distance *wh*-movement must target intervening Spec,CP positions. However, our approach might extend to the vP layer, if it is assumed that vP is a phase by virtue of being propositionally complete, since the gist of our proposal is that only complete syntactic objects can remain label-less. Obviously, vPs typically do need to be embedded, unlike CPs, which can be root structures. However, if vPs are phases, embedding of a vP will take place just as embedding of a subordinate CP does (see below), and nothing crucial will change in our account.

But let us be concrete. Take a sentence like (11) and its simplified derivation (12) given the classical PIC in (10). In (12), we indicate in gray type the structure that is inaccessible to computation.

(11) Which student do you think that John met?

(12) a. [$_C$ that [$_{TP}$ John met which student]]
      b. [which student] [$_C$ that [$_{TP}$ John met which student]]
      c. [$_{CP}$ [which student] do [$_{TP}$ you think [$_{CP}$ [which student] [$_C$ that [$_{TP}$ John met which student]]]]]

In (12b), the *wh*-phrase *which student* can move out of the embedded TP before this object becomes inaccessible. If it does so, then given the PIC, being the edge of the phase it remains accessible to the computation in the next phase and can move further, as in (12c).

Two questions immediately arise. First, the PIC does not say why the intermediate step of *which student*'s movement *must* be vacated. For example, it does not say why a sentence like **You think that which student John met* is ungrammatical. Second, the PIC says that it is *possible* for *which student* to move to the edge of the lower phase (and then be free to move further), but what *forces* this initial step? Certainly, this movement has welcome consequences, since it allows the *wh*-phrase not to get trapped in the cycle before checking of *wh*-features has taken place. Still, there is no obvious trigger for this beneficial movement, since the intermediate C is not interrogative, so it does not qualify as a probe for the *wh*-phrase. Assuming that the intermediate movement takes place only because it will eventually allow *wh*-feature checking to take place when the matrix C enters the derivation violates one of the basic tenets of Minimalist theorizing: that the derivation cannot "look ahead."

Chomsky (2000) deals with this problem by giving the head of the phase an "EPP feature," which is satisfied by filling its Spec position. This feature thus triggers movement to the Spec of the phase. However, it is apparent that postulating an EPP feature at best gives the problem a name, rather than fixing it. (The term *EPP* ultimately derives from Chomsky's (1982) Extended Projection Principle, which requires that all clauses have a subject, but Chomsky's

(2000) "EPP feature" is not exactly the same feature, as it is not restricted to subjects.)

In fact, postulating an EPP feature might pile problem upon problem, because it must be assumed that the embedded C is given the EPP feature just in case the embedded clause contains a *wh*-phrase. If the embedded C were always given an EPP feature, a sentence like (13) would be ruled out, because that feature would not be satisfied.

(13) You think that John met Mary.

Chomsky's (2000) proposal, then, boils down to postulating an EPP feature on the head of the phase when (and only when) an intermediate movement step takes place. Clearly, this is not satisfactory.

Summarizing so far, successive-cyclic movement, while well-motivated within a framework that takes seriously the issue of computational complexity, is still poorly understood. It relies on a stipulation (the PIC) and involves a movement step that is both untriggered and unstable.

The no-labeling approach mentioned in section 4.1 (see Blümel 2012, Chomsky 2013, Thoms 2011 for related but distinct proposals) represents clear progress, in that it explains in a principled way the instability of the intermediate step: the object created by the intermediate step, being unlabeled, is only temporarily tolerated in the derivation and needs to be destroyed within the next cycle. While this idea is very intuitive, the details of the various proposals are still insufficient to provide a proper theory of successive-cyclic movement. Let us detail here what we consider the problematic aspects of the proposal. The first concerns the reason why the intermediate step is unlabeled to begin with. According to Chomsky (2013), this is due to the configuration XP, YP, which is too flat to be able to provide a clear candidate for a label (see the discussion in section 2.7). But this cannot be the whole story, since specifier-head relations, in X-bar terms, are among the most stable configurations in the grammar, as typically instantiated in positions that (Rizzi 2011, 2013) calls "criterial."[2] (Using traditional terminology, a criterial position can be defined as the specifier position of a maximal projection in which the specifier and the head share a major interpretable feature; these include interrogative, topic, and focus features.) The second problematic aspect of the proposal concerns the mechanics of the derivation, which seems to run into a paradox, at least under an *internal* definition of labels (see the discussion in section 2.6). Consider again the derivation for (11). Suppose it has reached the step in (14), a label-less structure.

(14) [ø which student [c John met ~~which student~~]]

If the syntactic object in (14) remains label-less, it cannot be visible and thus cannot merge with other material. The derivation is interrupted. In order for this syntactic object to be labeled, *which student* must move out of it (at which point its trace will no longer count for the sake of labeling, and C will provide the label). The paradox is that, in order for the derivation to proceed, the label-less layer must be vacated, but the label-less layer can be vacated only if the derivation has already proceeded, providing a landing site for movement.[3] We will return to this crucial problem shortly.

Finally, no-labeling approaches proposed up to now make no progress in providing a trigger for the intermediate step. It is thus unmotivated, gives rise to an unlabeled structure for unclear reasons, and runs into a computational paradox.

Given this situation, we propose a radical simplification of the theory, claiming that intermediate steps in long-distance movement should be taken for what they look like: they are unprobed. Is this problematic? In section 4.2, we argued that unprobed movement does take place, but the resulting structure is unlabeled (because of the Probing Algorithm in (2)). We also suggested that root clauses are probably the only syntactic objects that can remain label-less, as they are already completed, and there is no harm in making them inaccessible to computation, as label-less objects are (because of the definition of label in (1)). By the same reasoning, it is expected that a label-less layer can be created on top of the root clause, and in fact we discussed several special cases of topicalization/dislocation that can occur only at the root. Finally, we mentioned that there is a stage of the derivation in which an embedded clause *is* a matrix clause (namely, when this clause has not yet been embedded).

With this in mind, consider again (14). Suppose *which student* has moved unprobed. By (2), this movement will have created a label-less syntactic object. If (14) remains label-less, by the definition in (1) it is no longer accessible to the computation, and the derivation is simply interrupted: the result is a root clause. But suppose the numeration contains the verb *think*. In order to be visible to *think*, (14) needs a label, and this label needs to be kept in the computation.

Before proceeding, we need to be more explicit about what it means to be "kept in the computation." Any computation must clearly include a numeration, definable as the set of words that will be used in the syntactic derivation, plus the structure that is being built cyclically. But this cannot be all. The computation must also include a workspace that contains syntactic objects built in a parallel and independent way. This must be the case, for example, each time the derivation gets to a point where two syntactic objects are merged: in this case, the numeration and the root structure cannot be the only source for Merge, which must be able to access the syntactic object built in parallel with the root structure. This notion of workspace is not controversial (although it is often implicit), since it plays a role in virtually any account of complex structures.

With this clarification about the workspace in mind, let us now return to embedded clauses. Suppose we simplify the PIC as follows:

(15) *Simplified Phase Impenetrability Condition*
When a phase is concluded, only its label remains accessible to further syntactic computation.

Not only is this version of the PIC simpler than the traditional version in (10), it is also derivable straightforwardly from the way the computation works: the label needs to be accessible for the derivation to continue.

Suppose there is some extra material merged at the root above the label, as in (14). (16a) illustrates the stage where the *wh*-phrase has been internally merged as a case of unprobed Merge. No label results. (16b) illustrates the next step, when cyclic transfer has taken place. Under the simplified PIC in (15), any material inside the CP stops being visible to the computation and only the label C is accessible. In (16), gray type indicates the material that has become inaccessible.

(16) a.

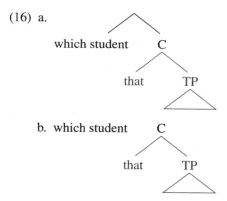

In (16b), we have left the *wh*-phrase and the label disconnected on purpose (this is graphically indicated by the fact that they are not sister nodes). In fact, if we take seriously the idea that a phase disappears from the computation when it is completed, what remains after cyclic Spell-Out is just a label, *not the syntactic object under the label*. So, *which student* and the label C cannot form a constituent in the new phase, since the syntactic object to which *which student* was attached in the former cycle has disappeared. C and *which student* now belong to the workspace of the new phase. Under the reasonable assumption that by the end of the computation all material in the workspace needs to be merged to the structure, both of these elements need to be integrated into the new structure under construction.

The label of the (now inaccessible) clause, C, is probed by the selecting verb, *think* in the present example. The label C merges with *think*, and the structure receives a label from the probe (V). What about *which student*? It is not probed locally (assuming that this is not an indirect question; we return below to the simple case of embedded interrogatives), so it must be kept in the workspace until a suitable probe becomes available, which it can merge with (or until the end of the phase, where free Merge is again available given that labels are not needed at the root). This is illustrated in (17).

(17) [c [which student] do you think [which student] [c John met ~~which student~~]]

Notice that we are now saying that there is no such thing as "real" successive-cyclic movement: in (17), the so-called intermediate step does not properly involve movement. Rather, since *which student* survives in the computation when the structure it was merged to disappears, it is kept in the workspace, ready to be merged in the new phase.

Interestingly, this entails that there is no proper three-link chain relating the positions of *which student* in (17): only the lowest position and the highest one are proper copies of the *wh*-element merged into the syntactic structure (a similar claim was made by Frank (2002) in a Tree Adjoining Grammar framework). We will return to this point in section 5.2.

As a side comment, let us clarify that, if issues of computational complexity must be taken seriously, there must be limitations on how big the workspace can be and how long a category can stay in the workspace without being integrated into the main clausal spine. Unfortunately, there is little discussion of these issues in the current literature. However, for present purposes, we need to assume very little: namely, that a single category can remain "hanging" in the workspace until the next higher phase is accessed. The issue of the upper limits of the workspace might be more deeply investigated in languages that allow multiple *wh*-fronting out of an embedded clause. We cannot explore this line of research here, though.

Let us doublecheck what happens in other embedded structures. Embedded *wh*-questions, like (18), do not constitute a problem given the assumptions we have made so far. Consider the relevant point of the derivation in (19), gray type again marking inaccessible material.

(18) I wonder [CP which student [John met ~~which student~~]].

(19)

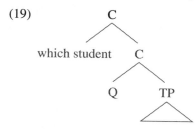

Here the operation of merging *which student* at the root is probed by the embedded C, which is interrogative. As a result, having a probe, the structure receives a label. Given the Probing Algorithm (2), the probe C "projects." When *wonder* is taken from the numeration and the clause needs to be embedded, by the simplified PIC in (15) the label is kept in the new cycle while the clause disappears from the computation. The *wh*-phrase disappears as well, being lower than the label itself and thus included in the completed phase: as a consequence, it is stable, and "trapped" in its position inside the indirect question.

Notice this important difference between our formulation of the PIC in (15) and the traditional one in (10): we do not ascribe any special status to the edge of the phase per se. Elements merged to the root of an embedded clause come in two very different varieties, depending on whether they are probed or not. If they are probed, they are stably located in the phase and disappear from the computation together with the clause when the phase is completed; if they are not probed, they escape the phase and are instable, since they need to be merged again in the next cycle. We believe that avoiding a special stipulation for syntactic objects located at the edge of the phase, in addition to deriving the facts more accurately, is much more in the Minimalist spirit.

Our approach also yields the correct results for the structures discussed in section 3.2, involving *wh*-head movement.

(20) a. I wonder [C what [you read ~~what~~]].
     b. I read [D what [you read ~~what~~]].

When *wh*-head movement is involved, there are indeed two labeling possibilities: either C provides the label (it is the probe of the movement operation) and the structure is a clause, as in (20a), or the word provides the label (by virtue of being a word) and the structure ends up being a nominal clause (a DP), as in (20b). In both cases, the *wh*-head can remain at the edge of the embedded CP.

We conclude this section by pointing out an important consequence of this approach: it offers a solid basis for deriving the condition that Rizzi (2011, 2013) calls Criterial Freezing. Criterial Freezing captures the fact that, once a phrase enters into a criterial configuration, it becomes unavailable for further movement.

(21) *Criterial Freezing*
      An element satisfying a criterion is frozen in place.

As noted earlier, if a category moves to the C area and its movement is probed by a feature in C, C will provide the label. Under the simplified PIC in (15), the entire category CP, except for the label C, will disappear from the derivation. Crucially, the object that disappears from the derivation includes the category that has been moved (in traditional terms, Spec,CP). Therefore, this category is frozen in place (see Rizzi 2013 for a derivation of Criterial Freezing from labeling, which is similar in spirit to the current proposal).

Having pinned down the nature of successive-cyclic movement, we are now equipped to show how our approach to (re)labeling can shed light on island constraints. Our starting point is the observation that, while there is a well-established line of attack for explaining *weak* island effects in terms of Relativized Minimality (or the Minimal Link Condition), there is no consensus in the Minimalist literature on how *strong* islands, including relative clauses, should be explained. Let us start with the Complex NP Constraint.

4.4   The Complex NP Constraint

In this section, we show how our (re)labeling approach to relativization, together with our account of successive-cyclic movement, allows us to explain an important property of relative structures—namely, that they are strong islands for extraction. That relatives are islands is captured by the Complex NP Constraint (Ross 1967). However, the Complex NP Constraint also bans extraction from a configuration where a noun takes what is standardly considered a clausal complement (see section 3.3.3). We discuss these cases in turn.

4.4.1   Part 1: Free Relatives
Mainly for expository reasons, we start developing our explanation of strong island effects with free relatives. We do so because in this case the role of (re)labeling in creating an island effect will be immediately apparent. A premise is that, as shown in (22) and already underlined in section 3.2, free relatives with *chi* 'who' are totally acceptable in Italian, as in many other languages, English being an exception (see Caponigro 2003 for a crosslinguistic survey).

(22) Chi ha telefonato sarà   punito.
     who has phoned   will.be punished
     'The person who made a phone call will be punished.'

Rizzi (1982) observed that while extraction of an argument out of an embedded question leads to marginality (see (23)), extraction of the same argument out of the corresponding free relative leads to sharp ungrammaticality (see (24)). (Sentences (23)–(24), showing this sharp contrast, are modeled after examples in Rizzi 1982, 68.)

(23) ?[A quale ragazzo]$_i$ sai   chi ha telefonato t$_i$?
     to which boy   (you) know who has phoned
     'Which boy is such that you know the person who made a phone call to him?'

(24) *[A quale ragazzo]$_i$ punirai   chi ha telefonato t$_i$?
     to which boy   (you) will.punish who has phoned
     Intended meaning: 'Which boy is such that you will you punish the person who made a phone call to him?'

A similar contrast arises in English with *what*-structures. (25), an indirect question, is degraded, but it is much better than (26), a free relative.

(25) ? [To whom]$_i$ did you know what John sent t$_i$?
(26) * [To whom]$_i$ did you destroy what John sent t$_i$?

This contrast shows that (strong) islandhood is immediately connected with labeling. Both (23) and (24) (and the English pair (25)–(26)) display an embedded *wh*-movement probed by the same C head. In embedded interrogatives, where the *wh*-word does not provide the label, the structure is only mildly deviant. For the time being, we make the standard assumption that this deviance is due to a Relativized Minimality violation. As the extracted category is an argument, the island effect is weak (see Rizzi 1990). (We return to Minimality and labeling in chapter 5, where we introduce some qualifications.) However, in free relatives, where the *wh*-word relabels the structure, the sentence is completely unacceptable. In this case, then, the island effect is strong. The same difference explains the English contrast illustrated in (25) and (26). So the key to explaining the strong islandhood of free relatives lies in answering this question: why does relabeling block extraction?

If *wh*-movement is successive-cyclic, in both (23) and (24) *a quale ragazzo* 'to which boy' has moved, passing through an intermediate step at the edge of the embedded clause. So the question can be further sharpened: why is successive-cyclic movement blocked by relabeling?

We have assumed that successive-cyclic movement temporarily unlabels the structure. When the clause is embedded and the phase disappears from the computation, the *wh*-phrase is kept in the new workspace and needs a probe in order to be later integrated. In (23), this is unproblematic (except for a mild Relativized Minimality violation): we have been assuming that a label-less layer can be found at the top of *a clause*, as long as the clause is not further embedded. So *a quale ragazzo* 'to which boy' can move unprobed to the edge of the (not yet embedded) clause. When the clause is embedded, its label remains visible and the *wh*-element remains in the workspace, while the syntactic object it was merged to disappears. As mentioned above, the *wh*-element will then be merged to the matrix C, its probe, when the latter enters the derivation, as in (27).

(27) a quale ragazzo sai [ø ~~a quale ragazzo~~ [$_{CP}$ chi [$_{TP}$ ~~chi~~ ha telefonato ~~a quale ragazzo~~]]]

In (24), on the other hand, *chi* 'who' provides the label to the embedded structure, so the embedded structure is not a clause but a DP. We have been making the natural assumption that clauses are the only objects that can remain unlabeled, as they are the only objects that do not need to be further selected, being complete. As a DP cannot be a root, it is not the type of object that can tolerate a label-less layer (recall that label-less syntactic objects are inaccessible to further computation, and a DP is not complete enough to be interpreted on its own).

The consequence is that the derivation for (24) in (28), in which *a quale ragazzo* 'to which boy' moves unprobed to the edge of the DP, is illegitimate. What is wrong with (28) is that there is an unlabeled layer on top of a DP node.

(28) *[ø ~~a quale ragazzo~~ [$_{DP}$ chi [$_{TP}$ ~~chi~~ ha telefonato ~~a quale ragazzo~~]]]

Another possible derivation for (24) needs to be excluded—namely, the one illustrated in (29).

(29) *chi [ø ~~a quale ragazzo~~ [$_{CP}$ [$_{TP}$ ~~chi~~ ha telefonato ~~a quale ragazzo~~]]]

In (29), first *a quale ragazzo* 'to which boy' moves unprobed to the edge of the clause. This step is possible since a clause is the type of object that can be a root and thus tolerates being unlabeled. However, things go wrong when we try to move *chi* 'who': if the structure created by movement of *a quale ragazzo* 'to which boy' has no label, no further computation is allowed inside it, given the definition of label in (1). This means that the embedded C cannot probe for *chi* 'who'. More generally, recall that we are assuming the simplified form of the PIC in (15), which states that when a phase is concluded, its internal structure stops being visible for further syntactic computation. In (29), unprobed movement of *a quale ragazzo* 'to which boy' has taken place to the edge of the phase. So, whatever material is found inside the phase CP is not available for any syntactic computation: *chi* 'who' is trapped.

Summarizing, successive-cyclic movement is not allowed in free relatives, owing to the conspiracy of two factors:

(i) If the *wh*-phrase ultimately targeting the matrix C moves first, the *wh*-D within the embedded clause is trapped inside a phase.
(ii) If the *wh*-D moves first, the *wh*-phrase ultimately targeting the matrix C cannot move, since its unprobed movement would create an unlabeled layer on top of a nominal structure.

Notice that, in order to derive the island effect in free relatives, the only assumption we need to make, in addition to the simplified PIC in (15), is that (root) clauses are special, since they can be label-less and can tolerate a label-less layer. This is a very natural assumption. Once this is granted, the system automatically derives the fact that (re)labeling is not compatible with absence of labeling. So, in the structure where (re)labeling takes place, successive-cyclic movement is blocked and a strong island effect arises.

Since our analysis of full relatives also involves a (re)labeling step, it is not difficult to extend to full relatives our account of the strong islandhood of free relatives. We do so in the next section.

4.4.2   Part 2: Full Relatives

A relevant aspect of the (re)labeling analysis is that it makes full and free relatives alike in a fundamental respect. Both are cases in which a word that moves "projects"; that is, it relabels the target of movement. The fundamental differences are that (i) what moves and labels the target is D in free relatives but N in full relatives, and (ii) the category that does the relabeling is a *wh*-word in free relatives but not in full relatives. The parallelism between full and free relatives is nevertheless important, because it will allow us to use the same logic to explain island effects in both structures. To illustrate how island effects arise, we look at the representative sentence in (30).

(30) *Which book did you meet the student who read ~~which book~~?

There are two derivations that we need to consider (and exclude). The first is (31).

(31) [ø [which book] [$_N$ student [$_C$ who ~~student~~ [$_T$ [~~who student~~] read ~~which book~~]]]]

In (31), the relabeling movement of the noun *student* takes place before successive-cyclic movement of *which book*. What is wrong with (31) is that a nominal structure is unlabeled. This goes against our working assumption that (root) clauses are the only category that tolerates being unlabeled, as they are the only objects that do not need to be further selected. NPs cannot be roots, so they are not the type of category that can temporarily be label-less.

The second derivation of (30) that needs to be excluded is (32).

(32) [N student [ø [which book] [C who ~~student~~ [T [~~who student~~] read ~~which book~~]]]]

In this derivation, first *which book* undergoes (so-called) successive-cyclic movement and then relabeling movement of *student* takes place. The problem with (32) is that it violates the simplified version of the PIC in (15). Successive-cyclic movement of *which book* takes place at the edge of the phase, when the phase is completed. This means that the material inside the phase is invisible by the time successive-cyclic movement has taken place. Therefore, *student* is trapped and cannot move out of the phase. (Re)labeling movement becomes impossible.

It should be clear that the explanation for the strong islandhood of full relatives is exactly parallel to the explanation for the strong islandhood of free relatives, as is desirable. We mention this because the free relative case makes it clear that the (re)labeling operation associated with relativization is what triggers the island effect by blocking successive-cyclic movement. Recall that (23) and (24) differ only because (re)labeling takes place in the latter. Accordingly, (24) shows a strong island effect, while (23) does not.

Before moving on to other types of islands, we note that the reasoning that explains the strong islandhood of free relatives and *wh*-relatives straightforwardly extends to *that*-relatives, since they also involve (re)labeling. We leave the proof of this to the reader.

4.4.3 Part 3: The Clausal "Complement" of the Noun

As is well-known, the Complex NP Constraint was designed to capture the fact that island effects are also observed when a *wh*-phrase is extracted out of what looks like the complement clause of a noun. To indicate the clausal modifier of the noun *claim* in sentences like (33), we will use the term *"complement"* within quotation marks. We do this to express our skepticism that nouns really take complements the way verbs do (see section 3.3.3). Be that as it may, it has been a standard observation starting from Ross's (1967) seminal work on islands that sentences like (33) are degraded.

(33) *Which person did you make the claim that Mary offended *t*?

Does our account for the islandhood of relatives extend to structures like (33)? No, it does not. This should be apparent if one thinks that in our account the (re)labeling step is a fundamental trigger of island effects and that there is no relabeling movement in (33) (in fact, there seems to be no dependency involving the noun *claim* at all). To doublecheck this, consider how a sentence like (33) might be derived. Successive-cyclic movement must take place in (34), and this involves the creation of a label-less layer on top of the embedded CP.

(34) [ø [which person] [$_C$ that [$_T$ Mary offended ~~which person~~]]]

Although (34) contains a label-less layer that is not at the root, this is not a problem, since the label-less layer is evacuated when *which person* is returned to the workspace that assists the derivation. The N *claim* is merged with the label, C, and the derivation can proceed, as the N *claim* provides the label by virtue of being a word, in accordance with the Probing Algorithm. The *wh*-element will be merged into the structure when the matrix C probing it eventually enters the derivation. This derivation for (33) parallels the derivation of licit cases of long-distance *wh*-movement like *Which student do you think that John met?*, illustrated above.

So, clausal "complements" of nouns pose a challenge to our approach to islandhood. There are two ways to go here. The first would be to assume that complement clauses, or at least clausal "complements" of nouns, must be analyzed as relative clauses. In fact, this has been proposed on independent grounds (see Arsenijević 2009a, Kayne 2010, Krapova and Cinque 2012). Although this is an interesting proposal, we will not adopt it here. One problem with this type of account is that in sentences like (33) it is hard to identify the position that would correspond to the gap in relative clauses.

The second way to go, which we will develop here, is to deny that there is a genuine island effect in sentences like (33). We do not simply refer to the anecdotal observation that extraction out of clausal "complements" of nouns produces less deviant results than extraction out of relatives. We advance a more specific proposal by capitalizing on the observation that relative clauses and clausal "complements" of nouns give rise to a temporary structural ambiguity. In fact, a sentence starting with (35a) admits either of the continuations (35b) or (35c).

(35) a. The claim that...
     b. John made a mistake (is false).
     c. John made (is a mistake).

A well-attested fact in the psycholinguistic literature is that, when there is a temporary structural ambiguity, the parser does not wait until the end of the sentence before analyzing it, but bets on one analysis. This is the basis of so-called garden path effects—cases where the parser reanalyzes a structure when its initial choice turns out to be wrong.

Here is our way of handling the apparent island effects when extraction takes place out of clausal "complements" of nouns. We assume that, each time the parser processes a structure like (35), it opts for the relative clause interpretation. If *that* turns out to be followed by a clausal "complement" of the noun, as in (35b), this initial choice needs to be revised. In other words, we claim that each clausal "complement" of a noun introduces a garden path effect. In section 4.5, we will describe two eye-tracking experiments that tested this hypothesis.

Importantly, the fact that clausal "complements" of nouns are associated with a garden path effect has consequences for the issue of their islandhood. Consider again a sentence like (33). Not only does processing this sentence prompt a garden path effect—the analysis that is initially chosen and that later needs to be revised involves computing an island violation. For example, given the preference for the relative clause parse, a string like (36) will be initially interpreted as having a continuation like (37). But of course (37) displays a strong island effect, because it involves extraction out of a relative clause.

(36) Which person did you make the claim that...

(37) *Which person did you make the claim that offended *t*?

So, the processing cost with clausal "complements" of nouns is very serious, because it involves reanalysis after an island effect has been triggered. We assume that this can explain the degraded status (or *pseudoisland effect*, as we will call it) of sentences like (33).

Our processing account for the pseudoisland effect in (33) makes a precise prediction. The degradation of the structure involving extraction out of clausal "complements" of nouns should disappear if the structure is *not* temporarily ambiguous with a relative clause. This prediction is borne out. Clear supporting evidence comes from Modern Greek, in which a clausal "complement" of the noun and a relative clause are not temporarily ambiguous because they are introduced by two distinct complementizers. Vassilios Spyropoulos has pointed out to us that, while extraction out of a relative clause is totally ungrammatical in Greek (see (38b)), extraction out of the clausal "complement" of a noun is much better (see (38a)). Crucially, the clausal "complement" of the noun in (38a) is introduced by the complementizer *oti*, while the relative clause in (38b) is introduced by the complementizer *pu*.[4]

(38) a. Pjon   akuses   ti fimi   oti   apelisan?
       who.ACC hear.PAST.2SG the rumor.ACC that$_{Comp}$ fire.PAST.3PL
       'Which person is such that you heard the rumor that they fired
       him?'
   b. *Pjus   akuses   ti fimi   pu   tha
       who.PL.ACC hear.PAST.2SG the rumor.ACC that$_{Rel}$ FUT
       stigmatisi?
       stigmatize.3SG
       Literally: 'Who did you hear the rumor which will stigmatize?'

Greek is not the only language showing no pseudoisland effect when no
temporary ambiguity arises. English also lacks this effect, although in a more
restricted set of circumstances. For example, (39) does not exhibit a (strong)
island effect, although extraction takes place from the clausal "complement"
of the noun *order*.

(39) Which car did you give the order to drive?

The absence of island effects in (39) cannot be attributed to the fact that extraction from an infinitival clause is better than extraction from a finite clause in
the general case, given the strong deviance of sentences like (40).

(40) *Which car did John know the right person to drive?
    (cf. John knows the right person to drive that car)

From our perspective, the acceptability of (39) is expected. It is a case of
extraction out of a clausal "complement" that is not ambiguous with a relative
clause. Hence, no garden path effect is triggered and the pseudoisland effect
is not observed.

Similar evidence is available in Italian as well, as the following contrast
shows:

(41) a. *Quale paese   hanno   dato l'ordine che
        which country (they) have given the order that
        invadessero   ~~quale paese~~?
        (they) invade.SUBJ
        'Which country did they give the order that they invade?'
   b. ?Quale paese   hanno   dato l'ordine di
        which country (they) have given the order to
        'Which country did they give the order to invade?'
        invadere ~~quale paese~~?
        invade

This contrast shows that it is more acceptable to extract from an *infinitival*
clausal "complement" of a noun than from an inflected one. The garden path

account we are proposing here provides a simple reason: (41a) displays the familiar pseudoisland effect elicited by temporary ambiguity with a relative clause structure. In (41b), which is sharply better, the clausal "complement" of *ordine* 'order', being an infinitival clause, is introduced by the complementizer *di*. Crucially, in Italian, infinitival relative clauses cannot be introduced by *di*, as shown in (42).

(42) Ho   comprato il libro da/*di leggere con attenzione.
    (I) have bought   the book to/*if read   with attention
    'I bought the book to read carefully.'

Since (41b) is not temporarily ambiguous with a relative clause, no garden path is triggered and no pseudoisland effect arises, just as in Modern Greek (and English).

Finally, notice that the contrast between (41a) and (41b) cannot be explained in terms of a general fact concerning extractability from infinitival clauses, as the data in (43) show.

(43) a. *Cosa cerchi   l'uomo   a cui   avevi   affidato *t*?
        what (you) look.for the man to whom (you) had given
    b. *Cosa cerchi   l'uomo   a cui   affidare *t*?
        what (you) look.for the man to whom to.give

Relative clause constructions display no asymmetry in extraction possibilities: extracting from a relative clause is simply not grammatical, whether the clause is infinitival or inflected.

Let us take stock. We have proposed that some Complex NP Constraint violations—those involving extraction out of the so-called clausal "complement" of a noun—are pseudoisland effects. The underlying derivation does not violate any grammatical constraint, but a degradation is observed because the structure is initially analyzed as a case of extraction out of a relative clause. Our approach predicts that extraction from a clausal "complement" of a noun should be accepted when the structure is not temporarily ambiguous with a relative clause. We have provided supporting evidence from Modern Greek, English, and Italian.

We are now equipped to return to another difference between relative clauses and clausal "complements" of nouns: Lebeaux's (1989) famous contrast illustrated in (44).

(44) a. ?? Which report that John$_i$ is incompetent did he$_i$ submit?
    b. ? Which report that John$_i$ revised did he$_i$ submit?

Classically, the data in (44) are interpreted in terms of an antireconstruction effect exhibited by relative clauses but not by complement clauses.

Chomsky (1995b) and Lebeaux (1989) argue that (44b) is better because the R-expression is contained in a relative clause and relative clauses, being adjuncts, can be late-merged. In (44a), the R-expression is contained in a complement clause and this, in their view, blocks late merging. Clearly, the Chomsky/Lebeaux type of explanation is not compatible with (any version of) the raising analysis, since the relative clause is nothing like an adjunct under this perspective (in fact, the relative clause is the *necessary* source position of the external head). This type of explanation also contrasts with our account of clausal "complements" of nouns, in which they are not complements at all, but adjuncts (see section 3.3).

The contrast between (44a) and (44b) is not that sharp, and it has even been proposed that antireconstruction effects in general are spurious (Lasnik 2003, chap. 9). Although we think there is something real in the contrast between (44a) and (44b), we believe it has nothing to do with reconstruction or antireconstruction; rather, it has to do with the parsing overload involved in clausal "complements" of nouns discussed above. The idea is that both structures indeed exhibit a mild Principle C effect, but that (44a) sounds more degraded because it involves a garden path effect on top of a weak Principle C effect. This parsing explanation is compatible with the fact observed by Lasnik (2003, 129) that with other pairs of sentences the contrast exemplified in (44a) and (44b) disappears.

Returning to islands, we should comment on one case in which, surprisingly enough, extraction out of a relative construction seems to be acceptable. Constructions of this type have been described for French and Italian by Siloni (1995) and Sleeman (2005). These are a special type of infinitival relative, illustrated for French in (45a) and for Italian in (46a), that is introduced by the complex determiner 'the first (one)' / 'the only (one)'. That these infinitival relatives are transparent for extraction is shown by the contrast with (45b) and (46b), which are garden-variety cases of extraction out of finite relative clauses. ((45) is from Sleeman (2005, 334), who attributes the identification of this type of structure to Siloni (1995), and (46) illustrates the same phenomenon in Italian.)

(45) a. les sommets$_i$ qu'il   a   été   le seul Français
         the tops   that he has been the only Frenchman
         à   atteindre t_i
         to   reach

    b. *les sommets$_i$ qu'il   a   été   le seul Français
         the tops   that he has been the only Frenchman
         qui   ait   atteints t_i
         who   has.SUBJ   reached

(46) a. [Quale libro]ᵢ è   stata la prima   a leggere t_i?
          which book (she) is been the first.FEM to read
          'For which book was she the first person who read it?'
      b. *[Quale libro]ᵢ è   stata la prima   che ha   letto t_i?
          which book (she) is been the first.FEM that (she) has read

Although we cannot enter into the specifics of these quite special, albeit very interesting, relatives, we can note that our approach seems to be equipped for explaining the contrast between the (a) and the (b) sentences in (45) and (46). In the (a) sentences, the gap inside the relative construction is likely to be occupied by PRO, since it corresponds to the subject position of an infinitival clause. If so, relativization results from a control configuration rather than from a movement configuration. Since, in our approach, the islandhood of relative clauses is ultimately due to the conflict between (re)labeling *movement* and *wh*-extraction, it is no surprise that an island effect does not arise if the (re)labeling movement is not instantiated in the relevant structure.

4.5 Clausal "Complements" of Nouns Give Rise to Garden Path Effects: An Experimental Confirmation

In this section, we report two experiments that support, albeit indirectly, the hypothesis that the degraded status of extraction out of a clausal "complement" of a noun is in fact due to a garden path effect. The experiments support the pseudoisland effect hypothesis because they indicate that when experiment participants read a sentence that is temporarily ambiguous between having a relative clause reading and having a clausal "complement" reading, they initially assume that the structure they are reading will include a relative clause. So, clausal "complements" involve some form of garden path.

We describe only the basic aspects of the experimental setting and the main results (for a more detailed description, see Cecchetto, Donati, and Vernice 2012).

4.5.1 Garden Path Effects and Their Possible Sources

As already mentioned, when there is a temporary structural ambiguity, the parser does not wait until the end of the sentence before analyzing it, but bets on one analysis, as garden path effects teach us. For example, when English speakers reach the word *fell* in the famous garden path sentence *The horse raced past the barn fell*, they become puzzled, as various behavioral measures (e.g., longer reading times) clearly show. This happens because the verb *raced* is initially interpreted as a main verb, whereas it should have been interpreted as a past participle forming a reduced relative clause ('The horse *which was raced* past the barn fell').

One legitimate question is why the parse in which *raced* is interpreted as a main verb is favored. The literature offers diverging answers. For example, Frazier (1978) suggests that the structure associated with the preferred (but ultimately wrong) interpretation of *The horse raced past the barn fell* is initially chosen because the parser is guided by formal principles like Minimal Attachment, which states that the parse using the fewest nodes consistent with the rules of the language should be preferred. So-called constraint-based models (e.g., MacDonald, Pearlmutter, and Seidenberg 1994, Trueswell 1996, Trueswell and Tanenhaus 1994) capitalize on the role of lexical frequency and argue that the main reason why *The horse raced past the barn fell* is so difficult to parse is that the form *raced* occurs much more frequently as a main verb than as a past participle. As a result, the parse in which *raced* is a main verb is ranked much higher than the alternative parse. Keeping this important debate in mind, we proceed to describe the specific garden path effects that are our main object of investigation.

4.5.2 Experiment 1: Object Relatives as opposed to Clausal "Complements"

As Experiment 1 was conducted in Italy, we used minimal pairs like (47a) and (47b), contrasting object relatives and clausal "complements." (Each experimental stimulus was presented to participants on a single line, not divided at the end of a line as shown here.) We monitored eye movements while 33 participants read sentences like (47a) and (47b). Because of poor or lack of eye-tracking data, 4 participants were excluded from the analysis, so the results that we report come from 29 participants.

	1	2	3	4
(47) a.	Il progetto che	il sindacato	*sosteneva fra*	gli operai
	the plan that	the unions	supported among	the workers

5
irritò la Confindustria.
annoyed the tycoons
'The plan that the trade unions supported among the workers annoyed the tycoons.'

	1	2	3	4
b.	Il progetto che	il sindacato	*sostenesse*	gli operai
	the plan that	the unions	supported.SUBJ	the workers

5
irritò la Confindustria.
annoyed the tycoons
'The plan that the trade unions would support the workers annoyed the tycoons.'

Participants read 48 sentences like (47a) and (47b) as well as 48 filler sentences. We used seven nouns for which clausal "complement" continuations and relative clause continuations are both natural (these nouns are the Italian counterparts of *order, fear, plan, command, doubt, insinuation,* and *desire*). To make sure that participants read and understood the sentences they were reading, we included 6 comprehension questions that required a *yes/no* response. In all the statistical models, the length (in characters) of the areas was included as a covariate, so the results that we will describe cannot be explained as an effect of the differing length of Area 3 in (47a) and (47b).

Crucially, (47a) and (47b) differ only in the italicized Area 3, which disambiguates between the object relative structure (47a) and the clausal "complement" structure (47b). As a matter of fact, up to the point when the affix on the verb in Area 3 is read, there is a structural ambiguity.

In eye-tracking experiments, there are two principal measures that may reveal a garden path effect. The first is reading times. The rationale is that if the relative clause parse is initially chosen, reading times in Area 3 should be longer in (47b) than in (47a), since at that stage readers must reconsider their first choice. The second measure is regressions—that is, eye movements back to an area that has already been explored. The rationale is that more regressions are expected into (or from) the area where readers are forced to change their first choice.

The main results of Experiment 1 are as follows. At Area 3, reading times did not differ. However, sentences like (47b) caused significantly more regressions out of Area 3 than sentences like (47b).

We interpret this as an indication that, when readers find a temporarily ambiguous structure, they opt for the relative clause interpretation. If readers are reading (47b), at Area 3 they find evidence that this was the incorrect analysis, and the higher number of regressions to earlier parts of the sentence indicates that reanalysis occurs.

4.5.3 Experiment 2: Subject Relatives as opposed to Clausal "Complements"

Experiment 2 was identical to Experiment 1 except that we compared subject relatives and clausal "complements." Italian being a pro-drop language, it is possible to devise minimal pairs like (48a) and (48b).

```
            1          2          3        4
(48)  a.  Alla fine  l'ordine che  convinse  l'ufficiale
          at.the end  the order that  led       the officer
          5
          a dare l'allarme fu cruciale.
          to give the alarm was critical
          'All in all, the order that led the officer to give the alarm was critical.'
```

<table>
<tr><td>1</td><td>2</td><td>3</td><td>4</td></tr>
</table>

b. Alla fine l'ordine che *convincessero* l'ufficiale
   at.the end the order that (they) lead.SUBJ the officer
   5
   a dare l'allarme fu cruciale.
   to give the alarm was critical
   'All in all, the order that they should convince the officer to give the alarm was critical.'

As in Experiment 1, the two structures differ only in the critical Area 3 (italicized). The main result of Experiment 2 was that at Area 3, reading times were longer for sentences like (48b) than for sentences like (48a). We interpret this result as evidence supporting the hypothesis that participants initially choose the relative clause parse even in the case of subject relatives, so they must revise their initial choice when the structure is disambiguated in favor of the clausal "complement" interpretation. In fact, we found evidence of longer reading times in (48b) even in Area 4, and this is naturally interpreted as a spillover effect deriving from the manipulation in Area 3.

Another significant difference was detected in Area 2 when we looked at the "Regression in" variable ("Regression in" indicates the probability that the relevant area will receive at least one regression from later parts of the sentence). This measure indicated that Area 2 was more likely to receive regressions in sentences like (48b) than in sentences like (48a). This is consistent with our interpretation. If clausal "complements" force a revision of the initial analysis, participants reading Area 3 and following areas in (48b) are more likely to go back to Area 2.

Still another significant difference was detected in Area 2 when we looked at the "Regression out full count" variable ("Regression out full count" indicates regression(s) from the relevant area to an earlier one, regardless of whether later areas have been visited or not). Sentences like (48b) were more likely than sentences like (48a) to elicit regressions from Area 2 backward. Since the only area preceding Area 2 is Area 1, this means that participants reading sentences containing clausal "complements" were more likely to start rereading the sentence from the very beginning. Needless to say, this is consistent with the hypothesis that clausal "complements" force some type of reanalysis.

4.5.4 Comments on the Experimental Results
The results summarized above support our treatment of island effects with clausal "complements." However, these results are also potentially relevant for the general proposal about relativization/complementation that we have been developing in this book.

There is a sense in which the results of Experiments 1 and 2 are surprising. Relative clauses are paradigmatic complex-to-process structures, since they contain a filler-gap dependency. This is especially true for object relatives, which are acquired and produced quite late by children, as we will discuss in detail in section 5.4. So why do experiment participants opt for what seems to be the more difficult structure? One possible answer, in line with constraint-based models, capitalizes on the fact that relatives are much more frequent than clausal "complements." In particular, constraint-based models predict that the more a certain noun x is biased toward a clausal "complement" continuation, the easier the clausal "complement" parse should be. For example, reading times in Area 3 should be lower and/or regressions should be fewer for nouns that more frequently occur with a clausal "complement" continuation. We show elsewhere (Cecchetto, Donati, and Vernice 2012, Vernice et al. 2014) that this prediction is not correct. The frequency biases of the seven nouns used in Experiments 1 and 2 do not explain the results.

Another possible explanation for the disadvantage of clausal "complements" is that in Italian they contain a subjunctive, and the subjunctive mood may be harder to process than the indicative. To control for this confound, we conducted Experiments 1 again with English stimuli like these:

(49) a. The information that she had discovered *the site* turned out

            to be important.

      b. The information that she had discovered *on the site* turned out

            to be important.

Numbering over (49a): positions 1 (The information that), 2 (she had discovered), 3 (the site), 4 (turned out), 5 (to be important). Numbering over (49b): positions 1 (The information that), 2 (she had discovered), 3 (on the site), 4 (turned out), 5 (to be important).

We found that the disadvantage of clausal "complements" is replicated in English (see Vernice et al. 2014).

So, it seems that a more structural type of explanation for this disadvantage is needed. This is where our general approach to relativization/complementation becomes relevant, as the following two important observations show.

First, assuming any version of the raising analysis, relative clauses are not adjuncts in the sense of phrase structure theory. Furthermore, in the specific version of the raising analysis proposed in chapter 3, relative clauses are treated as a canonical head-complement configuration: the fact that the relative clause head provides the label when it is merged with the relative clause makes relativization very similar to the configuration where a head provides a label when it is merged with its complement. At an abstract level, the only relevant difference is that the canonical head-complement configuration involves External Merge while the relative clause attachment involves Internal Merge.

Second, as we argued extensively in chapter 3, the "complement" of the noun has adjunct-like properties, despite its name (we return to this specific point in section 4.8).

Therefore, our approach simply reverses standard wisdom: we see complementation where canonical approaches see adjunction (relative clauses), and we see adjunction where more canonical approaches see complementation (clausal "complements"). We conjecture that this reversed perspective allows us to shed light on the preference for the relative clause parse that emerged both in Experiment 1 and in Experiment 2.

Assume that head-complement configurations are more transparent to the parser than adjunct-like configurations. If so, one might say that relative clauses are the initial choice of the parser because they instantiate the very basic head-complement configuration, despite the level of complexity that they introduce. If one adopts this perspective, the preference for the relative clause parse is due to the same principle (Late Closure in Frazier's (1978) garden path model) that triggers well-known garden path cases like *When Fred eats food gets thrown* by favoring the reading in which *food* is interpreted as the complement of *eats*.

We hypothesize that the parser's preference for the head-complement configuration is so strong that it holds even for relative clause formation, even though in this case the chosen parse involves creation of a filler-gap dependency (so that De Vincenzi's (1991) Minimal Chain Principle is violated).

In this section, we reported two experiments that support the pseudoisland effect account for the degradation observed with extraction out of the clausal "complement" of a noun. We also commented that these experimental results fit well with the approach to relativization/complementation that we have been pursuing.

4.6   Extending the Account to Other Strong Islands

In the previous sections, we have derived Ross's (1967) Complex NP Constraint from the interaction between the (re)labeling approach to relativization and the assumption that movement can take place without a probe only at the cost of creating an unlabeled structure. But of course the cases traditionally covered by the Complex NP Constraint are only a subset of the island effects described in the literature. Huang (1982) makes crucial use of the notion of (proper) government to propose a more general account for islandhood, which includes the Complex NP Constraint as a special case.

(50) *Condition on Extraction Domain* (Huang 1982)
      Extraction out of domain D is possible only if D is properly governed.

The idea of capturing all island effects under a single, very general constraint like the Condition on Extraction Domain (and more recent proposals;
see Boeckx 2008b for an overview) is certainly appealing. However, with the
simplification of the formal apparatus induced by adopting the Minimalist
requirement, attempting such a unification becomes more difficult. Furthermore, it is far from obvious that all islands are the same. For example, they
may vary in terms of their strength and crosslinguistic distribution. As we
showed in the preceding section, the Complex NP Constraint has proved to be
a spurious generalization, in that only relatives but not clausal "complements"
of nouns are strong and robust islands for extraction.

It is possible, then, that different types of islands must receive different
types of accounts. While the jury is still out, there are two observations we
would like to advance.

First, one should draw a line between islands whose effects can be explained
as Relativized Minimality or Minimal Link Condition effects (see Chomsky
1995b, Rizzi 1990, 2004, Starke 2001) and other islands. Although details of
implementation may vary, Relativized Minimality islands already have a satisfactory account, and one that fits Minimalist requirements. In a nutshell, if
copies need to be related to each other (forming a chain), a search procedure
must be involved when Internal Merge is at play. Any search procedure is
expected to obey economy considerations, hence to be sensitive to intervention
effects. *Wh*-islands and other weak islands descend naturally from this general
condition. In chapter 5, we will return to intervention effects, slightly revising
their account under our labeling approach.

Second, the unification quest that drove attempts like the Condition on
Extraction Domain should not be abandoned, since unification is to be preferred whenever possible on methodological grounds.

With this in mind, we will proceed as follows. In section 4.6.1, we show
that our account for the islandhood of relatives extends straightaway to adjunct
islands like *if*-clauses and *when*-clauses that prima facie may seem different
from relatives. In section 4.6.2, we discuss other islands that are more recal-
citrant to a free relative analysis. We then devote sections 4.7 and 4.8 to other
islands that cannot be analyzed as relatives but nevertheless descend from our
general labeling approach.

4.6.1 Adverbial Clauses That Are (Free) Relatives
In this section, we show that several types of adverbial clauses instantiate a
relativization structure. Given this fact, their strong island status can receive
the same explanation we have proposed for relatives in the strict sense.

We start from adverbial clauses that closely resemble free relatives, since they are introduced by a bare *wh*-element: these include *when*-clauses, *where*-clauses, and *how*-clauses. Exactly as free relatives can be paraphrased by using a full relative (*I like what you like* vs. *I like the thing that you like*), *when*-clauses, *where*-clauses, and *how*-clauses can be paraphrased by using a nominal plus a relative clause.

(51) a. I fell when she fell ~~when~~.
     b. I fell in the moment in which she fell.

(52) a. I fell where she fell ~~where~~.
     b. I fell in the place in which she fell.

(53) a. I fell how she fell ~~how~~.
     b. I fell in the way in which she fell.

A further parallelism among *when*-clauses, *where*-clauses, and *how*-clauses and strict-sense free relatives involves island effects. We have already discussed minimal pairs like (23) and (24), showing that islandhood depends on labeling. If the *wh*-word provides the label (free relative interpretation), extraction is totally impossible. If the embedded C provides the label (indirect question interpretation), extraction is possible, although it triggers a Relativized Minimality violation (the effect is mild if the extracted category is an argument).

Interestingly, *when*-clauses, *where*-clauses, and *how*-clauses display the same pattern, confirming that islandhood depends on labeling. The embedded question interpretation does not trigger a strong island effect (see (54)), while the free relative interpretation does (see (55)).

(54) a. ?Who do you know when she meets ~~who~~?
     b. ?Who do you know where she meets ~~who~~?
     c. ?Who do you know how she meets ~~who~~?

(55) a. *Who do you sweat when she meets ~~who~~?
     b. *Who do you sweat where she meets ~~who~~?
     c. *Who do you sweat how she meets ~~who~~?

If we assume that *when*-clauses, *where*-clauses, and *how*-clauses are indeed free relatives when they are interpreted as adverbial clauses, we can explain their strong islandhood as we did for free relatives in the strict sense. Take a *when*-clause like the one in (55a). In one possible derivation (see (56)), *when* moves first and provides the embedded clause with a suitable label, while *who* moves later and creates a label-less layer, since successive-cyclic movement of *who* is unprobed.

(56) *[∅ ~~who~~ [PP when [TP she meets ~~who~~ ~~when~~]]]

The problem with the derivation in (56) is that it violates the constraint that only root clauses can stay label-less: the syntactic object labeled by *when* is not a clause. A second derivation is shown in (57).

(57) *when [∅ ~~who~~ [TP she meets ~~who~~ ~~when~~]]

Here the problem is that, since the structure created by movement of *who* has no label, no further computation is allowed inside it, given the definition of label in (1). Therefore, *when* is trapped inside the island.

  Although we will not go through the derivation of these sentences step by step, it should be clear that our approach can derive island effects in adverbial clauses that are introduced by a full relative, such as the one in (58). These adverbial clauses *are* full relatives, so the explanation for the islandhood of full relatives extends to them.

(58) *Who do you sweat in the moment in which she meets ~~who~~?

  A more interesting case is *if*-clauses, like the one in (59).

(59) If he talks to the president, I sweat.

The reason why it is not straightforward to extend the account for free relatives to (59) should be apparent: since *if* is not a plain *wh*-word, it is not clear which gap it could leave inside the *if*-clause. However, certain analyses in the literature suggest that the free relative account can indeed be extended to *if*-clauses (see, e.g., Arsenijević 2009b, Bhatt and Pancheva 2006, Haegeman 2010b). First of all, even though *if* is not a plain *wh*-word, it does have an interrogative use in (some varieties of) English: for example, *I wonder if....* In fact, Kayne (1991) has argued that the conditional *if* and the interrogative *if* are one and the same element. As Bhatt and Pancheva (2006) discuss, the fact that the "complementizer" introducing the protasis is a *wh*-word is even clearer in other languages. In many Romance varieties, the equivalent of *if* is the canonical complementizer of embedded *yes/no* questions (*si* in French and Spanish, *se* in Italian); in German, the equivalent of *if* is *wenn*, which also appears in *when*-clauses; Bulgarian also uses an interrogative complementizer to form a conditional clause.

  A second important observation is that, from an interpretive point of view, (59) is not fundamentally different from the corresponding sentence with a *when*-clause: *When he talks to the president, I sweat.* In fact, (59) can be roughly paraphrased by using a nominal + a relative clause.

(60) I sweat in the situations/possible worlds in which he talks to the president.

Starting from this type of observation, Bhatt and Pancheva (2006) propose that *if*-clauses are just another case of free relative, where a *wh*-word (or a null operator) binds a possible-worlds variable. So, while a canonical free relative such as *what John bought* is interpreted as the plural definite description ιx [John bought *x*], the *if*-clause *if he talks to the president* is interpreted as the plural definite description ιw [he talks to the president in the possible world *w*]. Haegeman (2010b) supports the analysis that posits an analogy between temporal clauses and *if*-clauses in a cartographic framework. If, as all these authors have proposed, *if*-clauses are free relatives, our account for strong islands extends to them.

4.6.2 Adverbial Clauses That Resist a Reduction to Relativization Structures

The natural question that arises at this point is how far our account of strong islandhood can be extended. Answering this question completely would require a detailed analysis of the syntax of all types of adverbial clauses and an in-depth analysis of how extraction works (or does not work) in all of them. We cannot provide such analyses here, but we can advance some general considerations. Certainly, there are other types of adverbial clauses that seem amenable to a relativization analysis. For temporal clauses like the one in (61a), the plausibility of the relativization analysis is confirmed by the fact that they can be paraphrased by a nominal + a relative clause.

(61) a. Caterina went to Chicago before/after Carlo did.
     b. Caterina went to Chicago before the moment in which Carlo went to Chicago.

We mention temporal clauses because they lead to a digression concerning reason clauses. Reason clauses cannot be analyzed as free relatives, as observed by Bhatt and Pancheva (2006), among others. This is why: although temporal, locative, and conditional clauses indicate that the events in the matrix and adjunct clauses take place at the same time, at the same place, or in the same situation, a reason clause does *not* say that the events in the matrix and adjunct clauses take place for the same reason. Rather, a reason clause like the one in (62) indicates that the event in the matrix clause takes place as a consequence of the event in the adjunct clause.

(62) I am sweating because he is talking to the president.

In other words, it is not likely that *because* binds a position inside the clause it introduces, and consequently a free relative analysis does not seem well-grounded in this case. Still, reason clauses are strong islands, as (63) shows.

(63) *To whom are you sweating because I am talking ~~to whom~~?

While we do not have a full account for the strong island effect in reason clauses like the one in (63), we can offer a speculation. A revealing hint is that crosslinguistically, reason clauses can be introduced by a temporal expression (*since* in English, *dal momento che* 'from the moment that' in Italian, etc.). This suggests that the causal meaning might be superimposed over the temporal one. If so, the syntactic structure of a reason clause might contain the variable of the temporal operator while the semantics of causality is derived pragmatically.

(64) I decided to go, since you went t_{since} there in the first place.

Should this line of reasoning turn out to be correct, an extension of the approach offered for relative clauses might be at hand, since, despite appearances, an operator-variable dependency would be present in (some) reason clauses as well.

   However, there are other adverbial clauses (including some types of reason clauses) that look different and cannot be reduced to free relatives either directly or indirectly. These are peripheral adverbial clauses, which we discuss next.

4.7   The Islandhood of Peripheral Adverbial Clauses

So far, we have considered a traditional classification of adverbial clauses into *if*-clauses, *when*-clauses, reason clauses, and so on. However, there is a way to divide adverbial clauses into two groups that is orthogonal to the traditional classification. This is the distinction drawn by Haegeman (2003, 2010a, 2012) between *central* and *peripheral* adverbial clauses (see Tsimpli, Papadopoulou, and Mylonaki 2010 for experimental results supporting this distinction in Greek).

   Examples of the structures that Haegeman would later call peripheral adverbial clauses were first mentioned by Austin (1956), who observed that *if*-clauses like the ones in (65) and (66) do not in any sense state conditions under which the consequent is true.

(65) There are biscuits on the sideboard, if you want them.

(66) I paid you back yesterday, if you remember.

This is also the case for the *if*-clause in sentences like (67), which have been reported by various authors in slightly different forms.

(67) If you're so clever, what's the capital of Kyrgyzstan?

   However, *if*-clauses are not the only ones with uses that cannot be reconciled with their primary function. The same is true in sentences like (68): the adverbial clause, despite having the form of a reason clause, does *not* express the reason why the state in the matrix clause holds.

(68) Since you're so smart, what's the capital of Kyrgyzstan?

Haegeman (2012) defines *central* adverbial clauses as those that modify the event expressed in the matrix clause and *peripheral* adverbial clauses as those that structure the discourse, typically by introducing an explicit premise for the assertion made in the main clause. For example, (69a) contains a central *if*-clause in Italian, and (69b) contains a central reason clause.

(69) a. Se non bevi,   puoi   disidratarti.
          if not (you) drink (you) can dehydrate
          'If you do not drink, you can dehydrate.'
      b. Gianni suda   perché parla   con me.
          Gianni sweats because (he) talks with me
          'Gianni is sweating because he is talking to me.'

(70a) contains a peripheral *if*-clause and (70b), a peripheral reason clause.

(70) a. Se hai   sete, c'è   una birra in frigo.
          if (you) have thirst there is a   beer in fridge
          'If you are thirsty, there is a beer in the fridge.'
      b. Gianni è a casa   perché la sua macchina è in cortile.
          Gianni is at home because the his car   is in backyard
          'Gianni is at home, because his car is in the backyard.'

Importantly, the distinction between central and peripheral adverbial clauses is not only based on the different contributions they make to the interpretation of the matrix clause. Haegeman identifies several formal tests that clearly set central and peripheral adverbial clauses apart. They involve both the internal syntax of these clauses and their external syntax—that is, their relation with the main clause. Here, we mention two tests elaborated by Haegeman concerning the external syntax of central/peripheral adverbial clauses, and we add a third one.[5]

The first test, adapted from Haegeman's work, is the possibility of clefting. Central adverbial clauses may be clefted.

(71) a. È   se hai   sete che puoi   disidratarti.
          (it) is if (you) have thirst that (you) can dehydrate
          'It is if you are thirsty that you can dehydrate.'
      b. È   perché parla   con me che Gianni suda.
          (it) is because (he) talks with me that Gianni sweats
          'It is because he talks to me that Gianni sweats.'

However, peripheral adverbial clauses cannot be clefted. In fact, in order to be acceptable, the sentences in (72) must lose their "peripheral" meaning. For example, (72a) is only acceptable under the weird interpretation that it is when you are thirsty that a beer becomes available in the fridge. Similarly, (72b) strongly suggests that the presence of his car in the backyard causes Gianni's being at home.

(72) a. #È   se hai   sete che c'è   una birra in frigo.
        (it) is if (you) have thirst that there is a   beer in fridge
        'It is if you thirsty that there is beer in the fridge.'
    b. #È   perché la sua macchina è in cortile   che Gianni è
        (it) is because the his car   is in backyard that Gianni is
        a casa.
        at home
        'It is because his car is in the backyard that Gianni is at home.'

Another test discussed by Haegeman involves variable binding. A pronoun in a central *if*-clause may be bound by the matrix subject (see (73)). This is expected if the matrix subject c-commands the *if*-clause.

(73) Nessuno$_i$ arriva mai   in orario se pro$_i$ non viene controllato.
     nobody   arrives never on time   if (he) not is   monitored
     'Nobody$_i$ ever arrives on time if he$_i$ is not monitored.'

However, a pronoun in a peripheral *if*-clause cannot be bound by the matrix subject. Consider the discourse in (74). The subject pronoun in the peripheral *if*-clause cannot be bound by the negative quantifier in the matrix subject position.

(74) (Il capo$_j$ sta facendo un'indagine sui ritardatari.)
     '(The boss$_j$ is investigating people who arrive late at work.)'
     Nessuno$_i$ arriva mai   in orario, se proprio pro$_{j/*i}$ vuole saperlo.
     nobody   arrives never on time   if really   (he)   wants to.know.it
     'Nobody$_i$ ever arrives on time if he$_{j/*i}$ really wants to know.'

The contrast between (73) and (74) suggests that the peripheral/central character is responsible for the difference in variable binding. The same contrast can be observed with reason clauses. In (75), which includes a central reason clause, the embedded subject pronoun can be bound by the negative quantifier in matrix subject position.

(75) Nessuno$_i$ suda   perché pro$_i$ parla con me.
     nobody   sweats because (he) talks with me
     'Nobody$_i$ sweats because he$_i$ is talking to me.'

However, variable binding is blocked in (76), at least if the reason clause receives the "peripheral" reading in which it introduces a premise rather than expressing a causal link. In fact, the bound variable reading forces a "central" interpretation (for no person, the reason why this person left is the presence of his car in the backyard).

(76) #Nessuno$_i$ è uscito perché la sua$_{*i}$ macchina è in cortile.
      nobody is left because the his car is in backyard
      '#Nobody$_i$ left because his$_{*i}$ car is in the backyard.'

The examples discussed so far are modeled after Haegeman's examples. We would like to mention a further test, which involves Principle C of binding theory. Only an R-expression in a central adverbial clause triggers a clear Principle C effect. While the sentences in (77) have the status of Principle C violations, the sentences in (78) are much better, although prima facie the R-expression is c-commanded by an offending pronoun in both pairs of sentences.

(77) a. *pro$_i$ si   stanca, se Gianni$_i$ lavora troppo.
         (he) gets tired if Gianni works too.much
     b. *pro$_i$ suda, perché Gianni$_i$ parla con me.
         (he) sweats because Gianni talks with me

(78) a. ?pro$_i$ ha lavorato molto se Gianni$_i$ ha le   occhiaie.
         (he) has worked a.lot if Gianni has the shadows
         'He$_i$ must have worked hard, if Gianni$_i$ has rings under his eyes.'
     b. ?È   a casa, perché la   macchina di Gianni è in cortile.
         (he) is at home because the car   of Gianni is in backyard
         'He$_i$ is at home, because Gianni$_i$'s car is in the backyard.'

What is the source of these differences between central and peripheral adverbial clauses? Haegeman claims that, while central adverbial clauses are fully integrated (subordinated in a standard sense), peripheral adverbial clauses have a much looser relation to the main clause. In particular, she claims that central adverbial clauses are merged somewhere in the IP area, before the matrix IP is completed. Peripheral adverbial clauses, on the other hand, are merged after the derivation of the matrix CP is completed. Haegeman's analysis can explain the differences we just illustrated. For example, if the peripheral clause in (78) is merged on top of the CP area, the R-expression in the peripheral adverbial clause will never be c-commanded by the matrix subject, so no Principle C violation is expected. Similarly, one can say that variable binding does not obtain in (76) because the peripheral adverbial clause is merged higher than the potential binder of the pronoun. Finally, clefting a peripheral adverbial clause would involve subordinating it, but this is not possible if the position of peripheral adverbial clauses must be atop the CP of the matrix clause.

Having introduced the distinction between peripheral and central adverbial clauses, we can return to islandhood. In previous sections, we gave several examples showing that adverbial clauses are strong islands. Although we were not explicit about this, the examples we analyzed were all central adverbial clauses. However, peripheral adverbial clauses are strong islands as well. This is shown by the sharp ungrammaticality of (79) and (80).

(79) *What does he hate his situation if you want to know t_{what}?
     (cf. He hates his situation, if you want to know the truth)

(80) *What car is Gianni at home because he parked $t_{\text{what car}}$ in the backyard?
     (cf. Gianni is at home, because he parked his car is in the backyard)

We proposed an account for the islandhood of relative structures and extended it to *if*-clauses and other adverbial clauses that are all "central" in Haegeman's sense. It should be clear that we cannot extend this account to peripheral adverbial clauses, given the clear structural differences between the two types of adverbial clauses. However, we think that a different approach, still in terms of labeling, can explain the islandhood of peripheral adverbial clauses. A revealing observation is that they seem to introduce an independent illocutionary speech act and are not subordinate in any obvious sense. Embedding them is in fact quite difficult. First, clefting a peripheral adverbial is infelicitous (see (72)). Second, a peripheral adverbial clause cannot occur inside the complement position of a verb like *claim* or *think* (81).

(81) a. #Maria sostiene che se hai   sete c'è   della birra
        Maria claims   that if (you) have thirst there is of.the beer
        in frigo.
        in fridge
        'Maria claims that if you are thirsty, there is some beer in the fridge.'
     b. #Maria pensa che se hai   sete c'è   della birra
        Maria thinks that if (you) have thirst there is of.the beer
        in frigo.
        in fridge
        'Maria thinks that if you are thirsty, there is some beer in the fridge.'

These sentences suggest that peripheral adverbial clauses cannot be embedded: here, the only interpretation available is the (awkward) "central" one. The only exception appears to be sentences with the verb *say*, where the peripheral reading of the adverbial clause is more easily maintained. However, this might be due to the interference of the direct speech construction. We conclude that peripheral adverbial clauses cannot be embedded.

With this is mind, let us briefly return to labeling and Merge. We have identified cases of unprobed Internal Merge—namely, successive-cyclic movement and topicalization-like movement that target the root. As we discussed in section 4.2, under the definition of label in (1) and of the Probing Algorithm in (2), unprobed Merge produces a label-less object.

If we take seriously the strong unification thesis according to which Internal Merge and External Merge are the same operation except that Internal Merge "remerges" a copy already present in one of the two objects that are merged, we expect there should be cases where External Merge is not triggered (not probed), either.

We propose that peripheral adverbial clauses instantiate unprobed External Merge (see Hornstein 2009 for a similar proposal about adjuncts in general). Since the operation that merges a peripheral adverbial clause to the matrix clause is unprobed, the node created by this operation has no label under the Probing Algorithm in (2). This explains the fact that peripheral adverbial clauses cannot be subordinated, as subordination requires some type of selection and in turn selection requires the selectee to have a label. So, the only position available to peripheral adverbial clauses is attachment to the external boundary of the matrix clause (the root, once more), where no further derivation takes place.

Crucially, if this analysis is assumed, we have a very natural explanation for the islandhood of peripheral adverbial clauses: if a peripheral adverbial clause is attached to the extreme boundary of the matrix clause, *wh*-movement out of it (see (79) and (80)) will be a case of lowering movement, since the head in the C area in the matrix clause that attracts the *wh*-phrase is lower than the peripheral adverbial clause, where *wh*-movement starts.

In this section, we discussed the distinction between central and peripheral adverbial clauses. While the literature on island effects mainly focuses on central adverbial clauses, we showed that peripheral adverbial clauses are strong islands as well. We argued that our approach, which assumes that a label-less node can be created, but only at the root, can explain the islandhood of peripheral adverbial clauses.

4.8 What about "Complements" of Nouns?

Before we conclude this chapter, there is one last type of adjuncts that we should examine in light of our proposed approach to successive-cyclic movement and islandhood. Recall that in chapter 3 we discussed and strongly motivated the conclusion that nouns do not take complements the way verbs do. A consequence of this claim is that so-called "complements" of nouns like the PP *of John* in the DP *pictures of John* are treated as adjunct-like categories in our approach. On the other hand, we showed in section 4.4.3 that *clausal* "complements" of nouns are not genuine islands. We called them pseudoislands because they yield a degradation only insofar they are temporarily ambiguous with relative clauses, since this ambiguity triggers a garden path effect.

If we are on the right track, then we are saying that "complements" of nouns that cannot be temporarily mistaken for relative clauses are adjuncts but not islands. A relevant case is a structure like (82).

(82) Di quale persona hai   comprato la foto   del   fratello *t*?
     of which person (you) have bought   the picture of.the brother
     'Of which person did you buy the picture of the brother?'

In Italian, (82) is acceptable, but we acknowledge that the possibility of extraction out of a PP interacts with many factors (definiteness/indefiniteness of the DP from which extraction take place, type of preposition that heads the PP, etc.).

Abstracting away from these factors, we are interested in the general question, Can there be adjunct-like categories that are *not* islands? The answer depends on the definition of adjuncts and complements. Let us return briefly to the minimal phrase structure theory that we are trying to stick to in this book. If by adjunction we mean unprobed Merge, then the absolute prediction is that adjuncts should be strong islands: as we discussed in detail in the previous section, unprobed Merge yields an unlabeled syntactic object, which is by definition inaccessible to any derivation. On the contrary, complements are the result of a probed Merge operation that involves selection: being embedded in a labeled structure, complements are predicted to be transparent to extraction, at least insofar as they do not host a relabeling movement, as we have shown.

PP "complements" of nouns, despite their adjunct-like properties, do not need to be embedded under a label-less layer, though. Let us consider why. In chapter 3, we argued that a PP "complement" is late-merged when the noun has already been merged with the D. In order to discuss the (non)islandhood of PP "complements," we need to be more precise than that. In fact, contrary to what we said in chapter 3, Grimshaw (1990) shows in detail that there is a class of nouns, which she calls *complex-event nominals*, that *do* require a "complement." *Assignment* is an example. It has two interpretations. In (83a), it can refer to a concrete entity; in (83b), it refers to an event.

(83) a. The assignment is on one page.

  b. The assignment of the problem took a long time.

The addition of *constant*, as in (84b), forces the complex-event reading of the noun. Crucially, on this reading *assignment* requires a "complement," as shown by the awkwardness of (85), which has a status similar to that of (86).

(84) a. The assignment is to be avoided.

  b. The constant assignment of unsolvable problems is to be avoided.

(85) *The constant assignment is to be avoided.

(86) *We constantly assign.

However, as Grimshaw discusses, there is evidence that even complex-event nominals do not assign a theta-role to their "complement." Therefore, despite appearances, this class of nouns is not a problem for the hypothesis that a PP "complement" is late-merged to the noun, at least if we stick to the standard assumption that late Merge to a certain node is possible if that instance of Merge does not involve theta-role assignment.

  Be that as it may, the reason why we mention complex-event nominals here is a different one: namely, they might tell us something about the trigger of the late Merge of the PP to the noun. The crucial observation is that the obligatoriness of the "complement" of the noun depends on the choice of the determiner. With an agent "possessor," it is easier to find examples in which the *of*-phrase cannot be omitted.

(87) a. John's destruction *(of the evidence) was done in secret.

  b. The destruction (of the evidence) was done in secret.

(88) a. Our reinstatement *(of the graduate student) was a big mistake.

  b. That reinstatement (of the graduate student) was a big mistake.

These data suggest that the trigger of the late Merge of the PP "complement" of the noun is in fact the entire D + N unit; alternatively, it is a property of the noun that is determined when N is selected by D. If this analysis is on the right track, late Merge does not imply that the Merge operation lacks a probe. On the contrary, it may be that Merge takes place late because it cannot take place before N has been selected by D. If Merge of the PP is probed, we expect that the probe (N, after being selected by D) provides the label.

  So, late Merge of the PP "complement" does not create a label-less layer. It follows that having adjunct-like properties (as the PP "complement" of the noun does) does not mean being an island, at least in this case.

  Taking stock, we relate the adjunct-like properties of the PP "complement" of a noun to the fact that it is late-merged. However, late Merge does not create a label-less layer in this case. On the contrary, Merge of the PP is late precisely because it must be postponed until D, a (co)selector, enters the derivation. So, our system does not predict that "complements" of nouns (be they PPs or CPs) are islands in general, although we do not exclude that extraction out of them can be degraded by other factors, most notably the definiteness/indefiniteness of the DP from which extraction take place.

4.9 Conclusion

In this chapter, we have argued that a unified explanation for a large set of island effects is possible if one takes seriously the theory of labeling and asks what the few configurations in which labels are *not* necessary have in common. (We put Relativized Minimality effects aside, assuming that they already receive a satisfactory account in Minimalist terms; we will return to them in chapter 5.)

We started by investigating the status of successive-cyclic movement. Since in most cases there is no evidence that the intermediate step of successive-cyclic movement is triggered, we assumed that it is in fact unprobed. Given the Probing Algorithm in (2), this implies that the intermediate step of successive-cyclic movement creates a label-less layer. The definition of label in (1) entails that a label-less layer can be tolerated only at the root. Assuming a derivational perspective, the node targeted by the intermediate step of successive-cyclic movement *is* the root by the time this movement occurs, so successive-cyclic movement can take place. However, the label-less node disappears when the phase exits the computation, and the category whose movement has created the label-less node must be merged again in the new phase. This explains how long-distance movement takes place, when this is possible, without any need to posit an ad hoc edge feature.

We then turned to free relatives and argued that the relabeling step necessary to derive them blocks successive-cyclic movement, since a label-less layer and the relabeling operation are incompatible for reasons that we explained. This derives the strong island status of free relatives.

Next, we considered the cases captured by the Complex NP Constraint, starting with the ban on extracting from headed relatives. Given that our analysis of headed relatives is an extension of the one proposed for free relatives and that they also involve a relabeling step, the islandhood of full relatives is straightforwardly explained.

We then considered the other case captured by the Complex NP Constraint: the ban on extracting from what has been traditionally analyzed as the clausal complement of a noun. Our approach predicts that extraction should be possible in this case, as no relabeling takes place. In fact, we argued that this prediction is correct, despite standard claims in the literature. Extraction seems unacceptable, we argued, only because structures like *the claim that*... are initially analyzed as relative clauses, so extraction out of this structure automatically triggers the strong island effect associated with extraction out of relatives. The gist of our explanation is that when reanalysis takes place, the island effect has already been computed. However, extraction is possible out of the clausal "complements" of nouns that are not temporarily ambiguous with relative clauses, as shown by examples in English, Italian, and Modern Greek. We therefore concluded that the Complex NP Constraint is a spurious condition, and we offered experimental evidence supporting this analysis.

Next, we considered adverbial clauses, arguing that many of them have the syntax of (free) relatives. These include central (in Haegeman's (2003, 2010a, 2012) sense) *when*-clauses, *if*-clauses, and *how*-clauses. Hence, our approach explains their status as strong islands.

Adverbial clauses that are not amenable to a (free) relative analysis do exist, however. These include peripheral adverbial clauses (in Haegeman's sense). We proposed that they are merged to the matrix clause by an application of unprobed External Merge. This implies that they are attached to the root, as this is the only place where a label-less layer is tolerated. This explains their islandhood, since moving a category out of a peripheral adverbial clause would be a case of lowering.

We finally returned to "complements" of nouns, which have adjunct-like properties but are not islands (or at least not systematically so). Although late-merged, they are still probed by the constituent they modify; hence, they are labeled and potentially transparent to extraction.

We conclude with a general comment. Even if we are on the right track, one might ask why our approach (and other Minimalist approaches as well) should be an improvement over famous Government-Binding accounts of islands—say, the Condition on Extraction Domain in (50). We believe that those accounts were powerful and explicit empirical generalizations about the phenomena under consideration but fell short of deriving those generalizations from the primitives of the theory, at least if the notion of government is no longer accorded the status of a primitive.

We have built our account of islands on a specific theory of labeling and on the familiar idea that the derivation must proceed by cycles in order to reduce the computational burden associated with it. Therefore, our account of islands, if successful, is to be preferred, since the data are explained only by the interaction of these two factors.

We are aware that there are island cases that our approach does not apply to. For example, we did not say anything about subject island effects, extraction from coordinated structures, or a few adverbial clauses that are typically neglected in the literature on islands (e.g., purpose clauses). Reviewing all these cases is not possible in a monograph that focuses on (re)labeling. In principle, however, there are several ways to approach these cases. For example, some of these islands might be empirically different phenomena, as suggested by the fact that they have a more limited crosslinguistic distribution (this has been proposed for subject islands; see Stepanov 2007). If so, they might deserve a different explanation from the one offered for the strong islands considered in this chapter. Or they might be reduced to strong islands, for which we offered an explanation (we conjectured that this is the case for a particular type of reason clause). Or perhaps a more careful analysis of the data might reveal that these cases are not islands at all, as we proposed for clausal "complements" of nouns that traditionally motivated the Complex NP Constraint. Although this work still needs to be done, a significant nucleus of island effects has been explained in this chapter by invoking the interaction of basic principles, and we take this to be a significant step forward in the theory of movement.

5 Gross Minimality

5.1 Introduction

Let us open this chapter by summarizing once again some of our basic assumptions. We have proposed that Merge is a free operation applying to any pair of items. We have shown that the simplest Merge is symmetric and yields a syntactic object that is equal to the sum of its parts. We have claimed that the fundamental asymmetry of most syntactic objects, which can be described as the property of having a label, comes not from Merge itself but from the independent operation of Probing, by which a feature (the probe), in order to be to be valued, searches for another feature (the goal). When Merge results from a Probing operation, it yields a labeled syntactic object. Nothing in the system prohibits free (unprobed) Merge; however, unprobed Merge yields unlabeled syntactic objects, and they are not easily usable by the computation.

All this derives directly from the two basic definitions of label (1) and the Probing Algorithm (2), repeated here.

(1) *Label*
   When two objects α and β are merged, a subset of the features of either α or β become the label of the syntactic object $\{\alpha, \beta\}$. A label
   a. can trigger further computation, and
   b. is visible from outside the syntactic object $\{\alpha, \beta\}$.

(2) *Probing Algorithm*
   The label of a syntactic object $\{\alpha, \beta\}$ is the feature(s) that act(s) as a probe of the merging operation creating $\{\alpha, \beta\}$.

Given the definition in (1), unlabeled syntactic objects are predicted to be very restricted in their distribution. Since they lack a label that can make them visible from outside, they can only appear where selection is not playing any role, namely, at the root. This is why we claim that unprobed Merge can only occur at the periphery of root clauses. This is true both for External Merge, accounting for the peripheral position of real unprobed adjuncts (section 4.7), and for Internal Merge, which can only occur at the edge of root clauses (or be destroyed, as in successive-cyclic movement; see section 4.3).

This chapter is devoted to exploring Minimality effects in a framework where unprobed movement, although severely restricted, is not excluded. Our starting point, following the considerations put forward by Chomsky (2008, 2013), is the hypothesis that all linguistic operations conform to "third factor principles": very general principles of efficient computation that are not specific to the language faculty. In this perspective, conditions like c-Command (intended as "Search inside the object you merge with") and Minimality (intended as "Find the closest suitable category") should ultimately be analyzed as specific instantiations of third factor principles.

With this in mind, let us start with probed movement. There are two aspects of the computation of probed movement where locality considerations in principle may be involved. The first aspect is of course *Probing*, which applies cyclically when structure building takes place. Rizzi's (1990, 2004) Relativized Minimality, when applied to the notion of Probing, might be rephrased as follows: Y can probe X if and only if there is no Z such that (i) Z has the same feature that is probed in X, and (ii) Z intervenes between X and Y (i.e., Z c-commands X and is c-commanded by Y). Relativized Minimality, if so rephrased, can be seen as a theory of intervention effects on Probing.

However, if Merge and Probing are two distinct—although often related—operations, and especially if some room is left for unprobed Merge, this cannot be the end of the story. There must be a second aspect of the computation involved in Internal Merge, at least when no Probing is involved. This is *Chain Identification*, the operation by which, if a newly merged element has already been merged once, it must be related to its internal copy. Chain Identification is dissociable from Probing and may be seen as a postcyclic LF mechanism. Now the question arises: is Chain Identification sensitive to locality constraints? The answer is that it should be, if third factor considerations are important, hence principles of efficient computation apply across the board.

Obviously, probed movement is not the right case for studying whether intervention effects arise at the Probing level, the Chain Identification level, or both. Unprobed movement is more telling in this respect, because, if intervention effects arise, by definition they cannot be due to Probing; they can only be ascribed to the Chain Identification mechanism.

In this chapter, we will show that intervention effects do arise in cases of unprobed Merge, but they are different from cases traditionally analyzed as Relativized Minimality violations. Although in probed movement the probing feature restricts the class of interveners (say, only a category with a *wh*-feature counts as an intervener when a *wh*-category is probed), unprobed movement does not work in this way, since there is no probing feature to begin with. Although this could in principle yield instances of unconstrained movement, where nothing blocks it, this is not how unprobed movement works. Quite the opposite. When Relativized Minimality does not hold because no feature is probed, thus restricting the class of interveners, intervention still holds but in a more general way: in principle, any feature shared by the moving category X and by the intervening category Z can create a Minimality effect. We will call this *Gross Minimality effects*. Since Gross Minimality cannot involve probing, because Gross Minimality effects arise when no probing takes place, these effects must arise at the LF level of copy identification.

To be fully explicit about this: in our system, intervention effects arise at two levels. They may arise cyclically, when Probing applies; here, intervention is restricted by the probed feature (this is Rizzi's Relativized Minimality, reinterpreted as applying to Probing). They may also arise postcyclically, at the level of Chain Identification; here, intervention is not restricted (this is Gross Minimality). One may legitimately ask whether this introduces a redundancy. Our answer is that, if the mechanisms of Probing and Chain Identification cannot be identified, as shown by the existence of unprobed movement, and if third factor considerations apply, we do expect locality effects to emerge with both mechanisms. Crucially, however, the third factor principle "Find the closest suitable category" operates differently depending on the specific linguistic operation involved. If the operation manipulates only some specific features (the ones that are probed), search is restricted to those features and intervention is accordingly restricted. If the search is not limited to a specific feature, anything can interfere with the search mechanism and cause intervention.

The concept of Gross Minimality is reminiscent of Grillo's (2008, 2009) Generalized Minimality, which was developed (building on suggestions by Starke (2001)) to account for so-called canonicity effects in the aphasic population. (Some) patients with Broca's aphasia display a deficit in comprehending semantically reversible sentences with noncanonical order of theta-role assignment (these include passives, object relatives, and object clefts). Grillo's insight is that patients with agrammatic aphasia may have an impoverished representation of morphosyntactic features, so they detect a Minimality effect whenever one category crosses over another and the two categories differ only in features that are lost to the patient. While our account is consistent with Grillo's Generalized Minimality approach to canonicity effects in aphasia, we will use a distinct term (Gross Minimality) to stress the fact that we think that, even in the absence of pathology, Minimality is not selective (or relativized, in Rizzi's terms) *if movement is unprobed.*

This chapter is organized as follows. We first define the domain of Gross Minimality (section 5.2): since unprobed movement is restricted to root environments, Gross Minimality phenomena are predicted to tease apart root clauses from embedded clauses. We describe subject intervention in Italian direct questions along these lines (section 5.3). We then address children's well-known tendency to treat embedded clauses as if they were root clauses: given this general tendency, we analyze delays in the acquisition of object relative clauses and object *which*-questions as Gross Minimality effects (section 5.4). Since there is no restriction on the class of interveners with unprobed movement, Gross Minimality is expected to be not only gross, but also cumulative in its effects: the more features the moving category and the intervener share, the stronger the effect is expected to be. These cumulative effects, which result in gradient difficulties for children, are discussed in detail (section 5.5). Finally, we turn once again to the syntax of free relatives, which (in Romance) display intervention effects comparable to those observed in direct questions. We reduce them to Gross Minimality effects, given the relabeling and hence potentially unprobed nature of the movement they host (section 5.6). A conclusion closes the chapter (section 5.7).

5.2   Gross Minimality

Recall that in our proposals, Probing plays a much larger role than standardly assumed. In particular, we have extended the notion of Probing to selection, claiming that selection can trigger direct (External) Merge of a word from the numeration or from a parallel derivation in the workspace. Probing appears to be rather different when it involves Internal Merge—that is, when the newly merged element is part of the element it merges with.

However, it is possible to assume that indeed the operation Merge is always the same, and combines two unrelated syntactic objects. So-called Internal Merge then requires an extra step: when the merged element has already been merged once, it is necessary to relate the newly merged element to its internal copy, or, in traditional terms, to the foot of the chain. This, as we just claimed, can give rise to intervention effects. In other words, intervention effects do not need to be the direct output of Probing; they can also be associated with the presence of copies and with the necessity of relating them. This entails that intervention effects arise every time *Internal* Merge takes place, no matter whether it is probed or not.[1] Suppose that each time a copy is merged, it needs to be paired with its foot, and suppose that this pairing is feature-based, as seems to be generally the case in computation. When there is a probe, the feature that is probed naturally restricts the searching of the copy. So, only an element bearing the probed feature and c-commanding the copy intervenes and disrupts the derivation. This is classical Relativized Minimality, as illustrated in (3) with Italian examples.

(3) a. Cosa hai   detto che Paolo deve cucinare *t*?
        what (you) have said that Paolo must cook
        'What did you say that Paolo must cook?'
   b. ??Cosa ti   chiedi chi debba cucinare *t*?
        what you wonder who must cook
        'What do you wonder who must cook?'

The DP *Paolo* intervening between the two copies does not disrupt the dependency in (3a) because it does not bear the relevant, probed feature—namely, the *wh*-feature. However, the DP *chi* 'who' in (3b) does share this feature, resulting in a Relativized Minimality effect.

Suppose no Probing is involved, though. We are assuming that the copy-copy dependency must still be established for the copies to be correctly interpreted as part of the same chain. If no feature can restrict the range of intervening objects because no Probing is involved, any element intervening and sharing *any* feature with the highest copy should disrupt the computation. This is what we have called Gross Minimality. For example, the categorial feature that marks any word and any syntactic object will count. A consequence of this approach is that unprobed movement is much more restricted than probed movement not only with respect to contexts of application (being acceptable only in root contexts, as discussed in chapter 4), but also with respect to locality. A first prediction of our approach is that unprobed movement should be disrupted by any c-commanded element belonging to the same category as the moved element. Let us check whether this hypothesis is empirically supported.

5.3 Subject Intervention in Root Questions

Our prediction is even more precise: Minimality should work differently in embedded and in root contexts. In root contexts, in fact, it is always possible to move an element unprobed, while this option should be excluded (or dramatically restricted) in nonroot contexts, which need a label in order to be embedded. This implies that we should observe Relativized Minimality effects in embedded contexts, but Gross Minimality effects at the root. This prediction appears to account for a well-known asymmetry between direct and indirect questions in Italian and other Romance languages.

Italian is often described as a "free inversion" language, as the subject can freely occur postverbally, as shown in (4). (See, for example, Kayne and Pollock 1978, 2001; see also Belletti 2001 for evidence that "free inversion" is not really free, being in fact regulated by discourse factors like Topic and Focus, and for an analysis that incorporates these notions.)

(4) (Un treno) è arrivato (un treno).
    a   train is arrived a   train
    'A train has arrived.'

Prima facie, frequent occurrences of subject inversion in questions might be described in the same terms: as instances of the "free inversion" mechanism that is operative in declarative sentences. However, as Guasti (1996) and Rizzi (1996) observe for Italian, on closer inspection things are quite different. First of all, object extraction in direct questions without subject inversion is considerably awkward, as illustrated in (5a) and (6a).

(5) a. ?*Cosa Gianni ha fatto?
        what Gianni has done
   b. Cosa ha fatto Gianni?
        what has done Gianni
        'What did Gianni do?'

(6) a. ?*Quale libro Gianni ha letto?
        which book Gianni has read
   b. Quale libro ha letto Gianni?
        which book has read Gianni
        'Which book did Gianni read?'

Notice that, since Italian is a pro-drop language, this compulsory inversion can give rise to strong ambiguity with reversible predicates, as illustrated in (7).

(7) a. Quale bambino bacia Maria?
      which child   kisses Maria
      'Which child is Maria kissing?'
      'Which child is kissing Maria?'
  b. ?*Quale bambino Maria bacia?
      which child   Maria kisses

Still, avoiding the ambiguity of (7a) is not sufficient to make the noninverted version in (7b) felicitous. This shows that inversion, far from being free, is indeed a strong condition in direct questions. Similar obligatory subject inversion in direct questions is attested in other Romance languages, such as Romanian, European Portuguese, Spanish, and French (see, e.g., Ausín and Martí 2001, Barbosa 2001, Dobrovie-Sorin 1994, Goodall 1993, 2004, Ordóñez 1997, Poletto and Pollock 2004, Suñer 1994, Torrego 1984, Zubizarreta 1998, 2001). The examples in (8), (9), and (10) illustrate the phenomenon in French, Catalan, and Romanian, respectively.

(8) a. ?*Où   Yves va?
       where Yves goes
       'Where is Yves going?'
    b. ?*Qui Paul a   vu?
       who Paul has seen
       'Whom did Paul see?'

(9) ?*Què en Joan farà?
    what the Joan will.do
    'What will Joan do?'

(10) ?*Unde Ion s'a dus?
     where Ion has gone
     'Where did Ion go?'

The degraded status of direct questions with an intervening subject sharply distinguishes them from indirect questions, where the same word order results in a much better output (see Rizzi 1996, where this contrast was first noted). We illustrate the phenomenon only for Italian (see (11)–(12)) and French (see (13)); but see Barbosa 2001 for a discussion of how Romance languages differ with respect to it.

(11) a. Mi   chiedo cosa Gianni abbia   fatto.
        to.me (I) ask what Gianni has.SUBJ done
     b. Mi   chiedo cosa abbia   fatto Gianni.
        to.me (I) ask what has.SUBJ done Gianni
        'I wonder what Gianni did.'

(12) a. Mi   chiedo quale libro Gianni abbia   letto.
        to.me (I) ask which book Gianni has.SUBJ read
     b. Mi   chiedo quale libro abbia letto   Gianni.
        to.me (I) ask which book has.SUBJ read Gianni
        'I wonder which book Gianni read.'

(13) Je me   demande quel livre Jean a   lu.
     I to.me ask   which book Jean has read
     'I wonder which book Jean read.'

The Relativized/Gross Minimality approach we have just introduced can explain these facts in a very simple way. The data show that a subject intervenes in object extraction in direct questions ((5)–(6), (8)–(10)), but not in indirect questions. This is predicted if Minimality is Relativized to the probe only when there is a probe, and otherwise it is Gross. In indirect questions, where the clause needs a label since it is embedded, only instances of probed movement are allowed; as a result, only Relativized Minimality effects arise. A non-*wh* subject does not intervene in a *wh*-dependency, so (11a), (12a) and (13) are acceptable.

In direct questions, where the clause is a root clause and, as such, does not need a label, it can host instances of unprobed movement. As a result, Minimality is not Relativized to a probe, and it is therefore Gross: any element looking similar enough to the moved one and crucially belonging to the same category (DP in the cases seen so far) acts as an intervener. This is why *wh*-movement in (5a), (6a), and (8)–(10) cannot skip the non-*wh* subject.

An investigation by Greco (2013b), who conducted a magnitude estimation acceptability-rating task involving 77 speakers of Italian, reveals some previously unnoticed facts that are even more interesting from the perspective that assumes Gross Minimality. Greco shows that sentences like (14) and (15) do *not* display subject intervention effects, corresponding to the fact that what moves is a PP, not a DP.

(14) Di quale città Gianni ha conosciuto il   sindaco?
     of which city Gianni has met   the mayor
     'Of which city did Gianni meet the mayor?'

(15) In quale città Gianni ha conosciuto il   sindaco?
     in which city Gianni has met   the mayor
     'In which city did Gianni meet the mayor?'

This is explained if we assume that Gross Minimality is still an instance of Minimality, and that it is constrained by the categorial feature of the moved element: when what moves is a PP, the presence of a c-commanding DP subject on the way to the foot of the chain can be ignored.

As Greco (2013a) points out, however, the facts are slightly more complicated.[2] In particular, only a PP headed by a "real" preposition can safely move over a preverbal subject, as shown in (14) and (15). With dummy prepositions such as *a* 'to' and *di* 'of', subject intervention effects may show up again, as shown in (16). See Cardinaletti (2014) for a partially different view.

(16) ?*A chi   Gianni ha parlato?
     to whom Gianni has talked
     'Who did Gianni talk to?'

Assuming a Gross Minimality approach, this pattern can be explained if dummy prepositions do not head a phrase with label P, not being "real" (i.e., categorial) prepositions, but case markers (see Demonte 1987 and the references cited there for an analysis of dummy-headed "PPs" as pseudoprepositional NPs).

At this point, we need to introduce an important proviso. We are *not* saying that *wh*-movement cannot be probed in direct questions. We assume that it can, and in that case it triggers standard Relativized Minimality effects. What we are saying is that in root questions, movement of a *wh*-phrase could *also* be unprobed, triggering Gross Minimality effects. The awkwardness of (5a), (6a), and (8)–(10) is an effect of the latter derivation. We assume that the fact that these sentences are clearly degraded but not completely ungrammatical is due to the availability of the alternative probed derivation (which, being constrained by *Relavized* Minimality, does not trigger a locality violation).

Of course, we are well-aware that it is not generally the case that an ungrammatical derivation interferes with the acceptability rating of a sentence that can also be derived grammatically. In fact, each grammatical sentence can be associated with many ungrammatical derivations, and these do *not* interfere with its acceptability, as long as there is *one* acceptable derivation that produces the sentence as an output. Direct questions are special, however, since the grammatical and ungrammatical derivations differ only at the very end, so the completed sentence is associated with both of them. Informally speaking, there is no time for the ungrammatical derivation (the one where unprobed movement takes place) to be thrown out in favor of the grammatical one (the one in which probed *wh*-movement takes place), since the movement of the *wh*-phrase is the last step of the derivation. The presence of two derivations associated with the final output, one of them triggering a Gross Minimality violation, results in degradation.

An interesting case from this point of view is exclamatives, which exhibit the same subject intervention effect just described for direct questions, only stronger (see Greco 2013a).

(17) a. Cosa non ha   combinato!³
      what (he) NEG has done
      'What things he did!'
   b. *Cosa Gianni (non) ha   combinato!
      what Gianni NEG has done
      'What Gianni did!'

This sharper effect correlates with another difference: while indirect questions are readily available, "indirect exclamatives" are much harder or impossible (see Zanuttini and Portner 2003 for the claim that exclamatives can be embedded only under factive predicates). So, there cannot be a step beyond (17) where the clause is embedded and thus needs a label. As a result, the alternative (grammatical) derivation involving probed movement is never forced.

The opposite effect is associated with the use of the subjunctive in indirect questions. As Poletto (1997) has stressed, Italian exhibits a contrast in indirect questions between indicative and subjunctive clauses. While subjunctive clauses display no effect of subject intervention whatsoever (18a), some vestige of that effect still shows up when the clause is indicative (18b).

(18) a. Mi   chiedo dove   Gianni abbia   vissuto.
         to.me (I) ask where Gianni has.SUBJ lived
     b. ?Mi   chiedo dove   Gianni ha   vissuto.
         to.me (I) ask where Gianni has.IND lived
         'I wonder where Gianni lived.'

The subtle contrast between (18a) and (18b) is likely to be related to the fact that the subjunctive is a dependent mood, while, of course, indicative verbs may occur in main clauses. So, the string of words *dove Gianni ha vissuto* 'where Gianni has.IND lived', which happens to be an embedded question in (18b), can also be used as a matrix question, as in (19).

(19) ?*Dove Gianni ha   vissuto?
        where Gianni has.IND lived
        'Where did Gianni live?'

Therefore, there is a derivation associated with the string of words *dove Gianni ha vissuto* 'where Gianni has.IND lived' in which movement of *dove* 'where' is unprobed and a Gross Minimality effect is triggered. Assuming any version of the theory of phases, the embedded CP in (18) is a point of access to the interfaces. So, the illicit derivation (containing unprobed movement of *dove* 'where') and the licit derivation (containing *wh*-movement of the same category) compete at this point, since they differ only in the last step (informally speaking, the illicit derivation cannot be thrown out before the interface is cyclically accessed). Obviously, only the derivation that produces a labeled object can be selected by the verb *chiedere* 'wonder'. Still, in (18b) the presence at a previous point of access to the interfaces of a derivation triggering a Gross Minimality effect occasions mild interference, so (18b) is slightly worse than (18a), although it is better than (19).

Crucially, at no point in the derivation of (18a) can *dove* 'where' move unprobed, since subjunctive is a dependent mood, so the information that the structure needs embedding is already present before C is selected by *chiedere* 'wonder'. Since unprobed movement of *dove* 'where' would create a label-less layer (therefore an unembeddable structure), it is not allowed.

We now turn to the unacceptability of (19) and other direct questions like (20)–(21), in which what is extracted is an adjunct-like *wh*-category (Greco (2013a) observes the subject intervention effect in these cases).

(20) ?*Quando Gianni è andato?
      when   Gianni is gone
      'When did Gianni leave?'

(21) ?*Come Gianni è andato?
      how   Gianni is gone
      'How did Gianni leave?'

If we consider the most normal answers to the questions in (19)–(21), which involve a PP, as illustrated in (22), we might be inclined to think that these *wh*-elements are indeed PPs.

(22) a. In Brasile.
      in Brazil
   b. Dopo due mesi.
      after two months
   c. In bicicletta.
      by bicycle

If so, the presence of subject intervention is not clear, as a PP should not block unprobed movement of a DP. However, nothing in their morphological shape indicates that the Italian counterparts of *where*, *when*, and *how* are prepositional themselves. Nothing prevents us from analyzing them as DPs and explaining the facts in (19)–(21) as Gross Minimality effects. This is particularly clear for temporal adjuncts, which do not need to be PPs in Italian at all. Some DP temporal adjuncts are listed in (23).

(23) stamattina 'this morning', stasera 'tonight', il mese scorso 'last month', la prossima estate 'next week',...

Notice that when the *wh*-element is clearly prepositional in itself, as is the case with *perché* 'why', which is recognizably made up of *per* 'for' and *che* 'what', the subject does not intervene, just as in the other cases of PP-extraction illustrated in (14)–(15).[4]

(24) Perché Gianni è partito?
      why   Gianni is left
      'Why did Gianni leave?'

This confirms that what really counts for Gross Minimality is the category of the moved element and of the potential intervener.

Another fact that requires discussion is illustrated in (25).

(25) Cosa ha   fatto?
      what (he) has done
      'What has he done?'

In (25), a null pronominal subject does not disrupt the movement dependency. Why? Notice first of all that only a null pronoun can intervene, not an overt pronominal: with an overt pronoun in subject position, (26) is degraded, exhibiting a clear Gross Minimality effect.

(26) *Cosa lui ha   fatto?
       what he   has   done

Assuming the perspective of Gross Minimality, these data suggest that null subjects do not count as interveners when DP-movement is involved. This seems to go in the direction of Alexiadou and Anagnostopoulou's (1998) analysis of null subjects. They claim, and argue with a wealth of evidence, that the null subject of pro-drop languages is not pronominal at all, and that there is no pro element in the numeration. What happens in these languages is that the Extended Projection Principle (EPP (Chomsky 1982, 10); also called Narrow EPP in more recent works, beginning with Chomsky 1995b), which requires that all clauses have a preverbal subject, is directly checked through V-movement to Inflection (Agr in Alexiadou and Anagnostopoulou's terminology). The verb itself is endowed with a nominal feature able to check the EPP feature, hence exempting these languages from filling the relevant position with a nominal category.[5]

Let us now return to the fact that null subjects do not cause intervention effects. Given Gross Minimality, object movement as in (25)–(26) is predicted to be disrupted by any intervening element endowed with the *same categorial feature* as the moving element: the overt pronoun in (26) qualifies as such, but the nominal feature of V itself in (25) does not.

The repairing effect of subject dislocation, illustrated in (5b) and (6b) with subject inversion and in (27) with topicalization, can be described along the same lines.

(27) Gianni, cosa ha   fatto?
      Gianni what has   done
      'As for Gianni, what did he do?'

In both cases, given that both dislocations are typical of null subject languages (Cardinaletti 2002, Cecchetto 1999a, among many others), it is reasonable to assume that the EPP feature is checked by the verb itself; there is therefore no DP category in the relevant position, which might potentially intervene in the movement dependency.[6]

Of course, it remains to be explained what happens in languages like English, where no Minimality asymmetry is displayed in direct and indirect questions, and only Relativized Minimality effects appear in both contexts. In fact, (28) is a grammatical object extraction question, and no intervention is observed.

(28) What did John say?

Our approach to the problem is to deny, despite appearances, that English questions lack subject intervention effects. We start from the obvious observation that the contrast between (29) and (30) strongly invites an interpretation in terms of subject intervention, much as with the Romance counterparts of these sentences: there is a way to create root questions in English that is possible with subject extraction (30) but impossible with object extraction (29).

(29) *What John said?

(30) Who said this?

The explanation for this contrast in terms of subject intervention is only confirmed by the grammaticality of (31).

(31) I wonder what John said.

Recall that a distinctive feature of subject intervention in Romance is that it is a matrix phenomenon; in embedded questions, no such effect is observed (see (11)–(13), (18)). Therefore, the fact that the subject intervention effect detected in the matrix object question (29) disappears in the embedded object question (31) matches the Romance pattern and invites a unified explanation.

We interpret these facts by assuming that English, as well, allows for unprobed movement of wh-elements, restricted to root contexts and constrained by Gross Minimality. This account has an important advantage: it can explain the otherwise poorly understood fact that auxiliary inversion is not observed in subject direct questions and in embedded questions.

Of course, English has ways to ask object questions, much as Italian and other Romance varieties do. As mentioned above, the Romance way typically involves replacing a lexical subject with a null one or with a clitic, when possible (see (25)), or topicalizing the lexical subject (see (27)). The English way involves auxiliary inversion (see (28)). But why does auxiliary inversion avoid the subject intervention effect? Recall that in our system, intervention effects arise when the unprobed movement derivation competes with the *wh*-movement derivation. So, if we can explain why unprobed movement of *what* is not possible in (28), we will have an explanation for the lack of subject intervention effects in this sentence. Indeed, we do have a way to block the derivation of (28) where unprobed movement of *what* takes place. Let us go through the two potential derivations for this sentence step by step,

We assume, rather uncontroversially, that auxiliary inversion activates the C layer and that CP is a phase. At this stage, there are two possibilities. The first is that C attracts the *wh*-category and, being the probe, provides the label. In this derivation, only Relativized Minimality (not Gross Minimality) effects are expected. This is the legitimate derivation of (28), of course. The second possibility is that *what* moves unprobed. If it does, though, no label is provided for the resulting object. By itself, this would not be a problem in our system, since (28) is a root structure and label-less objects are tolerated at the root. The problem arising from the hypothetical unprobed movement derivation is different. Since the object to which *what* is merged when it moves unprobed (namely, CP) is a phase, under the definition of the PIC we adopted in section 4.3 (repeated here), only the label C is maintained, while the object under the label becomes inaccessible.

(32) *Simplified Phase Impenetrability Condition*
     When a phase is concluded, only its label remains accessible to further syntactic computation.

This has a consequence for the hypothetical unprobed movement derivation of (28). Much as in the case of successive-cyclic movement discussed in section 4.3, after the PIC applies, the category that has moved unprobed no longer forms a constituent with the object it was merged with, because that object has disappeared from the derivation (only its label remains). While in the case of successive-cyclic movement the *wh*-category that has moved unprobed has a chance to be integrated (this happens when the matrix interrogative C enters the derivation), in (28) the *wh*-category, if it moved unprobed, would remain unintegrated with the clausal spine. Therefore, the derivation with unprobed movement in fact cannot have as an output the question in (28).

We cannot systematically survey direct questions in every language here, but in a nutshell we predict that Gross Minimality will only be visible as a root phenomenon in those languages displaying no obligatory activation of the C layer in direct questions. French is a very interesting case in this respect because subject intervention effects arise when there is no evidence that the C layer has been activated, as in (33), but intervention effects do not arise when the C layer *is* activated, as in the clefted question (34).

(33) ??Quel livre Jean a acheté?
    which book Jean has bought

(34) Quel livre est-ce que Jean a acheté?
    which book is it that Jean has bought
    'Which book did Jean buy?'

Let us take stock. We are assuming that subject intervention effects in matrix questions are not limited to (a subset of) Romance languages. Despite appearances, they can be observed in other languages, including English. They have not been noted up to now, because languages develop ways to ask object questions without triggering subject intervention effects. These strategies, including obligatory auxiliary movement to C in matrix nonsubject questions in English, can be seen as "tricks" to circumvent subject intervention effects.

Before we turn to child grammar, let us briefly consider successive-cyclic movement again. Recall our assumption (section 4.3) that the intermediate step of successive-cyclic movement, which is not locally probed and is obligatorily evacuated, is indeed an instance of unprobed movement. It might appear, then, that we predict Gross Minimality effects at the intermediate step level. For example, one might expect a non-*wh* subject to create an intervention effect for a *wh*-object that moves successive-cyclically. However, this is not what is observed, since, as is well-known, successive-cyclic movement is subject to *Relativized* (not Gross) Minimality effects.

We believe this does not go against our account, though. Recall that we also claimed that the *wh*-element that has moved unprobed to the edge of the clause is not *moved* further; rather, it is returned to the workspace when the clause it was merged with is sent to the interfaces. The *wh*-element is then merged again when a probing element, the root C, enters the derivation. Strictly speaking, then, in our approach there is no intermediate copy that needs to be related to the upper and lower copies. The only two copies available by the end of the derivation, when Chain Identification takes place, are the upper and lower ones. Crucially, the upper copy *is* probed, and there is thus a feature (the *wh*-feature) that can restrict the searching of the copy. As a result, Relativized Minimality (not Gross Minimality) holds.

This presupposes that, as already anticipated, the mechanism of Chain Identification is an LF phenomenon that takes place postcyclically. We explained in section 5.1 why we think that locality constraints similar to those holding for Probing apply to Chain Identification as well. In a nutshell, this happens because locality is a third factor principle, which is expected as such to affect all (linguistic) computations.

Finally, we note that Gross Minimality effects created by subject intervention are not restricted to questions. As Greco (2013a) discusses in detail, the
same kind of effect is observed in several other root contexts: exclamatives
(as mentioned earlier), focus fronting, topic resumptive preposing, and free
relatives. In our view, all these constructions can be described as contexts
involving or allowing unprobed movement, hence constrained by Gross
Minimality. We will return to free relatives in section 5.6; regarding the others,
see Greco 2013a.

5.4 Subject Intervention in Child Grammar

The kind of Gross Minimality effects discussed in the preceding section are
not an isolated phenomenon. They are strongly reminiscent of what happens
in child grammar with object extraction in relatives and other constructions.
In this section, we will review what is known about this aspect of language
acquisition, since Gross Minimality could be the key to explaining it.

It is well-known that children up to age 5 are more accurate on subject than
on object relative clauses both in comprehension and in production (for Italian,
see Adani 2008, Adani et al. 2010, Arosio, Adani, and Guasti 2009, Arosio,
Guasti, and Stucchi 2010, Belletti 2014, Belletti and Contemori 2010; for
Hebrew, see Arnon 2005, Friedmann and Novogrodsky 2004, Friedmann, Belletti, and Rizzi 2009; for European Portuguese, see Friedmann and Costa 2010;
for German, see Arosio et al. 2012; for Greek, see Guasti, Stavrakaki, and
Arosio 2012).

However, this asymmetry does not hold true for all types of object relatives.
Friedmann, Belletti, and Rizzi (2009) show that it holds in (36), where both
the relative head and the embedded subject are full noun phrases, but not in
(37), where the subject is a (null) pronominal. (We illustrate the phenomenon
with Italian examples, although it holds more generally and Friedmann, Belletti, and Rizzi illustrate it mainly with Hebrew examples.)

(35) *Subject relative*
      la   fatina che ~~la fatina~~ tira   il   cavallo
      the fairy that   pulls the horse

(36) *Object relative*
      il   cavallo che la   fatina tira   ~~il cavallo~~
      the horse   that the fairy pulls

(37) *Object relative with a null subject*
      il   cavallo che tirano   ~~il cavallo~~
      the horse   that (they) pull

To explain this pattern, Friedmann, Belletti, and Rizzi appeal to Relativized Minimality. Both subject and object relatives feature an Ā-movement. They differ in that in object but not subject relatives, a nominal expression (the embedded subject) intervenes between the antecedent and the gap. To account for the fact that intervention is operative in child but not adult grammar, Friedmann, Belletti, and Rizzi rely on maturation of how Relativized Minimality works. In their account, lexical restriction plays the crucial role. A DP element is lexically restricted if it contains a full NP. Nonlexically restricted DPs are those formed only by a bare *wh*-word or by a pronoun. Crucially, Friedmann, Belletti, and Rizzi claim that this reflects a featural difference: [+/−NP]. The generalization is that intervention disrupts children's comprehension and production whenever the antecedent and the intervener are both lexically restricted, as they share the [+/−NP] feature. This yields a Relativized Minimality violation. However, this feature does not count for adults' computation of Relativized Minimality, for reasons that Friedmann, Belletti, and Rizzi explain.

The greatest advantage of Friedmann, Belletti, and Rizzi's account is that it recognizes that children's difficulty with object relatives is a problem with subject intervention. This is clearly on the right track, especially in light of other, often ignored phenomena of child grammar. The problem with object relatives is *not* restricted to relativization, but extends to any object extraction. In particular, while object *what*-questions are acquired at the same age as or earlier than subject *who*-questions (Stromswold 1995),[7] comprehension and production of object *which*-questions like (38) is delayed with respect to comprehension and production of subject *which*-questions like (39) (e.g., Avrutin 2000, Friedmann, Belletti, and Rizzi 2009).

(38) Dimmi quale bambina il   pupazzo accarezza.
      tell.me which girl   the puppet caresses

(39) Dimmi quale bambina accarezza il   pupazzo.
      tell.me which girl   caresses the puppet

The strong uniformity of subject intervention phenomena in child grammar was confirmed by an experiment we conducted with Maria Teresa Guasti. Thirty-four Italian-speaking children, with mean age 6.6 and age range between 5 and 7, were given two picture-matching tasks, one associated with relative clauses (e.g., the Italian equivalent of *Show me the dragon that is chasing the magician*) and the other with indirect 'which'-N-questions (e.g., the Italian equivalent of *Tell me which dragon is chasing the magician*). Examples of the sentences administered to the children are given in (40) and (41); for the picture associated with these sentences, see figure 5.1.

Figure 5.1
Picture corresponding to the sentence *Dimmi quale drago il mago segue* 'Tell me which dragon the magician follows'.

(40) a. Fammi   vedere il   drago che segue   il   mago.
       make.me see   the dragon that follows the magician
      'Show me the dragon that follows the magician.'
    b. Fammi   vedere il   drago che il   mago   segue.
       make.me see   the dragon that the magician follows
      'Show me the dragon that the magician follows.'

(41) a. Dimmi quale drago segue   il   mago.
       tell.me which dragon follows the magician
    b. Dimmi quale drago il   mago   segue.
       tell.me which dragon the magician follows

The same pictures were presented two weeks apart. Half of the children were first presented with the relative clause task and two weeks later with the 'which'-question task. The reverse held for the other half of the children. The results were very clear. Those children who had trouble with object relatives also had trouble with object questions, and vice versa, those who were at ease with object questions proved to have acquired object relatives as well.

This result confirms that the intuition underlying Friedmann, Belletti, and Rizzi's proposal is on the right track, and that children have trouble with subject intervention in Ā-dependencies in general. However, we see two problems with the way they implement their intuition. The first is theoretical and has to do with the notion of a [+/−NP] feature, which plays a crucial role in their account. The introduction of a [+/−NP] feature has a stipulative flavor. "NP feature" is not a morphological feature, and it is difficult to think that it is listed as such in the lexicon. Therefore, it should be introduced in the derivation only when D merges with N. This seems to violate the Inclusiveness Condition, according to which narrow syntax merely operates on words and cannot "add" material, like features, during the derivation.

The second problem is empirical and has to do with the facts discussed in the previous section: even adult grammars display cases of Ā-dependencies disrupted by subject intervention. It would be highly desirable to account for all these cases in a unified way, explaining why in adult grammar object relatives and object indirect questions with an overt subject are possible while direct questions with an overt subject are still degraded. This kind of unification is difficult under Friedmann, Belletti, and Rizzi's approach, since they assume a parameter in the way Relativized Minimality is computed: either the [+/−NP] feature counts (in children) or it does not count (in adults). Italian root question facts remain unexplained without some independent assumption.

Suppose now that the child data above are interpreted as instances of *Gross* Minimality. Recall from chapter 3 that in our account every relative clause involves a *wh*-movement step. Assume that children treat *wh*-movement as unprobed in direct and indirect questions as well as in relative clauses. This would yield Gross Minimality, hence intervention of an overt subject (but, crucially, not of a null subject) whenever the object is *wh*-extracted, as in the cases discussed above. Under this assumption, the peculiarity of child grammar would not reside in Minimality, which would be computed exactly the same way as in adult grammar: namely, in its Relativized form with probed movement and in its Gross form with unprobed movement. Rather, the difference would reside in the availability of unprobed movement. In adult grammar, unprobed movement is restricted to root clauses because only root clauses can be unlabeled (but see section 5.5 for an exception). Child grammar, we claim now, is more liberal with unprobed movement. Still, the question becomes: why are children more liberal? Furthermore, we know that structures created by unprobed movement are label-less. So, how do children manage these structures?

Starting from the first question, a key observation is that, under our approach, children have problems with object relatives because they treat them as if they were root clauses. Crucially, it is a well-documented fact that children tend to treat embedded clauses as root clauses. Ultimately, this has to do with the fact that children acquire embedded clauses at a much later stage than main clauses (e.g., Bloom et al. 1989). So, when embedded clauses start being produced and comprehended, they often display properties restricted to root clauses in adults, as if children inferred their grammar from the earlier-acquired structure, root clauses. An example of this kind of extension is verb-second phenomena in some varieties of child German, which children up to age 4 or 5 extend to subordinate clauses (e.g., Schönenberger 2001, Westergaard 2007).

The second question is how children handle label-less structures produced by unprobed movement. Let us start with relative clauses. Prima facie, it is hard to explain how a child handles a subject relative, if, as we have been assuming, it is unlabeled because children extend unprobed movement to this embedded context. However, consider example (40a). In our framework, a possible derivation for (40a) *in child grammar* is (42).

(42) [$_D$ il [$_{NP}$ drago [$_ø$ [che drago] [$_{TP}$ ~~che drago~~ segue il mago]]]]

By hypothesis, unprobed movement of the *wh*-phrase *che drago* 'which dragon' creates a label-less layer (as in chapter 4, for convenience we indicate this layer with the empty set symbol, though the use of this symbol has no theoretical significance). The unlabeled node cannot be selected and no further movement can take place inside it, given the definition of label in (1). However, suppose that unprobed movement of the noun *drago* 'dragon' out of the *wh*-phrase takes place. By itself, this movement would create a label-less layer, like any other instance of unprobed movement. However, given the Probing Algorithm in (2), the noun, being a word, is an intrinsic probe and can provide the structure with the label N. The result is an NP, which can be selected by the external determiner.

Of course, we can maintain our explanation for the fact that object relatives are not allowed in child grammar: as the derivation involves unprobed movement of the *wh*-phrase, a violation of Gross Minimality will occur with object relatives.

In fact, one can speculate that at a certain stage children move to the adult analysis precisely *because* they have evidence that the derivation in (42) is not compatible with object relatives.[8]

Now, how do children compute embedded questions if they have a preference for treating *wh*-movement as unprobed? The facts are clear, as we mentioned. Embedded *which*-questions on the subject are not problematic for children at age 5 (in fact, earlier than that), while *which*-questions on the object are still problematic at that age. When the child processes the embedded question in (43), (i) both the derivation where *quale drago* 'which dragon' moves unprobed and the derivation where it undergoes *wh*-movement are activated and (ii) the first derivation is more prominent.

(43) Voglio   sapere   quale   drago   il   mago   segue.
        (I) want   to.know   which   dragon   the   magician   follows

When *sapere* 'to know' enters the derivation, the first derivation is abandoned, since it leads to a label-less object, which cannot be selected by *sapere* 'to know'. However, we have evidence from adult grammar that an abandoned derivation that has accessed the interfaces at a previous phase interferes with the grammaticality judgment on the completed sentence. This is responsible for the better status of embedded subjunctive clauses over indicative clauses, since the former do not allow unprobed movement to begin with (see (18)). So, in the object question (43) the Gross Minimality effect arising in the derivation where movement of *quale drago* 'which dragon' is unprobed still affects the status of the sentence. This interference effect is particularly strong for children, since there is a stage in child grammar where the derivation with unprobed movement is preferred.

In the subject question (44), however, the abandoned derivation does not result in any Gross Minimality effect, so no interference arises.

(44) Voglio   sapere   quale   drago   segue   il   mago.
     (I) want   to.know   which   dragon   follows   the   magician

If we are on the right track, adults should also find (44) easier to process than (43). This prediction agrees with the psycholinguistic literature showing that object dependencies are harder than subject dependencies, although adults' difficulty with the former manifests itself not in comprehension problems but in more subtle effects (longer reading times, more regressions in eye-tracking experiments, etc.; see, e.g., Gibson 1998, Gordon, Hendrick, and Johnson 2001, 2004, King and Just 1991).

Notice finally that this approach might extend to another group of people who display limited cognitive resources and comparable syntactic peculiarities: agrammatic individuals with Broca's aphasia. These individuals have particular problems in comprehending sentences in which a DP has moved over an intervening DP (see Avrutin 2006, Caplan and Waters 1999, Caplan, Waters, DeDe et al. 2007, Caplan, Waters, Kennedy et al. 2007, Friederici and Gorrell 1998, Grodzinsky 2000, Kolk 1998, Mauner, Fromkin, and Cornell 1993, Piñango 1999; and see Caramazza et al. 2005 for a partially different view).

As mentioned earlier, Grillo (2008, 2009) has proposed a Minimality approach that is very close in spirit to our Gross Minimality hypothesis. We suspect that Grillo's Generalized Minimality explanation could easily be reframed by assuming that individuals with Broca's aphasia treat these instances of movement as being unprobed, hence giving rise to Gross Minimality effects.

5.5   Gradient Gross Minimality Effects

We have slightly simplified our discussion of Gross Minimality so far, assuming that it works categorically, just as Relativized Minimality does: either the subject shares the categorial feature of the extracted object and thus disrupts the dependency, or it does not share the feature and thus does not intervene. However, a closer look at the data reveals a more fine-grained picture. The similarity/dissimilarity of the intervening subject appears to be gradient: the more features the subject shares with the extracted object, the more severe the disruption; or, vice versa, the fewer features the subject shares with the extracted object, the more acceptable the object extraction (both in comprehension and in production). However, and most crucially for our purposes, only *projecting* features on the intervening category modulate the Gross Minimality effect. We illustrate this general fact with some examples.[9]

Let us start with person features. Person features are clearly part of the label of a given DP: person is computed in verbal agreement, which is clearly a relation external to the DP itself. A look at subject pronouns shows that the person feature makes a difference in producing intervention effects. As we have already discussed, a third person pronoun acts as an intervener in adult direct questions. The situation is partially different in child grammar: in a study with French-speaking children, Christe (2011) shows that a third person pronoun acts as an intervener in children's relative clauses, but a first or second person pronoun does not. Sentences like (45) are much more problematic for children than sentences like (46a–b).

(45) Montre-moi le   crocodile qu'il   poursuit.
       show me   the crocodile that he chases
       'Show me the crocodile that he is chasing.'

(46) a. Montre-lui le   crocodile que je poursuis.
          show him   the crocodile that I   chase
          'Show him the crocodile that I am chasing.'
    b. Montre-lui le   crocodile que tu   poursuis.
          show him   the crocodile that you chase
          'Show him the crocodile that you are chasing.'

Incidentally, the unacceptability of (45) in child grammar is prima facie problematic for Friedmann, Belletti, and Rizzi's (2009) approach, because if Minimality effects are due to the [+/−NP] feature, the nonlexically restricted pronoun should *not* disrupt the dependency of the lexically restricted relative head. We can describe the difference between (45) and (46) by saying that the person feature adds to the Gross Minimality effect triggered by the categorial feature. When the categorial feature is the only feature that the subject intervener shares with the moved object, as in (46), the effect is milder. When the intervener shares the person feature in addition to the categorial feature, as in (45) and in all other cases discussed so far, the effect is stronger. In other words, matching in two features between the intervener and the moved category, as in (45), creates a more severe Gross Minimality violation than matching in just one feature, as in (46). This description is consistent with the Gross Minimality account: since no Probing takes place, intervention is not restricted to a specific set of features. As a result, any feature counts, insofar as it is visible from outside the category—that is, insofar as it is part of the category's label. Person is one such feature.[10]

The same holds for number. As Adani et al. (2010) have shown in a study with Italian-speaking children, there is a difference in object extraction depending on whether or not the extracted object and the intervening subject have the same number feature. If they do (as in (47)), children's comprehension of the relevant object relative is much worse. If they do not, as in (48), children's comprehension is better.

(47) Il   leone   che il   gatto   sta toccando è seduto per terra.
     the lion.SG that the cat.SG is touching is sitting on the ground
     'The lion that the cat is touching is sitting on the ground.'

(48) Il   leone   che i   coccodrilli   stanno toccando è seduto
     the lion.SG that the crocodiles.PL are   touching is sitting
     per terra.
     on the ground
     'The lion that the crocodiles are touching is sitting on the ground.'

Again, a feature represented on the label of the intervening category (in this case, number) modulates the Minimality effect created by the categorial feature.

As for gender, it does not appear to play a role, at least in Italian: children's comprehension of (49) and (50) does not differ significantly (Adani et al. 2010, Belletti et al. 2012).[11]

(49) Il   gatto   che il   topo   sta lavando è salito   sullo
     the cat.MASC that the mouse.MASC is washing is climbed onto.the
     sgabello.
     stool
     'The cat that the mouse is washing climbed onto the stool.'

(50) Il   gatto   che la   capra   sta lavando è salito   sullo
     the cat.MASC that the goat.FEM is   washing is climbed onto.the
     sgabello.
     stool
     'The cat that the goat is washing climbed onto the stool.'

This can be explained if gender is a feature that is not part of the label of nominal expressions in Italian. An indirect piece evidence for this proposal comes again from verbal agreement, as the finite verb never agrees in gender with the subject in Italian. Interestingly, in Hebrew (see Belletti et al. 2012), where gender *is* part of inflectional agreement, gender plays a role in the computation of intervention. This crosslinguistic variation is important because it shows that Gross Minimality effects, though cumulative and not categorical like Relativized Minimality effects, are still grammatical effects, since they are structurally constrained. In particular, once more, the crucial fact is that the relevant feature is represented in the label.

Finally, case features have the same modulating effect: in languages like Modern Greek, morphological case matching between subject and object in object relatives is associated with worse comprehension rates than case mismatching (Arosio et al. 2012, Guasti, Stavrakaki, and Arosio 2012). As case is represented in the label of the nominal category in Modern Greek, this fact is consistent with the Gross Minimality account.

In this section, we have shown that the categorial feature is not the only feature that counts for the Gross Minimality effect observed in object relatives in child grammar. Match or mismatch in morphosyntactic features like person, number, gender, and case augments or alleviates—in other words, modulates—the intervention effects of the subject. Critically, this happens when these features are present in the label of the intervening category and are thus computed by Gross Minimality.

5.6 Drawing the Threads of the Argument Together: Back to (Free) Relatives

Let us summarize. We have claimed that unprobed movement is restricted by a wider Minimality condition than probed movement, and we called this condition Gross Minimality. Gross Minimality is responsible for the many, partly cumulative subject intervention effects found with object extraction. Having the consequence of unlabeling the structure hosting it, unprobed movement—and its symptom, Gross Minimality—is predicted to be very constrained. Putting children (and maybe agrammatic patients) aside, unprobed movement is only possible when a label-less structure is acceptable. This is true at the root, as we have discussed in detail. But we are now ready to consider yet another possibility.

Consider an instance of unprobed movement of a word. As should be clear by now, the resulting dependency is predicted to be constrained by Gross Minimality (since there is no probe restricting the search of the foot of the chain). An important twist, which we have not yet stressed, is that unprobed movement of a word should be possible in embedded contexts as well, since a word can always provide the label for the structure.

Returning to free relatives, which are indeed structures involving the movement of a word, we might wonder whether the probed *wh*-movement derivation discussed in section 3.2 is the only possibility, or whether the alternative with no probe is also available to the computation. A fact pointing to the latter possibility is the observation, due to Greco (2013a), that free relatives in Italian display subject intervention phenomena.[12] It is useful to compare an object free relative (51a) and an object indirect question (51b), both with a preverbal lexical subject.

(51) a. ?*Ho   incontrato chi Gianni ha   colpito.
         (I) have met   who Gianni has hit
     b.   Mi   domando chi Gianni abbia   colpito.
         to.me (I) wonder who Gianni has.SUBJ hit
         'I wonder who Gianni hit.'

(51a) is clearly worse than (51b). This suggests that the free relative in (51a) can be derived via unprobed movement: in principle, in (51a), *chi* 'who' can move unprobed and still label the structure, since it is a word. This derivation does not need to be abandoned, because the resulting object (a DP) can be selected by the verb *incontrare* 'meet'. The consequence is that a Gross Minimality effect is triggered. In (51b), on the other hand, the label-less structure created by the unprobed movement cannot be rescued, since, even if *chi* 'who' provides the label, the resulting DP cannot be selected by the interrogative verb, which requires a CP. Therefore, the unprobed movement derivation must be abandoned. The only derivation leading to (51b) is the one in which movement of *chi* 'who' is probed, and this derivation is of course not affected by Gross Minimality.[13]

As we suggested for the similar case of direct questions, the reason why (51a) is marginal but not utterly ungrammatical is that there is a licit derivation for (51a)—namely, the one in which *chi* 'who' moves by regular *wh*-movement. As *wh*-movement obeys Relativized, not Gross, Minimality, no subject intervention effect arises in that parallel derivation.

We can now return to an important point we left open in our account of full relatives in section 3.3. Our analysis of *wh*-relatives is illustrated in (52).

(52) [$_D$ the [$_{NP}$ man [[$_{DP}$ who ~~man~~] I love [$_{DP}$ ~~who man~~]]]]

In section 3.3, we asked what triggers the relabeling movement of *man* in a sentence like (52). We briefly mentioned that this short movement might be analyzed as unprobed, but we did not discuss this possibility further since we had not yet introduced the concept of unprobed movement. Now it should be clear that nothing prevents us from adopting that analysis. After the internal DP has undergone *wh*-movement to the edge of the clause, the final N-raising can take place without a trigger because *man* can nominalize the structure, being a word. No Gross Minimality effect arises since the unprobed movement step is very short, and nothing intervenes between the *wh*-phrase *who man* in the C area and the edge of the clause to which the noun *man* raises.[14]

5.7 Conclusion

In chapter 4, we proposed that unprobed Merge must be possible given our basic assumptions about the nature of Merge and Probing, and that its distribution should be very restricted since it yields unlabeled syntactic objects. In particular, we argued, unprobed Merge can only apply at the root, where labels are not necessary because there is no "outside" that needs to see the syntactic object.

This chapter has focused on another predicted property of unprobed *Internal* Merge, concerning locality. What differentiates Internal Merge and External Merge is that when the merged element has already been merged once, it must be related to the internal copy, or, in traditional terms, to the foot of the chain. This gives rise to intervention effects, which may obtain every time Internal Merge holds, whether it is probed or not.

When there is a probe, it naturally restricts the searching of the copy, and only an element bearing the probed feature and c-commanding the copy intervenes and disrupts the derivation. This is classical Relativized Minimality (Rizzi 1990, 2004). If no feature is probed, on the other hand, any element intervening and sharing *any* feature with the highest copy disrupts the computation. This is what we call Gross Minimality. After defining the concept of Gross Minimality, we showed that direct questions in Italian and other Romance languages, object extraction in child grammar, and free relatives in Romance are all instances of unprobed movement restricted by Gross Minimality.

6 Conclusion (and Openings)

Two themes link the chapters of this book. First, we investigated the process by which a word provides the label when it is merged with another category. This process takes place in cases of External Merge (e.g., when V merges with a DP to form the most embedded layer of the VP), but it also takes place when a word is internally merged with a phrase. In the latter case, the resulting structure typically receives a label different from the one it had before the word moved; this is the configuration we have called *relabeling*. Accordingly, we claim that words have a relabeling power.

Of course, saying that words have a relabeling power presupposes some notion of word. Although we acknowledged that "word" is a slippery concept, we argued that what is not negotiable in the relabeling approach—namely, that some units already equipped with a category are delivered from the morphological component to syntax—is made highly plausible by linguistic arguments as well as by results emerging from the neurolinguistic and psycholinguistic literature.

We claimed that relabeling is responsible for one of the most complicated puzzles in the theory of syntax: the fact that sometimes clausal constituents are turned into nominal constituents, that is, relative clauses. In particular, we claimed that relabeling is involved in all the cases of relativization considered in this book: free relatives, externally headed relatives, reduced relatives, and at least some cases of internally headed relatives. What all these cases of relativization have in common is that a word is merged with the relative structure that it comes from and provides the label by virtue of being a word. What changes in the different cases of relativization is the type of word that moves and the type of category that the word merges with. The relabeling word can be a D (as in free relatives and in Italian Sign Language (LIS) internally headed relatives) or an N (as in externally headed relatives). The category that is relabeled by the word can be a CP (as in full relatives) or a VP/vP (as in reduced relatives).

This analysis, although very simple, has been precluded for externally headed relative clauses by the observation that the external head does not need to be a word, since a phrase can be freely modified by a relative (as in *the chapter of this book that I like most*). However, we overcame this obstacle by providing a wealth of independent evidence that any modifier of the relative clause head (*of this book*) is late-merged after the noun (*chapter*) has moved and relabeled the structure, and thereby claiming that modifiers of the noun can only be adjuncts.

On the other hand, under the relabeling approach, the configuration from which relativization emerges has much in common with the head-complement configuration. In this sense, our approach makes apparent what was already implicit in other types of raising analyses for relative clauses: relatives cannot be adjunction structures. We investigated this point by comparing relative clauses having a structure exemplified by *the agreement that they had reached at the end of the book* with minimally different structures that have been traditionally analyzed as complement clauses of a noun, like *the agreement that they had reached the end of the book*, and testing experimentally the garden path effect that this temporary structural ambiguity gives rise to.

The other (albeit strictly related) theme that links the chapters in this book is the assumption that phrase structure building is governed by what we called the Probing Algorithm, according to which the probe of the merging operation provides the label for the resulting structure. In fact, we explained that words have a relabeling power precisely because they are intrinsic probes. We then explored an issue that naturally emerges if one takes the Probing Algorithm seriously. Suppose that in principle Merge can be unprobed, since it is the fundamental structure-building operation and, if it could not apply freely, silence should be preferred to speech or a short sentence should always be preferred to a long one. Still, it is a fact that Merge is typically connected to a probe, and the systematicity of this connection cannot be coincidental. The Probing Algorithm can shed light on this. Clearly, under the Probing Algorithm, no Probe means no label, so unprobed Merge comes with a cost, since unlabeled objects are very special and it is not even obvious that they can be tolerated in the derivation.

Clarifying whether unlabeled objects are permissible or not required disentangling two possible concepts of label. On the one hand, a label can be seen as an instruction about how a syntactic object should be interpreted in the semantic component (external definition). On the other hand, a label can be seen as the information that determines what a syntactic object selects and what it is selected by (internal definition). The first view emphasizes the semantic role of labels; the second emphasizes the role of labels in determining the possible distribution of a category inside the clause. We argued in favor of the internal definition and, on this basis, we concluded that there is one special type of object that can remain unlabeled. This object is the root, since it does not need to be selected or to trigger further computation.

Capitalizing on the special status of the root, we built a theory of successive-cyclic movement and of strong islands, in which labeling plays a crucial role. Finally, we asked what the locality conditions on unprobed movement can be, since the well-established theory of locality known as Relativized Minimality naturally applies only to cases of probed movement (a category intervenes between probe and goal if it has the same features as the probed category). We proposed a tighter locality condition on unprobed movement, Gross Minimality, and claimed that it can shed light on various phenomena including subject intervention effects in adult and child grammar.

This book is now finished, but we believe that our research into the mechanisms of probing and labeling is not. Many directions open quite naturally given the central role we have assigned to probing and labeling in syntactic computations, and we look forward to exploring them in future work.

We have extended the notion of Probing far beyond its initial borders. Probing was born as a notion related to mechanisms that trigger feature relations, such as movement and long-distance morphological agreement. But we have extended it to include selection. In all cases, what seems to hold is an asymmetric relation between an element in need of some featural "satisfaction" or valuation, the probe, and an element able to satisfy or value it, the goal. In all cases, the probe seeks the goal in its c-command domain, and probing reduces to a simple searching operation, quite naturally obeying third factor principles such as locality and intervention. In all cases, given the Probing Algorithm, the probe labels the structure it is located in.

There are many areas where we believe this extended notion of Probing could be relevant and where its labeling consequences might play an important role. We hope the reader will be willing to imagine these areas and try to figure out how a (re)labeling approach could shed light on them. One such area is the traditional realm of binding—that is, referential relations between nominal expressions, which we explored in a preliminary way in Cecchetto and Donati 2010. Pronouns are clearly elements missing something (call it referentiality) that may establish a relation with another element (a referential expression) in the syntactic context. Suppose referentiality is a feature. We can then imply that a pronoun is a probe searching for a goal that can referentially value it. If this is the case, our system makes a number of predictions concerning the distribution of pronouns and their interpretation, which are worth exploring in future research. Just to mention the clearest one, given that only labels can probe, we predict that a pronoun can probe into its c-command domain for referential valuation only when it can provide the label for the structure it is located in. This seems to be enough to derive the contrast in (1).

(1) a. *He$_i$ likes John$_i$.
    b. He$_i$ is John$_i$.

(1a) is a classical Principle C violation; it can be interpreted in our system as a symptom of mislabeling. *He* can obtain the same referential value as *John* by probing it. This implies that *he* labels the structure; however, (1a) is a clause, not a DP, and a D label thus yields unacceptability.

Under the standard definition of Principle C, (1b) *should* be a Principle C violation, but it is grammatical. This is explained in our system if the derivation of the copular sentence in (1b) includes a stage where a small clause step is relabeled by *he*. In that position, *he* can thus probe *John* without causing any harm. More generally, our system predicts that Principle C effects should be obviated in every context where a D label is acceptable. We leave to further research a systematic scrutiny of what happens in all the various contexts where this prediction is relevant, as well as the fundamental question of whether all anaphoric relations between nominal expressions can be reduced to Probing.

Notes

Chapter 1

1. Another antilexicalist approach is Borer's (2003, 2004) exoskeletal approach to categories. See also Boeckx 2008a, 2010 for a conceptual criticism of lexicalism and Adger 2013 for a coherent phrase structure theory based on an antilexicalist stand.

Chapter 2

1. Collins (2002) sketches a theory of syntax in which the notion of label can be dispensed with. However, what he tries to eliminate is really the notion of label as an extra object distinct from the two items that are merged, as in X-bar theory. In his system, what we call a *label*, which cannot be dispensed with, is called a *locus*.

2. Chomsky (2013) claims that *what* is indeed syntactically more complex than a word, being headed by a null Q. But his claim looks suspiciously like an attempt to reintroduce the X-bar stipulation that a word cannot enter a derivation without heading a phrase. Similar analyses have also been proposed for elements such as *he*. What we want to underline here is that if words exist and Merge assembles them, an element that looks like a word should be analyzed as such unless strong counterevidence is given.

3. Here, *relevant conditions* refers to locality conditions defined in terms of Relativized Minimality and Subjacency. We will set locality considerations aside for the time being, returning to discuss them in chapters 4 and 5.

Chapter 3

1. The term *relabeling* is a very useful shortcut for describing all the situations in which a movement operation produces a label different from the one the structure had before that operation. We will use this term although, as we noted in chapter 2, it is not entirely accurate from a technical point of view, since what really happens in what we call relabeling configurations is not that the old label is changed; rather, a new and different label is added on top of the old one.

2. A qualification is needed. In chapter 5, we will argue that in a restricted set of cases, including direct questions and free relatives, movement of a *wh*-category can take place without being probed. This is what we will call *unprobed movement*. However, even assuming that one of the possible derivations of free relatives involves unprobed movement, no featural difference needs to be assumed in the C area between a free relative and the corresponding interrogative.

3. Caponigro's (2003, 10) identification of free relatives in 29 languages is based on the following operative definition:

Free relatives are all and only those strings that satisfy the following properties: (i) they contain a *wh*-word, or a morphologically complex word with a *wh*-word as its root; (ii) they are clauses with a gap; and (iii) they can always be replaced with truth-conditionally equivalent DPs or PPs.

We basically agree with this working definition, although we will introduce an important caveat concerning morphologically complex words like *whatever/whichever* (see the discussion regarding (29)–(34)).

4. A reviewer asks what the relabeling approach has to say about correlatives. In section 3.5, we will offer a relabeling analysis of an Italian Sign Language (LIS) construction that in the previous literature has been described as a correlative structure. We will argue that this LIS construction is a case of an obligatorily extraposed internally headed relative, and we will discuss in more detail the issue of the nonexistence of in-situ free relatives. However, genuine correlatives that cannot be reduced to special cases of internally headed relatives are not a test case for the relabeling approach because correlatives by definition have a clausal (not a nominalized) nature.

5. A reviewer notes that for many speakers he or she consulted, (29a) is fully natural only with a restrictive coda. As the same reviewer notes, this is not particularly problematic for the analysis that takes *whichever* to be an external determiner introducing a full relative, since there are determiners that require a relative clause, such as *derjenige* 'the one' in German and possibly *the few* in English.

6. An intermediate case that we cannot explore here is Hebrew. In Hebrew, *wh*-words do introduce free relatives. However, free relatives are not ambiguous with questions because in free relatives the *wh*-word must be followed by the clitic complementizer *še-*, while this does not happen in interrogatives. Therefore, descriptively speaking, Hebrew free relatives share some properties with free relatives in English and Italian (use of a *wh*-word) and other properties with the "demonstrative + relative" construction that we do not assimilate to genuine free relatives (obligatory occurrence of a complementizer).

Another interesting case in this respect is the dialect of Chiavari (near Genoa), in which a clause like (i) is ambiguous between a relative and an interrogative reading (see Capello 2010 for more data and an analysis).

(i) kuelu ke   t'e   vistu
    this   that you have seen
    'what have you seen' (relative)
    'What you have seen?' (interrogative)

7. Analyzing the complementizer *that* as the internal determiner allows us to take a step forward in explaining *ever*-relatives as well. Recall from section 3.2 that there are

strong reasons to think that *ever*-relatives must be analyzed as full relatives, where the *ever*-item is the external determiner, as in (i).

(i) Bill will eat whichever dish (that) wins the contest.

However, subject *ever*-relatives contrast with garden-variety subject full relatives with respect to the possibility of omitting *that*: while *that* can be omitted in (i), it is obligatory in (ii).

(ii) Bill will eat the dish *(that) wins the contest.

Suppose there are actually two *whichever*s: one is a determiner that can be selected as such from the lexicon (and thus can head a *that*-relative and be used absolutely); the other is formed derivationally, when the determiner *which* heading a *wh*-phrase cliticizes onto *ever*, as in (iii).

(iii) Bill will eat [$_{DP}$ which-ever [$_{NP}$ dish [$_{CP}$ ~~which dish~~ wins the contest ~~which dish~~]]]

In (iii), *which dish* moves as a *wh*-phrase to the periphery of the relative clause. From here, *dish* moves and relabels the structure as usual; *which* is then attracted by the affix *ever*, and together they form the complex determiner *which-ever*. A similar derivation is blocked in (ii) because, under our analysis, if *that* is absent, the relative clause contains an NP (*dish*), not a DP (*that dish*). Ultimately, this leads to a violation of the Theta-Criterion and case theory.

A similar contrast does not arise between object *ever*-relatives and garden-variety object full relatives; see (iv) and (v). We assume that a phonologically null determiner can be licensed in (v), which cannot be licensed in (ii). We do not know whether this is a superficial phenomenon, akin to the fact that without *that* the relative clause in (ii) would have the same form as the declarative *the dish wins the contest*, or whether there is some deeper reason.

(iv) Bill will eat whichever dish (that) Mary is cooking.
(v) Bill will eat the dish (that) Mary is cooking.

8. This construction is not to be confused with the one we discussed at the end of section 3.2, illustrated here:

(i) lo que quiero
    it that (I) want
    'what I want'

In (i), the element introducing the clause is clearly a pronoun (*lo*), while it is a determiner (*el*) in the case discussed in the text.

9. Given the Probing framework adopted here, it is possible to define adjuncts as unprobed syntactic objects. As such, they might be inserted in the syntactic structure after the Probing-driven syntax has completed the phase. Notice that the idea that adjuncts are unprobed, which is very reasonable if we assume they are not selected and do not receive a theta-role, has an important consequence concerning labeling: if, as discussed in chapter 2, labels are given by Probing relations, when a merging operation is performed with no probe, no label should arise (see Hornstein 2009 for a very similar

approach to adjunction). But the facts concerning adjuncts are intricate. We will return to them in chapter 4.

10. This criterion is not as strong as usually claimed, even with verbs. Virtually any transitive verb allows some idiosyncratic object-less use. (We thank Leonardo Savoia for discussion of this fact.) Whether this observation should push us toward completely rethinking the notion of internal argument, we do not know and do not want to discuss here (see Adger 2013 for a proposal in this direction, though). What is essential for our analysis of relativization is a more limited claim, namely, that *nouns* do not take complements.

11. Grimshaw (1990) claims that there is a class of nouns that *do* require a "complement." Grimshaw labels them *complex-event nominals*. We discuss this class of nominals and their relevance for the status of noun "complements" in section 4.8. See also Donati and Cecchetto 2011 for extensive discussion.

12. More evidence for the fact that the determiner + noun form a constituent without the "complement" of the noun comes from idioms. The verbal domain exhibits a well-known asymmetry concerning idioms: there are idioms where the verb and the complement are fixed and the subject is variable, such as *kick the bucket* and *bite the dust*, but no idiom exists where the subject and the verb are fixed and the complement is variable. The same asymmetry is not found in the nominal domain: there are idioms where the noun and the "complement" are fixed and the determiner is variable (such as *flash in the pan*), *and* there are idioms where the determiner and the noun are fixed and the "complement" is variable: for example, in Italian, *due fili al ragù/al pesto/ai funghi* 'two strings Bolognese/with pesto/with mushrooms' (i.e., 'some spaghetti'); *quattro passi tra le nuvole/al parco...* 'four steps in the clouds/in the park' (i.e., 'a stroll...'). Similar examples are robustly attested crosslinguistically: for example, in French, *trois pas* 'three steps' (i.e., 'a stroll'); *(il n'y a pas) trente-six façons de le dire/de le faire/de...* '(there aren't) thirty-six ways of saying it/of doing it/of...' (i.e., 'there is only one way to do/to say /to...').

13. There is some variation on this judgment among speakers: while most sharply reject *ne*-cliticization with a relative clause, others are more tolerant. Thanks to Giorgio Graffi for pointing this out to us.

14. Bhatt (2002) points out that in (i), *longest book* can be interpreted in the scope of *say* (the so-called low reading). This leads him to assume reconstruction of the phrase *longest book* into a position c-commanded by *say*.

(i) The longest book John said Tolstoy had written was *Anna Karenina*.

However, Sharvit (2007) explains the low reading in (i) without assuming reconstruction of the entire phrase *longest book* (see also Bhatt and Sharvit 2005 and Heycock 2005, where it is shown that the low reading arises only with a restricted set of propositional attitude verbs). Furthermore, Bhatt and Pancheva (2012) argue that in (ii) the head noun *man* must be generated inside the relative clause, while *first* must be generated outside it.

(ii) the first man to walk on the moon

The semantic accounts proposed by Sharvit (2007) for (i) and by Bhatt and Pancheva (2012) for (ii) are consistent with the relabeling approach.

15. At first sight, this might seem to go against the generalization we discussed in section 3.2, where we claimed that the relabeling movement associated with relativization can never take place at LF because categories feed cyclic derivations. Things are more complicated in LIS, however: in PE-clauses, when the determiner PE appears in situ, the nonmanual marking associated with it obligatorily spreads over the relative clause. This spreading performs what we might call a "prosodic labeling," which is able to nominalize the structure, as required. This possibility appears to be unique to the signing modality (see Cecchetto and Donati, in press a for details and Cecchetto, Geraci, and Zucchi 2009 for the general mechanism).

16. This stranding of the head noun has interesting interpretive consequences that we cannot discuss here. See Shimoyama 1999, where the interpretation of internally headed relative clauses in Japanese was first explored, and also Cecchetto, Geraci, and Zucchi 2006 and Branchini and Donati 2009 for discussion.

Chapter 4

1. There are actually two very different interpretations of the notion of phase in the Minimalist literature. The "traditional" one, going back to Uriagereka's (1999) seminal work on cyclic Spell-Out and explicitly established in Chomsky 2001, relates phase inaccessibility to the idea of cyclic Spell-Out: the phase, when completed, exits syntax and is sent to the interfaces. More recently, Chomsky—still maintaining that phases are objects that cannot be modified by further computation—dissociates phase impenetrability from Spell-Out: a phase, while inaccessible, is claimed not to disappear (Chomsky 2013). As a consequence, for example, "if an SO containing [a phase] Z is raised by IM [Internal Merge], then Z will appear in the surface position (as in "the man who said that Z was elected") (Chomsky 2013, 42). Since this issue, though interesting, does not play a role in the present discussion, we will simply put it aside.

2. Chomsky (2013, 45) argues that when the structure is stable, as in criterial configurations, the stability is due to the feature-checking mechanism that gives "prominence" to the relevant feature, which can thus provide the label. But this amounts to saying that the crucial property allowing a configuration to receive a label is *not* whether or not two maximal projections are involved, but whether a probing relation is active. This is very much in line with what we are proposing in this book—namely, that probing relations determine labels.

3. Chomsky (2013) avoids this paradox by claiming that labels are not needed in syntax, but only at the interface: Merge can create a label-less object as long as this object obtains a label by the end of the cycle, when it is sent to the interface. We have already detailed our criticism of this external definition of label in section 2.6.

4. A clear contrast is detectable also in cases of adjunct extraction. Extraction from an *oti*-clause (a clausal "complement" of a noun), as in (ii), is not perfect, but it is much better than extraction from a relative clause, as in (iii). Sentence (i) illustrates extraction out of a finite clause. Many thanks to Vassilios Spyropoulos for discussion of these examples.

(i)   Me   pjon   tropo   akuses   oti   apelisan   to Jani?
      with what.ACC way. ACC hear.PAST.2SG that_{Comp} fire.PAST.3PL the John.ACC

Literally: 'In which way did you hear that they fired John?'

(ii) ?Me   pjon   tropo   akuses   ti fimi   oti   apelisan
      with what.ACC way.ACC hear.PAST.2SG the rumor.ACC that_{Comp} fire.PAST.3PL
      to Jani?
      the John.ACC

Literally: '*In which way did you hear the rumor that they fired John?'

(iii) *Me   pjon   tropo   akuses   ti fimi   pu   tha
      with what.ACC way.ACC hear.PAST.2SG the rumor.ACC that_{Rel} FUT
      stigmatisi   to Jani?
      stigmatize.3SG the John.ACC

Literally: '*In which way did you hear the rumor that (which) will stigmatize John?'

5. In fact, the category "peripheral clause" might be too general, as two subtypes can be identified (see Haegeman 2012, sec. 4.8.2). We gloss over this fine-grained classification, which is not crucial for our purposes.

Chapter 5

1. There is another possibility that follows from our hypothesis; we will only mention it briefly here because more research is needed. If we relate Minimality effects to Chain Identification, we predict that when movement is both unprobed (hence free) and not interpretable (hence not forming a chain), no Minimality effect should arise. Scrambling in Japanese, described by Saito (1989) and others as semantically vacuous, might be interpreted as such a case of zero Minimality.

2. Also see Greco 2013a for discussion of "argumenthood" of the PP as another factor that modulates the acceptability judgments.

3. Since in Italian an interrogative and an exclamative have the same word order, a simple heuristic to distinguish them is inserting an expletive negation, which is allowed only in exclamatives. We use this heuristic in (17). However, the judgments do not change if the expletive negation is omitted.

4. Possibly, subject intervention in (24) is absent because *perché*-clauses involve no movement at all (see Rizzi 2001 for the hypothesis that *perché* 'why' is generated in the left periphery, and Cecchetto and Donati 2012 for supporting evidence). That the lack of subject intervention with reason clauses is due to lack of movement is indirectly confirmed by the following examples discussed by Greco (2013a, 81):

(i) a. Perché Ezra ha   detto che Thomas ha   accettato l'incarico?
       why   Ezra has said that Thomas has accepted the assignment
       'Why did Ezra say that Thomas accepted the assignment?'
    b. Perché hai   detto che Thomas ha   accettato l'incarico?
       why   (you) have said that Thomas has accepted the assignment
       'Why did you say that Thomas accepted the assignment?'

In principle, the sentences in (i) should both be ambiguous, with *perché* 'why' interpreted either with wide scope, modifying the root clause, or with narrow scope, as a modifier of the embedded clause. Interestingly, only (ib), where no overt subject intervenes in the root clause, is ambiguous; in (ia), the presence of the subject (*Ezra*) blocks the movement operation associated with the narrow scope reading. Note that Cardinaletti (2014) discusses similar examples.

5. The same analysis can be extended to French subject clitics, which do not intervene in object extraction, unlike lexical subjects.

(i) ?*Qui Jean a   vu?
      who Jean has seen
(ii) Qui t'as   vu?
      who you have seen
      'Who did you see?'

6. We must of course assume that the subject does not act as an intervener for object extraction within the VP. But VP is always selected (it cannot be a root category), and thus it requires a label: no instance of unprobed movement is ever allowed within it and thus no Gross Minimality effect is expected.

7. This might be due to the availability of a simple "*what*=object" versus "*who*=subject" linear algorithm for interpreting these questions without any processing of a proper dependency.

8. One might ask what blocks derivation (42) in adult grammar. As sentence (40a) is grammatical, one cannot exclude that this derivation is indeed possible. The difficulty that adults exhibit in parsing object relative clauses might be interpreted as evidence of the persistence of this "childish" unprobed movement derivation. Adults appear to be sensitive to the same fine-grained distinctions in subject intervention that we discuss in section 5.5 (object relatives are better comprehended when there is a first or second person pronoun or a proper name in subject position; Garraffa and Grillo 2008, Gibson 1998, Gordon, Hendrick, and Johnson 2001, Grillo 2009, Reali and Christiansen 2007, Warren and Gibson 2002, 2005). We leave this interesting issue open here.

9. We disagree with the conclusions reached by Goodluck (2010, 1516), who claims that children's performance with object extraction "is not subject to Relativized Minimality," on the basis of facts not very different from the ones discussed in the text. In a nutshell, Goodluck shows that children's performance with object extraction in questions is also affected by some *semantic* similarity/dissimilarity between the moved element and the intervening subject. See Bentea and Durrleman 2013 for discussion.

10. As observed above (see (26)), in adult Italian an overt pronoun is never allowed in preverbal position in direct questions, even when the person feature of the pronoun is first or second person.

(i) *Cosa io ho   fatto?
      what I have done
(ii) *Cosa tu hai   fatto?
      what you have done

In this respect, adult direct questions are somewhat more constrained than child object relatives. Although it is not totally clear to us why this is so, we suspect that it involves the fact that a *wh*-phrase is a focused element in a question, and in Italian an overt pronoun can be used naturally only if it is focused (otherwise, pro is used).

11. To be more precise, Adani et al. (2010) do observe a slight effect of gender in Italian as well, but interestingly this effect is not restricted to object extraction: both in subject and in object relatives, the presence of a gender mismatch between the two arguments of the embedded clause improves children's comprehension. This mild effect, and crucially its nonselectivity, makes it very different from the intervention effects displayed in Hebrew, and Adani et al. (2010) discuss it in terms of working memory (elements that are more different are easier to remember), not Minimality.

12. This is an area where a clear crosslinguistic difference is observed. Friedmann, Belletti, and Rizzi (2009) report that 5-year-old Hebrew-speaking children, who still have problems with comprehending object full relatives (i), do not seem to have any problem with object extraction in free relatives (ii).

(i) Tare li   et   ha-pil   she-ha-arie martiv.
     show to.ME ACC   the-elephant that-the-lion wets
     'Show me the elephant that the lion is wetting.'
(ii) Tare li   et   mi   she-ha-yeled   martiv.
     show to.me ACC   who   that-the-boy   wets
     'Show me the one that the boy is wetting.'

Friedmann, Belletti, and Rizzi interpret this contrast as a strong argument in favor of their account: in (ii), they claim, a [−NP] element, *mi* 'who', is moved across a [+NP] element, *ha-yeled* 'the boy'. No Relativized Minimality effect is triggered.

We do not have a full-fledged analysis of the Hebrew construction in (ii), but we stress that the obligatory presence of the complementizer *she* makes Hebrew free relatives nonambiguous with *wh*-interrogatives, where *she* is impossible. Recall from section 3.2 that systematic ambiguity with an interrogative structure (as a case of labeling "conflict") is a crucial component of our analysis of free relatives. Be that as it may, Friedmann, Belletti, and Rizzi's account cannot be easily extended to Italian free relatives, which, as noted in the text, display a subject intervention effect even in adult grammar. Furthermore, Costa, Grillo, and Lobo (2012) find that as a group, children speaking European Portuguese do not show any preference for object free relatives over object full relatives. Interestingly, free relatives in European Portuguese are similar to free relatives in Italian and English, in that no complementizer is required, so they are systematically ambiguous with the corresponding interrogative structure. More research is needed here, but we suspect that the (non)ambiguity between free relatives and questions might play a role in the explanation of the crosslinguistic differences.

13. Note that by following the same logic, one would expect free relatives in English to display subject intervention effects. But this is not the case; witness the full acceptability of (i).

(i) What John said is horrible.

We offer an account for the absence of subject intervention effects in English free relatives in forthcoming work. In a nutshell, our account capitalizes on the fact that in Italian, free relatives are modeled after direct questions, which show intervention effects. In English, however, as the impossibility of auxiliary inversion in free relatives shows, the source of free relatives is *in*direct questions, which never show intervention effects. See Cecchetto and Donati, in press b, for a full account.

14. In Donati and Cecchetto 2011, we proposed an extension of this unprobed movement analysis to pseudorelatives in Romance, illustrated for Italian in (i).

(i) Ho   incontrato lui   che baciava Maria.
    (I) have met   him that kissed   Maria
    'I met him while he was kissing Maria.'

Pseudorelatives are indeed good candidates for the derivation we discuss in the text with respect to free relatives: like free relatives, they involve the movement of the word (*lui* 'him' in (i)); unlike free relatives, though, they have no possible derivation involving a probed movement, since the pronoun has no special morphological marking (it is not *wh*, for example). As predicted, pseudorelatives appear to strictly obey Gross Minimality and thus to be possible only on subjects; witness the ungrammatical object pseudorelative in (ii).

(ii) *Ho   incontrato lui   che Maria baciava ~~lui~~.
     (I) have met   him that Maria kissed

The syntax of pseudorelatives is very intricate, however, and an accurate analysis of this construction would take us too far away from our relabeling path in this book. See Donati and Cecchetto 2011 for more details.

References

Aboh, E. O. 2003. *The morphosyntax of complement-head sequences.* Oxford: Oxford University Press.

Ackema, P., and A. Neeleman. 2004. *Beyond morphology: Interface conditions on word formation.* Oxford: Oxford University Press.

Ackema, P., and A. Neeleman. 2007. Morphology ≠ syntax. In G. Ramchand and C. Reiss, eds., *The Oxford handbook of linguistic interfaces,* 325–352. Oxford: Oxford University Press.

Adani, F. 2008. The role of features in relative clause comprehension: A study of typical and atypical development. Doctoral dissertation, University of Milano-Bicocca.

Adani, F., H. van der Lely, M. Forgiarini, and M. T. Guasti. 2010. Grammatical feature dissimilarities make relative clauses easier: A comprehension study with Italian children. *Lingua* 120, 2148–2166.

Adger, D. 2003. *Core syntax: A Minimalist approach.* Oxford: Oxford University Press.

Adger, D. 2013. *A syntax of substance.* Cambridge, MA: MIT Press.

Albrecht, L., L. Haegeman, and R. Nye, eds. 2012. *Main clause phenomena: New horizons.* Amsterdam: John Benjamins.

Alexiadou, A., and E. Anagnostopoulou. 1998. Parametrizing AGR: Word order, V-movement and EPP-checking. *Natural Language and Linguistic Theory* 16, 491–539.

Ardila, A., and M. Rosselli. 1994. Averbia as a selective naming disorder: A single case report. *Journal of Psycholinguistic Research* 23, 139–148.

Arnon, I. 2005. Relative clause acquisition in Hebrew: Toward a processing-oriented account. In A. Brugos, M. R. Clark-Cotton, and S. Ha, eds., *Proceedings of the Twenty-ninth Boston University Conference on Language Development,* 37–48. Somerville, MA: Cascadilla Press.

Arosio, F., F. Adani, and M. T. Guasti. 2009. Grammatical features in the comprehension of Italian relative clauses by children. In J. M. Brucart, A. Gavarró, and J. Solà, eds., *Merging features: Computation, interpretation, and acquisition,* 138–158. Oxford: Oxford University Press.

Arosio, F., M. T. Guasti, and N. Stucchi. 2010. Disambiguating information and memory resources in children's processing of Italian relative clauses. *Journal of Psycholinguistic Research* 40, 137–154.

Arosio, F., K. Yatsushiro, M. Forgiarini, and M. T. Guasti. 2012. Morphological information and memory resources in children's processing of relative clauses in German. *Language Learning and Development* 8, 340–364.

Arregi, K. 1998. Spanish *el que* relative clauses and the Doubly Filled COMP Filter. Ms., MIT. Available at http://home.uchicago.edu/~karlos/Arregi-elque.pdf.

Arsenijević, B. 2009a. Clausal complementation as relativization. *Lingua* 119, 39–50.

Arsenijević, B. 2009b. {Relative {conditional {correlative clauses}}}. In A. Lipták, ed., *Correlatives cross-linguistically*, 131–156. Amsterdam: John Benjamins.

Ausín, A., and L. Martí. 2001. Subject-verb inversion and the status of preverbal subjects in Spanish. Paper presented at the 4th Hispanic Linguistics Symposium, Bloomington, IN.

Austin, J. L. 1956. Ifs and cans. *Proceedings of the British Academy* 42, 107–132.

Avrutin, S. 2000. Comprehension of *wh*-questions by children and Broca's aphasics. In Y. Grodzinsky, L. Shapiro, and D. Swinney, eds., *Language and the brain*, 295–313. San Diego, CA: Academic Press.

Avrutin, S. 2006. Weak syntax. In K. Amunts and Y. Grodzinsky, eds., *Broca's region*, 49–62. New York: Oxford University Press.

Baker, M. 1988. *Incorporation: A theory of grammatical function changing*. Chicago: University of Chicago Press.

Baker, M. 1996. *The polysynthesis parameter*. Oxford: Oxford University Press.

Baker, M. 2009. Language universals: Abstract but not mythological. *Behavioral and Brain Sciences* 32, 448–449.

Barbosa, P. 2001. On inversion in *wh*-questions in Romance. In A. Hulk and J.-Y. Pollock, eds., *Subject inversion in Romance and the theory of Universal Grammar*, 20–59. Oxford: Oxford University Press.

Barrie, M. 2011. *Dynamic antisymmetry and the syntax of noun incorporation*. Dordrecht: Springer.

Battye, A. 1989. Free relatives, pseudo-free relatives and the syntax of CP in Italian. *Rivista di Linguistica* 1, 219–250.

Belletti, A. 1999. Italian/Romance clitics: Structure and derivation. In H. van Riemsdijk, ed., *Clitics in the languages of Europe*, 543–579. Berlin: Mouton de Gruyter.

Belletti, A. 2001. Inversion as focalization. In A. Hulk and J.-Y. Pollock, eds., *Subject inversion in Romance and the theory of Universal Grammar*, 60–90. Oxford: Oxford University Press.

Belletti, A. 2014. Notes on passive object relatives. In P. Svenonius, ed., *Functional structure from top to toe*. Oxford: Oxford University Press.

Belletti, A., and C. Contemori. 2010. Intervention and attraction: On the production of subject and object relatives by Italian (young) children and adults. In J. Costa, A.

Castro, M. Lobo, and F. Patras, eds., *Language acquisition and development: Proceedings of GALA 2009*, 39–52. Newcastle upon Tyne: Cambridge Scholars Publishing.

Belletti, A., N. Friedmann, D. Brunato, and L. Rizzi. 2012. Does gender make a difference? Comparing the effect of gender on children's comprehension of relative clauses in Hebrew and Italian. *Lingua* 122, 1053–1069.

Bentea, A., and S. Durrleman. 2013. Children don't like restrictions: Evidence from the acquisition of object A'-dependencies in French. Poster presented at Boston University Conference on Language Development 38.

Bhatt, R. 2002. The raising analysis of relative clauses: Evidence from adjectival modification. *Natural Language Semantics* 10, 43–90.

Bhatt, R. 2006. *Covert modality in non-finite contexts*. Berlin: Mouton de Gruyter.

Bhatt, R., and R. Pancheva. 2006. Conditionals. In M. Everaert and H. van Riemsdijk, eds., *The Blackwell companion to syntax*, 638–687. Oxford: Blackwell.

Bhatt, R., and R. Pancheva. 2012. Two superlative puzzles. Paper presented at GIST 5: Generalizing Relative Strategies, Ghent University. Available at http://www.gist.ugent.be/node/84.

Bhatt, R., and Y. Sharvit. 2005. A note on intensional superlatives. In E. Georgala and J. Howell, eds., *Proceedings of Semantics and Linguistic Theory (SALT) 15*, 62–79. Ithaca, NY: Cornell University, CLC Publications.

Bianchi, V. 1999. *Consequences of antisymmetry: Headed relative clauses*. Berlin: Mouton de Gruyter.

Bianchi, V. 2002. Headed relatives in generative syntax: Part I. *Glot International* 6, 197–204.

Bianchi, V., and M. Frascarelli. 2010. Is topic a root phenomenon? *Iberia* 2, 43–88.

Bloom, L., M. Rispoli, B. Gartner, and J. Hafitz. 1989. Acquisition of complementation. *Journal of Child Language* 16, 101–120.

Blümel, A. 2012. Successive cyclic movement as recursive symmetry-breaking. In N. Arnett and R. Bennett, eds., *Proceedings of the 30th West Coast Conference on Formal Linguistics*, 87–97. Somerville, MA: Cascadilla Proceedings Project.

Boeckx, C. 2003. *Islands and chains*. Amsterdam: John Benjamins.

Boeckx, C. 2008a. *Bare syntax*. Oxford: Oxford University Press.

Boeckx, C. 2008b. Islands. *Language and Linguistics Compass* 2, 151–167.

Boeckx, C. 2010. Defeating lexicocentrism. Ms., ICREA/Universitat Autònoma de Barcelona. Available at http://ling.auf.net/lingBuzz/001130.

Borer, H. 1984. *Parametric syntax: Case studies in Semitic and Romance languages*. Dordrecht: Foris.

Borer, H. 2003. Exo-skeletal vs. endo-skeletal explanations. In J. Moore and M. Polinsky, eds., *The nature of explanation in linguistic theory*, 31–67. Chicago: University of Chicago Press.

Borer, H. 2004. The grammar machine. In A. Alexiadou, E. Anagnostopoulou, and M. Everaert, eds., *The unaccusativity puzzle: Explorations of the syntax-lexicon interface*, 288–331. Oxford: Oxford University Press.

Borsley, R. D. 1997. Relative clauses and the theory of phrase structure. *Linguistic Inquiry* 28, 629–647.

Branchini, C. 2007. On relativization in Italian Sign Language. Doctoral dissertation, University of Urbino.

Branchini, C., and C. Donati. 2009. Relatively different: Italian Sign Language relative clauses in a typological perspective. In A. Lipták, ed., *Correlatives cross-linguistically*, 157–191. Amsterdam: John Benjamins.

Browning, M. A. 1987. Null operator constructions. Doctoral dissertation, MIT.

Bury, D. 2003. Phrase structure and derived heads. Doctoral dissertation, University College London.

Burzio, L. 1986. *Italian syntax*. Dordrecht: Reidel.

Capello, B. 2010. The interrogative pronominal status of *ce que* in French and *quello che* in Italian. Talk given at the workshop "The Diachronic Evolution of (Italo)-Romance Pronominal Systems," 10th Italian Dialectology Meeting, University of Bristol.

Caplan, D., and G. S. Waters. 1999. Verbal working memory and sentence comprehension. *Behavioral and Brain Sciences* 22, 77–94.

Caplan, D., G. S. Waters, G. DeDe, J. Michaud, and A. Reddy. 2007. A study of syntactic processing in aphasia I: Behavioral (psycholinguistic) aspects. *Brain and Language* 101, 103–150.

Caplan, D., G. S. Waters, D. Kennedy, N. Alpert, N. Makris, G. DeDe, J. Michaud, and A. Reddy. 2007. A study of syntactic processing in aphasia II: Neurological aspects. *Brain and Language* 101, 151–177.

Caponigro, I. 2003. Free not to ask: On the semantics of free relatives and *wh*-words crosslinguistically. Doctoral dissertation, UCLA.

Caponigro, I. 2004. The semantic contribution of *wh*-words and type shifts: Evidence from free relatives crosslinguistically. In R. B. Young, ed., *Proceedings of Semantics and Linguistic Theory (SALT) 14*, 38–55. Ithaca, NY: Cornell University, CLC Publications.

Caramazza, A., R. Capasso, E. Capitan, and G. Miceli. 2005. Patterns of comprehension performance in agrammatic Broca's aphasia: A test of the Trace Deletion Hypothesis. *Brain and Language* 94, 43–53.

Cardinaletti, A. 2002. Against optional and null clitics. Right dislocation vs. marginalization. *Studia Linguistica* 56, 29–57.

Cardinaletti, A. (2014). Cross-linguistic variation in the syntax of subjects. In C. Picalle, ed., *Linguistic variation in the Minimalist framework,* 82–107, Oxford: Oxford University Press.

Carlson, G. 1977. Amount relatives. *Language* 53, 520–542.

Caselli, M. C., P. Casadio, and E. Bates. 2001. Lexical development in English and Italian. In M. Tomasello and E. Bates, eds., *Language development: The essential readings*, 76–110. Oxford: Blackwell.

Cecchetto, C. 1999a. A comparative analysis of left and right dislocation in Romance. *Studia Linguistica* 53, 40–67.

Cecchetto, C. 1999b. Optionality and directionality: A view from leftward and rightward scrambling in Japanese. In K. Inoue, ed., *Researching and verifying an advanced theory of human language: Explanation of the human faculty for constructing and computing sentences on the basis of lexical conceptual features*, 49–83. Chiba: Kanda University of International Studies, Graduate School of Language Sciences.

Cecchetto, C. 2000. Doubling structures and reconstruction. *Probus* 12, 1–34.

Cecchetto, C. 2006. Reconstruction in relative clauses and the copy theory of traces. In P. Pica and J. Rooryck, eds., *Linguistic variation yearbook 5*, 5–35. Amsterdam: John Benjamins.

Cecchetto, C., and C. Donati. 2010. On labeling: Principle C and head movement. *Syntax* 13, 241–278.

Cecchetto, C., and C. Donati. 2012. "Perché" Rizzi is right. In V. Bianchi and C. Chesi, eds., *ENJOY LINGUISTICS! Papers offered to Luigi Rizzi on the occasion of his 60th birthday*, 54–62. Siena: CISCL Press.

Cecchetto, C., and C. Donati. In press a. Relativization in Italian Sign Language (LIS): The missing link of relativization. In A. Herrmann, R. Pfau, and M. Steinbach, eds., *Complex sentences and beyond in sign languages*. Berlin: Mouton de Gruyter.

Cecchetto, C., and C. Donati. In press b. Subject intervention in free relatives. In E. Di Domenico, C. Hamann, and S. Matteini, eds., *Structures, strategies and beyond*. Amsterdam: John Benjamins.

Cecchetto, C., C. Donati, and M. Vernice. 2012. Relative clauses vs clausal complements of nouns: Reversing the picture. Paper presented at NELS 2012.

Cecchetto, C., C. Geraci, and S. Zucchi. 2006. Strategies of relativization in Italian Sign Language. *Natural Language and Linguistic Theory* 24, 945–975.

Cecchetto, C., C. Geraci, and S. Zucchi. 2009. Another way to mark syntactic dependencies: The case for right peripheral specifiers in sign languages. *Language* 85, 1–43.

Chierchia, G. 2013. *Logic in grammar: Polarity, free choice, and intervention*. Oxford: Oxford University Press.

Chierchia, G., and I. Caponigro. 2013. Questions on questions and free relatives. Paper presented at Sinn und Bedeutung 19. University of the Basque Country. Available at https://docs.google.com/file/d/0B9lZn0JumEoyYkE1TElmSHlFdk0/edit?pli=1.

Chomsky, N. 1965. *Aspects of the theory of syntax*. Cambridge, MA: MIT Press.

Chomsky, N. 1970. Remarks on nominalization. In R. Jacobs and P. Rosenbaum, eds., *Readings in English transformational grammar*, 184–221. Waltham, MA: Ginn.

Chomsky, N. 1981. *Lectures on government and binding*. Dordrecht: Foris.

Chomsky, N. 1982. *Some concepts and consequences of the theory of government and binding*. Cambridge, MA: MIT Press.

Chomsky, N. 1986. *Barriers*. Cambridge, MA: MIT Press.

Chomsky, N. 1993. A minimalist program for linguistic theory. In K. Hale and S. J. Keyser, eds., *The view from Building 20*, 1–52. Cambridge, MA: MIT Press.

Chomsky, N. 1995a. Bare phrase structure. In H. Campos and P. Kempchinsky, eds., *Evolution and revolution in linguistic theory*, 51–109. Washington, DC: Georgetown University Press.

Chomsky, N. 1995b. *The Minimalist Program*. Cambridge, MA: MIT Press.

Chomsky, N. 2000. Minimalist inquiries. In R. Martin, D. Michaels, and J. Uriagereka, eds., *Step by step: Essays on Minimalism in honor of Howard Lasnik*, 89–155. Cambridge, MA: MIT Press.

Chomsky, N. 2001. Derivation by phase. In M. Kenstowicz, ed., *Ken Hale: A life in language*, 1–52. Cambridge, MA: MIT Press.

Chomsky, N. 2004. Beyond explanatory adequacy. In A. Belletti, ed., *Structures and beyond: The cartography of syntactic structure*, vol. 3, 104–131. Oxford: Oxford University Press.

Chomsky, N. 2005. Three factors in language design, *Linguistic Inquiry* 36, 1–22.

Chomsky, N. 2008. On phases. In R. Freidin, C. Otero, and M. L. Zubizarreta, eds., *Foundational issues in linguistic theory: Essays in honor of Jean-Roger Vergnaud*, 133–166. Cambridge, MA: MIT Press.

Chomsky, N. 2013. Problems of projection. *Lingua* 130, 33–49.

Christe, E. 2011. Rôle de l'interférence basée sur la similarité dans le traitement de structures linguistiques complexes: Les relatives objets. Mémoire de maîtrise, University of Geneva.

Cinque, G. 1977. The movement nature of left dislocation. *Linguistic Inquiry* 8, 397–411.

Cinque, G. 1978. La sintassi dei pronomi relativi 'cui' e 'quale' nell'italiano moderno. *Rivista di Grammatica Generativa* 3, 31–126.

Citko, B. 2008. Missing labels: Head movement as Project Both. In C. B. Chang and H. J. Haynie, eds., *Proceedings of the 26th West Coast Conference on Formal Linguistics*, 121–128. Somerville, MA: Cascadilla Proceedings Project.

Collins, C. 2002. Eliminating labels. In S. D. Epstein and D. Seely, eds., *Derivation and explanation in the Minimalist Program*, 42–64. Oxford: Blackwell.

Comrie, B. 1981. *Language universals and linguistic typology*. Oxford: Blackwell.

Costa, J., N. Grillo, and M. Lobo. 2012. Minimality beyond lexical restriction: Processing and acquisition of headed and free *wh*-dependencies in European Portuguese. *Revue Roumaine de Linguistique* 57, 143–160.

Crepaldi, D. 2007. Nouns and verbs in the brain: Neuropsychological, psycholinguistic and neuroimaging evidence. Doctoral dissertation, University of Milan-Bicocca.

Demonte, V. 1987. C-command, prepositions, and predication. *Linguistic Inquiry* 18, 147–157.

Deutsch, A., R. Frost, and K. I. Forster. 1998. Verbs and nouns are organized and accessed differently in the mental lexicon: Evidence from Hebrew. *Journal of Experimental Psychology: Learning, Memory, and Cognition* 24, 1238–1255.

De Vincenzi, M. 1991. *Syntactic parsing strategies in Italian: The Minimal Chain Principle*. Dordrecht: Kluwer.

Dobrovie-Sorin, C. 1994. *The syntax of Romanian: Comparative studies in Romance*. Berlin: Mouton de Gruyter.

Donati, C. 2006. On *wh*-head movement. In L. Cheng and N. Corver, eds., *Wh- movement: Moving on*, 21–46. Cambridge, MA: MIT Press.

Donati, C., and C. Cecchetto. 2011. Relabeling heads: A unified account for relativization structures. *Linguistic Inquiry* 42, 519–560.

Doron, E. 1982. The syntax and semantics of resumptive pronouns. *Texas Linguistic Forum* 19, 1–34.

Dowty, D. 2003. Thematic proto-roles and argument selection. In J. Gutiérrez-Rexach, ed., *Semantics: Critical concepts*, IV:221–244. London: Routledge.

Embick, D., and R. Noyer. 2007. Distributed Morphology and the syntax/morphology interface. In G. Ramchand and C. Reiss, eds., *The Oxford handbook of linguistic interfaces*, 289–324. Oxford: Oxford University Press.

Emonds, J. 1976. *A transformational approach to English syntax: Root, structure-preserving, and local transformations.* New York: Academic Press.

Frank, R. 2002. *Phrase structure composition and syntactic dependencies.* Cambridge, MA: MIT Press.

Frazier, L. 1978. On comprehending sentences: Syntactic parsing strategies. Doctoral dissertation, University of Connecticut, Storrs.

Friederici, A. D., and P. Gorrell. 1998. Structural prominence and agrammatic theta-role assignment: A reconsideration of linear strategies. *Brain and Language* 65, 253–275.

Friedmann, N., A. Belletti, and L. Rizzi. 2009. Relativized relatives: Types of intervention in the acquisition of A-bar dependencies. *Lingua* 119, 67–88.

Friedmann, N., and J. Costa. 2010. On children's difficulty in understanding coordination and relative clauses with crossing dependencies. *Lingua* 120, 1502–1515.

Friedmann, N., and Y. Grodzinsky. 1997. Tense and agreement in agrammatic production: Pruning the syntactic tree. *Brain and Language* 56, 397–425.

Friedmann, N., and R. Novogrodsky. 2004. The acquisition of relative clause comprehension in Hebrew: A study of SLI and normal development. *Journal of Child Language* 31, 661–681.

Garraffa, M., and N. Grillo. 2008. Canonicity effects as grammatical phenomena. *Journal of Neurolinguistics* 21, 177–197.

Geach, P. T. 1964. Referring expressions again. *Analysis* 24, 172–175.

Gibson, E. 1998. Linguistic complexity: Locality of syntactic dependencies. *Cognition* 68, 1–76.

Goldin-Meadow, S. 2011. Homesign: Gesture to language. In R. Pfau, M. Steinbach, and B. Woll, eds., *Sign language: An international handbook*, 601–625. Berlin: Mouton de Gruyter.

Goldin-Meadow, S., C. Butcher, C. Mylander, and M. Dodge. 1994. Nouns and verbs in a self-styled gesture system: What's in a name? *Cognitive Psychology* 27, 259–319.

Goodall, G. 1993. SPEC of IP and SPEC of CP in Spanish *wh*-questions. In W. Ashby, M. Mithun, G. Perissinotto, and E. Raposo, eds., *Linguistic perspectives on the Romance languages: Selected papers from the XXI Linguistic Symposium on Romance Languages*, 199–209. Amsterdam: John Benjamins.

Goodall, G. 2004. On the syntax and processing of *wh*-questions in Spanish. In B. Schmeiser, V. Chand, A. Kelleher, and A. Rodriguez, eds., *Proceedings of the 23rd West Coast Conference on Formal Linguistics*, 101–114. Somerville, MA: Cascadilla Press.

Goodglass, H., and E. Kaplan. 1983. *Boston Diagnostic Aphasia Examination* (BDAE). Distributed by Psychological Assessment Resources, Odessa, FL.

Goodluck, H. 2010. Object extraction is not subject to Child Relativized Minimality. *Lingua* 120, 1516–1521.

Gordon, P. C., R. Hendrick, and M. Johnson. 2001. Memory interference during language processing. *Journal of Experimental Psychology: Learning, Memory, and Cognition* 27, 1411–1423.

Gordon, P. C., R. Hendrick, and M. Johnson. 2004. Effects of noun phrase type on sentence complexity. *Journal of Memory and Language* 51, 97–114.

Greco, C. 2013a. Arguments and subjects in A'-syntax. Doctoral dissertation, University of Milan-Bicocca.

Greco, C. 2013b. A puzzle about subject position in *wh*-questions. Talk presented at Incontro di Grammatica Generativa 39, Modena.

Grillo, N. 2008. Generalized Minimality. Doctoral dissertation, Utrecht Institute of Linguistics OTS.

Grillo, N. 2009. Generalized Minimality: Feature impoverishment and comprehension deficits in agrammatism. *Lingua* 119, 1426–1443.

Grimshaw, J. 1990. *Argument structure*. Cambridge, MA: MIT Press.

Grimshaw, J. 1991. Extended projection. Ms., Brandeis University. [Reprinted in *Words and structure*, 1–69. Stanford, CA: CSLI Publications (2005).]

Grodzinsky, Y. 2000. The neurology of syntax: Language use without Broca's area. *Behavioral and Brain Sciences* 23, 1–71.

Grosu, A., and F. Landman. 1998. Strange relatives of the third kind. *Natural Language Semantics* 6, 125–170.

Guasti, M. T. 1996. On the controversial status of Romance interrogatives. *Probus* 8, 161–180.

Guasti, M. T., A. Gavarrò, J. De Lange, and C. Caprin. 2008. Article omission across child languages. *Language Acquisition* 15, 89–119.

Guasti, M. T., S. Stavrakaki, and F. Arosio. 2012. Crosslinguistic differences and similarities in the acquisition of relative clauses: Evidence from Greek and Italian. *Lingua* 122, 700–713.

Guimarães, M. 2000. In defense of vacuous projections in bare phrase structure. In M. Guimarães, L. Meroni, C. Rodriguez, and I. San Martin, eds., *University of Maryland working papers in linguistics* 9, 90–115. College Park: University of Maryland, Department of Linguistics.

Haegeman, L. 2003. Conditional clauses: External and internal syntax. *Mind and Language* 18, 317–339.

Haegeman, L. 2010a. The internal syntax of adverbial clauses. *Lingua* 120, 628–648.

Haegeman, L. 2010b. The movement derivation of conditional clauses. *Linguistic Inquiry* 41, 595–621.

Haegeman, L. 2012. *Adverbial clauses, main clause phenomena, and the composition of the left periphery.* Oxford: Oxford University Press.

Hale, K., and S. J. Keyser. 2002. *Prolegomenon to a theory of argument structure.* Cambridge, MA: MIT Press.

Heycock, C. 2005. On the interaction of adjectival modifiers and relative clauses. *Natural Language Semantics* 13, 359–382.

Higginbotham, J. 1985. On semantics. *Linguistic Inquiry* 16, 547–593.

Hillis, A. E., and A. Caramazza. 1991. Category-specific naming and comprehension impairment: A double dissociation. *Brain* 114, 2081–2094.

Hirschbühler, P., and D. Bouchard. 1985. French "quoi" and its clitic allomorph "que." In C. Neidle and R. A. Nuñez, eds., *Studies in the Romance languages*, 39–60. Dordrecht: Foris.

Hornstein, N. 2009. *A theory of syntax: Minimal operations and Universal Grammar.* Cambridge: Cambridge University Press.

Hornstein, N., and J. Nunes. 2008. Adjunction, labeling, and bare phrase structure. *Biolinguistics* 21, 57–86.

Huang, C.-T. J. 1982. Logical relations in Chinese and the theory of grammar. Doctoral dissertation, MIT.

Hulsey, S., and U. Sauerland. 2009. Sorting out relative clauses. *Natural Language Semantics* 14, 111–137.

Iatridou, S., E. Anagnostopoulou, and R. Izvorski. 2001. Observations about the form and meaning of the perfect. In M. Kenstowicz, ed., *Ken Hale: A life in language*, 189–238. Cambridge, MA: MIT Press.

Jackendoff, R. 1977. *X-bar syntax: A study of phrase structure.* Cambridge, MA: MIT Press.

Jacobson, P. 1994. Binding connectivity in copular sentences. In M. Harvey and L. Santelmann, eds., *Proceedings of Semantics and Linguistic Theory (SALT) 4*, 161–178. Ithaca, NY: Cornell University, Cornell Linguistics Circle.

Julien, M. 2007. On the relation between morphology and syntax. In G. Ramchand and C. Reiss, eds., *The Oxford handbook of linguistic interfaces*, 209–238. Oxford: Oxford University Press.

Kayne, R. 1975. *French syntax.* Cambridge, MA: MIT Press.

Kayne, R. 1976. French relative *que*. In F. Hensey and M. Luján, eds., *Current studies in Romance linguistics*, 255–299. Washington, DC: Georgetown University Press.

Kayne, R. 1991. Romance clitics, verb movement, and PRO. *Linguistic Inquiry* 22, 647–686.

Kayne, R. 1994. *The antisymmetry of syntax.* Cambridge, MA: MIT Press.

Kayne, R. 2009. Antisymmetry and the lexicon. *Linguistic Variation Yearbook 2008*, 1–32.

Kayne, R. 2010. Why isn't 'this' a complementizer? In *Comparisons and contrasts*, 190–227. New York: Oxford University Press.

Kayne, R., and J.-Y. Pollock. 1978. Stylistic inversion, successive cyclicity, and Move NP in French. *Linguistic Inquiry* 9, 595–621.

Kayne, R., and J.-Y. Pollock. 2001. New thoughts on stylistic inversion. In A. Hulk and J.-Y. Pollock, eds., *Subject inversion in Romance and the theory of Universal Grammar*, 107–162. Oxford: Oxford University Press.

Keenan, E. L. 1985. Relative clauses. In T. Shopen, ed., *Language typology and syntactic description*. Vol. 2, *Complex constructions*, 141–170. Cambridge: Cambridge University Press.

King, J., and M. A. Just. 1991. Individual differences in syntactic processing: The role of working memory. *Journal of Memory and Language* 30, 580–602.

Kolk, H. H. J. 1998. Disorders of syntax in aphasia: Linguistic-descriptive and processing approaches. In B. Stemmer and H. Whitaker, eds., *Handbook of neurolinguistics*, 249–260. San Diego, CA: Academic Press.

Koopman, H., and D. Sportiche. 1991. The position of subjects. *Lingua* 85, 211–258.

Krapova, I., and G. Cinque. 2012. "Clausal complements" of nouns as reduced relative clauses. Paper presented at GIST 5: Generalizing Relative Strategies, Ghent University. Available at http://www.gist.ugent.be/file/267.

Kratzer, A. 1996. Severing the external argument from its verb. In J. Rooryck and L. Zaring, eds., *Phrase structure and the lexicon*, 109–137. Dordrecht: Kluwer.

Kural, M. 1997. Postverbal constituents in Turkish and the Linear Correspondence Axiom. *Linguistic Inquiry* 28, 498–519.

Larson, R. 1998. Events and modification in nominals. In D. Strolovitch and A. Lawson, eds., *Proceedings* of Semantics and Linguistic Theory (SALT) 8, 145–168. Ithaca, NY: Cornell University, CLC Publications.

Lasnik, H. 2003. *Minimalist investigations in linguistic theory*. New York: Routledge.

Lasnik, H., and J. Uriagereka. 1988. *A course in GB syntax*. Cambridge, MA: MIT Press.

Lebeaux, D. 1989. Language acquisition and the form of the grammar. Doctoral dissertation, University of Massachusetts, Amherst.

Legate, J. A. 2003. Some interface properties of the phase. Linguistic Inquiry 34, 506–516.

Link, G. 1984. Hydras: On the logic of relative constructions with multiple heads. In F. Landmann and F. Veltmann, eds., *Varieties of formal semantics*, 245–257. Dordrecht: Foris.

MacDonald, M. C., N. J. Pearlmutter, and M. S. Seidenberg. 1994. Syntactic ambiguity resolution as lexical ambiguity resolution. In C. Clifton, L. Frazier, and K. Rayner, eds., *Perspectives on sentence processing*, 123–153. Hillsdale, NJ: Lawrence Erlbaum.

Manzini, M. R., and L. Savoia. 2003. The nature of complementizers. *Rivista di Grammatica Generativa* 28, 87–110.

Manzini, M. R., and L. Savoia. 2011. *Grammatical categories*. Cambridge: Cambridge University Press.

Marantz, Alec. 1997. No escape from syntax: Don't try morphological analysis in the privacy of your own lexicon. In A. Dimitriadis, L. Siegel, C. Surek-Clark, and A. Williams, eds., *Proceedings of the 21st Annual Penn Linguistics Colloquium*, 201–225. Pennsylvania Working Papers in Linguistics 4.2. Philadelphia: University of Pennsylvania, Penn Linguistics Club.

Mauner, G., V. A. Fromkin, and T. L. Cornell. 1993. Comprehension and acceptability judgments in agrammatism: Disruption in the syntax of referential dependencies. *Brain and Language* 45, 340–370.

McCloskey, J. 1997. Subjecthood and subject positions. In L. Haegeman, ed., *Elements of grammar*, 197–236. Dordrecht: Kluwer.

Miceli, G., L. Giustolisi, and A. Caramazza. 1991. The interaction of lexical and non-lexical processing mechanisms: Evidence from anomia. *Cortex* 27, 57–80.

Moltmann, F. 1992. Coordination and comparatives. Doctoral dissertation, MIT.

Moro, A. 2000. *Dynamic Antisymmetry*. Cambridge, MA: MIT Press.

Munn, A. 1994. A Minimalist account of reconstruction asymmetries. In M. Gonzàlez, *Proceedings of NELS 24*, 397–410. Amherst: University of Massachusetts, Graduate Linguistic Student Assocation.

Muysken, P. 1982. Parametrizing the notion 'head'. *Journal of Linguistic Research* 2, 57–75.

Nespor, M., and I. Vogel. 1986. *Prosodic phonology*. Dordrecht: Foris.

Nunes, J. 1998. Bare X-bar theory and structures formed by movement. *Linguistic Inquiry* 29, 160–168.

Obenauer, H.-G. 1994. Aspects de la syntaxe A-barre: Effets d'interventions et mouvements des quantifieurs. Thèse d'état, Université Paris 8.

Ordóñez, F. 1997. Word order and clause structure in Spanish and other Romance languages. Doctoral dissertation, City University of New York.

Perlmutter, D., and J. R. Ross. 1970. Relative clauses with split antecedents. *Linguistic Inquiry* 1, 350.

Pesetsky, D., and E. Torrego. 2006. Probes, goals and syntactic categories. In Y. Otsu, ed., *Proceedings of the Seventh Tokyo Conference on Psycholinguistics*, 25–60. Tokyo: Hituzi Syobo.

Piñango, M. M. 1999. Syntactic displacement in Broca's aphasia comprehension. In Y. Grodzinsky and R. Bastiaanse, eds., *Grammatical disorders in aphasia: A neurolinguistic perspective*, 75–87. London: Whurr.

Poletto, C. 1997. L'inversione interrogativa come "verbo secondo residuo": l'analisi sincronica proiettata nella diacronia. In P. Ramat and E. Roma, eds., *Atti del XXX convegno SLI*, 311–327. Rome: Bulzoni Editore.

Poletto, C., and J.-Y. Pollock. 2004. On the left periphery of some Romance *wh* questions. In L. Rizzi, ed., *The structure of CP and IP: The cartography of syntactic structures*, 251–296. New York: Oxford University Press.

Ramchand, G. 2008. *Verb meaning and the lexicon*. Cambridge: Cambridge University Press.

Reali, F., and M. H. Christiansen. 2007. Processing of relative clauses is made easier by frequency of occurrence. *Journal of Memory and Language* 53, 1–23.

Riemsdijk, H. van. 2006. Free relatives. In M. Everaert and H. van Riemsdijk, eds., *The Blackwell companion to syntax*, 2:338–382. Oxford: Blackwell.

Rizzi, L. 1982. *Issues in Italian syntax*. Dordrecht: Foris.

Rizzi, L. 1990. *Relativized Minimality*. Cambridge, MA: MIT Press.

Rizzi, L. 1996. Residual verb second and the *Wh*-Criterion. In A. Belletti and L. Rizzi, eds., *Parameters and functional heads: Essays in comparative syntax*, 63–90. Oxford: Oxford University Press.

Rizzi, L. 1997. The fine structure of the left periphery. In L. Haegeman, ed., *Elements of grammar*, 281–337. Dordrecht: Kluwer.

Rizzi, L. 2001. On the position "int(errogative)" in the left periphery of the clause. In G. Cinque and G. Salvi, eds., *Current studies in Italian syntax: Essays offered to Lorenzo Renzi*, 267–296. Amsterdam: Elsevier.

Rizzi, L. 2004. Locality and the left periphery. In A. Belletti, ed., *Structures and beyond: The cartography of syntactic structures, vol. 3*, 223–251. Oxford: Oxford University Press.

Rizzi, L. 2011. On some properties of Criterial Freezing. In E. P. Panagiotidis, ed., *The Complementizer Phrase*, 17–32. Oxford: Oxford University Press.

Rizzi, L. 2013. Cartography, criteria, and labeling. Paper presented at the Cartographic Workshop, University of Geneva, 7 June.

Rosenbaum, P. 1967. *The grammar of English predicate complement constructions*. Cambridge, MA: MIT Press.

Ross, J. R. 1967. Constraints on variables in syntax. Doctoral dissertation, MIT.

Safir, K. 1999. Vehicle change and reconstruction in Ā-chains. *Linguistic Inquiry* 30, 587–620.

Saito, M. 1985. Some asymmetries in Japanese and their theoretical implications. Doctoral dissertation, MIT.

Saito, M. 1989. Scrambling as semantically vacuous A'-movement. In M. Baltin and A. Kroch, eds., *Alternative conceptions of phrase structure*, 182–200. Chicago: University of Chicago Press.

Sapir, E. 1921. *Language: An introduction to the study of speech*. New York: Harcourt, Brace.

Sauerland, U. 2003. Unpronounced heads in relative clauses. In K. Schwabe and S. Winkler, eds., *The interfaces: Deriving and interpreting omitted structures*, 205–226. Amsterdam: John Benjamins.

Schönenberger, M. 2001. *Embedded V-to-C in child grammar: The acquisition of verb placement in Swiss German.* Dordrecht: Kluwer.

Selkirk, E. 1984. *Phonology and syntax: The relation between sound and structure.* Cambridge, MA: MIT Press.

Shapiro, K., and A. Caramazza. 2003. The representation of grammatical categories in the brain. *Trends in Cognitive Sciences* 5, 201–206.

Sharvit, Y. 1999. Functional relative clauses. *Linguistics and Philosophy* 22, 447–478.

Sharvit, Y. 2007. Two reconstruction puzzles. In P. Jacobson and C. Barker, eds., *Direct compositionality*, 336–359. Oxford: Oxford University Press.

Shimoyama, J. 1999. Internally headed relative clauses in Japanese and E-type anaphora. *Journal of East Asian Linguistics* 8, 147–182.

Siloni, T. 1995. On participial relatives and complementizer D^0: A case study in Hebrew and French. *Natural Language and Linguistic Theory* 13, 445–487.

Sleeman, P. 2005. The Com(p-)position of DP-internal infinitival clauses. In L. Brugè, G. Giusti, N. Munaro, W. Schweikert, and G. Turano, eds., *Contributions to the thirtieth Incontro di Grammatica Generativa*, 333–349. Venice: Libreria Editrice Cafoscarina.

Spears, A. 1990. Tense, mood, and aspect in the Haitian Creole preverbal marker system. In J. V. Singler, ed., *Pidgin and creole tense-mood-aspect systems*, 119–142. Amsterdam: John Benjamins.

Speas, M. 1991. Functional heads and inflectional morphemes. *The Linguistic Review* 8, 389–417.

Starke, M. 2001. Move dissolves into Merge. Doctoral dissertation, University of Geneva.

Starke, M. 2009. Nanosyntax: A short primer to a new approach to language. Ms., CASTL, University of Tromsø.

Stepanov, A. 2007. The end of CED? Minimalism and extraction domains. *Syntax* 10, 80–126.

Stowell, T. 1981. Origins of phrase structure. Doctoral dissertation, MIT.

Stromswold, K. 1995. The acquisition of subject and object *wh*-questions. *Language Acquisition* 4, 5–48.

Suñer, M. 1994. V-movement and the licensing of argumental *wh*-phrases in Spanish. *Natural Language and Linguistic Theory* 12, 335–372.

Suñer, M. 2001. The puzzle of restrictive relative clauses with conjoined DP antecedents. In J. Herschensohn, E. Mallén, and K. Zagona, eds., *Features and interfaces in Spanish and French: Essays in honor of Heles Contreras*, 267–278. Amsterdam: John Benjamins.

Sylvain, S. 1936. *Le créole haïtien.* Wetteren, Belgium: Meester.

Takano, Y. 2014. A comparative approach to Japanese postposing. In M. Saito, ed., *Japanese syntax in comparative perspective.* Oxford: Oxford University Press. DOI: 10.1093/acprof:oso/9780199945207.003.0006.

Tanaka, H. 2001. Right-dislocation as scrambling. *Journal of Linguistics* 37, 551–579.

Thoms, G. 2011. Getting rid of interpretable features: Blind *wh*-movement and Justification. Talk given at the 21st Colloquium on Generative Grammar, Seville.

Torrego, E. 1984. On inversion in Spanish and some of its effects. *Linguistic Inquiry* 15, 103–129.

Torrego, E. 1995. On the nature of clitic doubling. In H. Campos and P. Kempchinsky, eds., *Evolution and revolution in linguistic theory*, 399–418. Washington, DC: Georgetown University Press.

Travis, L. 1984. Parameters and the effects of word order variation. Doctoral dissertation, MIT.

Trueswell, J. C. 1996. The role of lexical frequency in syntactic ambiguity resolution. *Journal of Memory and Language* 35, 566–585.

Trueswell, J. C., and M. K. Tanenhaus. 1994. Towards a lexicalist framework of constraint-based syntactic ambiguity resolution. In C. Clifton, L. Frazier, and K. Rayner, eds., *Perspectives on sentence processing*, 155–179. Hillsdale, NJ: Lawrence Erlbaum.

Tsimpli, I., D. Papadopoulou, and A. Mylonaki. 2010. Temporal modification in Greek adverbial clauses: The role of aspect and negation. *Lingua* 120, 649–672.

Uriagereka, J. 1995. Aspects of the syntax of clitic placement in Western Romance. *Linguistic Inquiry* 26, 79–123.

Uriagereka, J. 1999. Multiple Spell-Out. In S. D. Epstein and N. Hornstein, eds., *Working Minimalism*, 251–282. Cambridge, MA: MIT Press.

Valian, V. 1986. Syntactic categories in the speech of young children. *Developmental Psychology* 22, 562–579.

Vergnaud, J.-R. 1974. French relative clauses. Doctoral dissertation, MIT.

Vernice, M., V. Moscati, C. Donati, and C. Cecchetto. 2014. Does frequency win over syntactic complexity? Cross-linguistic evidence from the processing of relative vs. noun-clausal complement structures. Poster presented at Second Interannual Meeting of the Italian Society of Linguistics on "Usage-based theories and approaches in linguistics." Freie Universität Bozen.

Warren, T., and E. Gibson. 2002. The influence of referential processing on sentence complexity. *Cognition* 85, 79–112.

Warren, T., and E. Gibson. 2005. Effects of NP-type on reading English clefts. *Language and Cognitive Processes* 20, 751–767.

Waxman, S., and A. Booth. 2003. The origins and evolution of links between word learning and conceptual organization: New evidence from 11-month-olds. *Developmental Science* 6, 128–135.

Westergaard, M. 2007. Learning and unlearning V2: On the robustness of the triggering experience in a historical perspective. In C. Picchi and A. Pona, eds., *Proceedings of the XXXII Incontro di Grammatica Generativa*, 193–207. Alessandria: Edizioni dell'Orso.

Williams, E. 2007. Dumping lexicalism. In G. Ramchand and C. Reiss, eds., *The Oxford handbook of linguistic interfaces*, 353–381. Oxford: Oxford University Press.

Zanuttini, R., and P. Portner. 2003. Exclamative clauses: At the syntax-semantics interface. *Language* 79, 39–81.

Zubizarreta, M. L. 1998. *Prosody, focus, and word order*. Cambridge, MA: MIT Press.

Zubizarreta, M. L. 2001. The constraint on preverbal subjects in Romance interrogatives: A Minimality effect. In A. Hulk and J.-Y. Pollock, eds., *Subject inversion in Romance and the theory of Universal Grammar*, 183–204. Oxford: Oxford University Press.

Index

Linguistic Inquiry Monographs

Samuel Jay Keyser, general editor